S0-AUD-004

Library
Western Wyoming Community College

DISCARDED

The Saloon on the
Rocky Mountain Mining Frontier

Give . . . wine unto them
that be of heavy hearts.
Proverbs 31:6

Rye whiskey, rye whiskey,
Rye whiskey, I cry,
If you don't give me rye whiskey,
I surely will die.
Western folk song

978
W52s
1979

The Saloon on the Rocky Mountain Mining Frontier

By ELLIOTT WEST

University of Nebraska Press

LINCOLN AND LONDON

Copyright © 1979 by the University of Nebraska Press
All rights reserved

Library of Congress Cataloging in Publication Data

West, Elliott, 1945-
  The saloon on the Rocky Mountain mining frontier.

  Bibliography: p. 183
  Includes index.
  1. Frontier and pioneer life—Rocky Mountain region.
  2. Hotels, taverns, etc.—Rocky Mountain region—History.
  3. Rocky Mountain region—Social life and customs.
  I. Title.
  F721.W37   978   78-24090
  ISBN 0-8032-4704-4

Manufactured in the United States of America

To Carolyn

Contents

Illustrations

MAP

Preface

FOR many modern tourists, a summer trip to the Western states is incomplete without a visit to a genuine saloon. Enough authentic places have survived—the Crystal Palace of Tombstone, Arizona, and the Silver Dollar of Leadville, Colorado, for instance—to preserve a feel for the past. Vacationers seem to believe that in these barrooms they can find something vital to the frontier experience—its freedom, its virility, a hint of bawdiness and of imminent violence. A band with electric guitars might be playing in the corner, and the bartender might be a college senior, but the resident of Akron or Jersey City cannot be fooled. When he walks in, the wooden floors creak and he smells the fragrance of a hundred years of spilt beer. He orders whiskey straight-up at the long bar or at an oak table worn smooth with use, and he knows the truth. The spirits of dusty cowpunchers and bewhiskered sourdoughs are here. Part of the ''real West'' has survived.

Fed on a diet of Western novels, films, and television shows, the public assumes the importance of the saloon in the history of the frontier, but historians have given the drinking house only passing attention. Most books on Western and Eastern saloons are superficial and sensationalized. They supply the popular demand for colorful stories, but with few exceptions they make no effort to assess the functions of the public drinking house and its place in American social history. These works tell a great deal about what the public would like to believe the past to have been, but they add little to our understanding of what in fact was true.

Some historians and sociologists recently have begun to give the retail liquor business a closer, more analytical look, but they have directed most of their efforts toward the drinking places of modern

America—cocktail lounges, neighborhood bars, and skid-row taverns. These writers have described the activities and elaborate codes of behavior in these institutions that often play an important part in the lives of their patrons. A few historians have turned their attention to saloons operating before national Prohibition, but almost without exception they have focused on the larger urban centers of the East and the Midwest. The early Western saloon remains virtually ignored.[1]

This study is an attempt to help redress that imbalance by examining the saloon in one part of the far Western frontier, the mining towns of the Rocky Mountains. This area today includes parts of Arizona, New Mexico, Colorado, Wyoming, Utah, Montana, and Idaho. It is a region characterized by immense distances and extremes of geography and climate. Curving gently from northwest to southeast, the Rocky Mountains in the United States cover more than 180,000 square miles. The northern, middle, and southern Rockies together form the backbone of a watershed feeding almost half of the nation, and from them flow the far West's four greatest rivers, the Missouri, the Columbia, the Colorado, and the Rio Grande. Coeur d'Alene in Idaho's northward-reaching arm is about as close as Paris to the Arctic Circle, while Tombstone in southern Arizona is nearer than Tunis to the equator. The rugged Rockies contain many peaks over fourteen thousand feet above sea level, but plateaus and high valleys, sometimes called "parks" or "holes," allow the cultivation of fruits and vegetables and the raising of cattle and sheep.

For all its beauty, this region was and remains a demanding land. The mean temperature of the mountaintops varies by as much as thirty-five degrees from that of the plains below, and the higher reaches of the Rockies have a summer only half as long as that of Alaska's Yukon Valley. By the end of October, a long winter has settled upon much of the high country. Storms moving east and south from the northern Pacific coast vent their greatest fury on Idaho and Montana, but even in the San Juan range of southwestern Colorado the average annual snowfall exceeds twenty feet. The climate and the lay of the land meant that during its early settlement much of the region remained difficult to reach. If two men had left Chicago simultaneously in the spring of 1863, one traveling east and the other west, the first probably would have arrived in London before the second reached Orofino in Idaho or Grasshopper Creek in Montana.

Yet men and women came by the thousands, drawn by the glitter of precious metals. The Rocky Mountain mining frontier lasted roughly a third of a century, from the first significant placer mining along Cherry Creek, now part of Denver, in the summer of 1858 until the last important strike not far to the southwest at Cripple Creek in the early 1890s. Most of the activity during the first decade was directed toward the discovery and extraction of gold, but eventually miners from Tombstone to Idaho's Owyhee district added vast amounts of silver to the wealth taken from the region.

The towns that sprang up on the mining frontier varied enormously in their prosperity and endurance, some appearing and vanishing in less than a year and others surviving until today. The more promising of them attracted Eastern and foreign investment capital, and some developed smelting and processing facilities and emerged as market centers for the smaller towns around them. By far the largest and wealthiest urban center was Leadville, high in the central Rockies west of Denver. Its relative accessibility and its rich deposits of both gold and silver drew thousands of persons after 1878 and made it at its peak around 1882 Colorado's largest population center. Leadville was the Rocky Mountains' only true gold and silver mining city.

Historians traditionally have concentrated on the economic impact, entrepreneurship, and technological achievements of the mining frontier. Social historians usually have described the evolution and stages of growth of mining towns and the development of government and urban services. Nonetheless, even the earliest of these histories give some attention to the entertainment and leisure time of the inhabitants, their search for diversion and fun and relaxation. And there is often at least some mention of the many low barrooms and resplendent saloons to be found in the mining camps. Some writers note only the great number of saloons. Others comment on the violence that sometimes occurred in them. At most, writers generally devote no more than a paragraph or so to the social prominence of the saloon as a gathering place for the men of the town.[2]

If miners enjoyed drinking in saloons, they were no different from many other Americans of that time. The high point of national alcoholic consumption seems to have come during the two or three generations immediately preceding the mining booms of the far West. Colonial Americans of whatever sex, age, class, or region drank substantial amounts of ale and wine, and later rum, gin, and corn whiskey. During the years between the birth of the Republic and the Civil War, however, citizens of the new nation began to consume much more, in part because of expanded production of distilled liquors, and perhaps, as one author recently has suggested, because geographical expansion and economic revolution created an unparalleled social disorder and encouraged mass compulsive drinking.[3]

Consumption of liquor in the United States declined somewhat and stabilized after 1860, but even then Americans drank enough wine, beer, and hard liquor annually to equal about two gallons of pure alcohol for every man, woman, and child in the country. European immigrants came from societies with even harder-drinking traditions. A report published at the turn of the century by the British Board of Trade showed that the per capita consumption of this nation was lower than those of all the countries of Western Europe. The drinking rate of Germany was twice that of the United States, while an American would have had to drink at a pace four times the national average to keep up with the typical toper of France.[4]

Many of the prospectors, speculators, merchants, and other men on the make who crossed the plains to the Rockies, whether they came from Saint Louis, Boston, Hamburg, or County Cork, likely had at least a nodding acquaintance with the drinking house and its products, proprietor, and customs. In part from simple social momentum, saloons appeared in the mining towns to serve the needs of the new arrivals, and they sprang up in numbers that amazed some observers and appalled others. "It seemed to me that over the front entrance of every other building one could read the word saloon," one of the first women to settle in Boise, Idaho, later recalled.[5] Her memory might well have been accurate. A business census taken in Sawtooth, Idaho, a year after the birth of the camp showed that of forty-one retail stores, twenty were barrooms. Other such surveys revealed that drinking places often outnumbered all other retail establishments. A Leadville journalist reported at the end of 1880 that the four million dollars in trade done by the city's 249 saloons exceeded that of any other kind of business except banking and mining itself. As late as 1893, the tourist Julian Ralph estimated that there was a tavern for every eighty inhabitants of Montana. Experienced mountaineers claimed they could gauge the prosperity of a town by using the number of its saloons as an economic barometer.[6]

For no other reason than their abundance, then, the saloons of the mining frontier deserve some attention. They obviously accounted for a large part of a camp's trade, and many persons in those acquisitive societies apparently believed that the barroom offered a genuine chance of financial advancement. Beyond that, the saloon was a significant institution because of its social impact upon the mining town. The saloonman and his place of business helped ease some of the immediate problems of a new camp, and they aggravated others. For good or ill, the tavern played an important part in the everyday lives of many inhabitants and in the development of their towns.

In this study I have gone beyond the spare generalizations of existing histories to describe in some detail various aspects of saloons and the liquor trade on the Rocky Mountain mining frontier. Above all, I have tried to place the saloon in the context of the mining town—its physical growth, social composition, and prevailing attitudes. What follows is a case study of an important business and its place in one part of the American frontier.

Although I have concentrated on the gold and silver mining towns of the Rockies, occasionally I have included references to supply centers such as Boise and Tucson. Furthermore, I have paid closest attention to the earliest period of each camp, for it was then that the saloon performed its most varied and important roles and had its greatest impact. The definition of a saloon could be a vague one, for whiskey was sold in many places. Most larger hotels had a taproom, and general stores traditionally had a barrel with a dipper for regular customers. I have given most of my attention to drinking houses called saloons by contemporary observers, places that seem to have relied on the sale of liquor by the drink for most of their income. When describing gambling halls, dance halls, and theaters, I have tried to refer to them as such. There have survived few personal papers and records of saloonmen—the diary of George Hand of Tucson is a revealing exception—so I have relied heavily upon published contemporary reports, unpublished reminiscences, manuscript censuses, some local town records, and, especially, mining town newspapers.

I have tried to avoid the emotional attacks upon, and defenses of, the barroom common to many past writers in favor of a functional approach that stresses the practical effects of the saloon trade. The first chapter examines the validity of the popular image of the hard-drinking mining frontier and discusses some of the ill effects of mass drinking on the society of the camps. The following three chapters describe the saloon and its physical development, consider the owner of the barroom and his most important characteristics, and assess the various social roles of the drinking house. Chapter five evaluates the economic possibilities of the business for those who entered it. The concluding chapter remarks briefly on the changing place of the tavern in those towns that survived and matured, and then offers an evaluation of the saloon's significance to the Rocky Mountain mining frontier.

Part of the research for this book was financed with funds provided by the Graduate School of the University of Texas at Arlington and the Penrose Fund of the American Philosophical Society. For that help I am most grateful. The staff members of several institutions gave invaluable assistance in locating the most useful material among their holdings. In particular I would like to thank Harriett C. Meloy and Brian Cockhill of the Montana Historical Society, Judith Austin of the Idaho State Historical Society, John C. Brennan of the Western History Collection of the University of Colorado Library, and the staffs of the Arizona Historical Society, State Historical Society of Colorado, Denver Public Library, and the Henry E. Huntington Library. The employees of the Lake County Clerk's Office in Leadville, Colorado, cheerfully dug out pertinent records and suffered without a murmur my disruptive presence. Mrs. Mary Alice Price of the interlibrary loan office of the University of Texas at Arlington Library was extremely helpful in obtaining material essential to this project.

Specifically, I would like to thank the following institutions for allowing me to quote directly from documents in their possession— the Idaho State Historical Society for the E. Lafayette Bristow Papers; the Arizona Historical Society for the Charles F. Bennett Reminiscence, Alexander Davidson Reminiscence, and the George Hand Diary; the Colorado Historical Society for the Auraria Town Company Records; the Lake County Public Library in Leadville, Colorado, for the George Elder Letters; and the Montana Historical Society for the Gilbert Benedict Papers, William Bertsche Collection, Thomas Conrad Letters, Cornelius Hedges Papers, George Herendeen Papers, Sallie R. Herndon Diary, Franklin L. Kirkaldie Papers, Bob Powell Reminiscence, W. R. Sellew Papers, Z. E. Thomas Reminiscence, Robert Thoroughman Reminiscence, Daniel Tuttle Letters, and Samuel William Carvoso Whipps Reminiscence.

Duane A. Smith of Fort Lewis College and George Wolfskill, Richard G. Miller, and John A. Hudson, all of the University of Texas at Arlington, read parts of the manuscript and made useful comments. For their suggestions and painful honesty I am especially thankful. I want to thank as well Clifford P. Westermeier and Robert G. Athearn for their encouragement, and particularly Thomas J. Noel for his criticisms, insights, and suggestions. I also appreciate the time spent by the office staff of the Department of History of the University of Texas at Arlington in typing part of this manuscript.

My oldest debt is to my grandmother, Virginia M. Page, who taught me to love the mountains almost as much as she did. My parents, Dick and Betsy West, have given me support and encouragement I can neither measure nor repay. My children, Elizabeth, Bill, and Richard, endured their father's neglect and accepted with amusement what must have seemed to them a mild lunacy. Above all, I thank my wife, Carolyn, for reasons I have told her, and will tell her again.

The Saloon on the
Rocky Mountain Mining Frontier

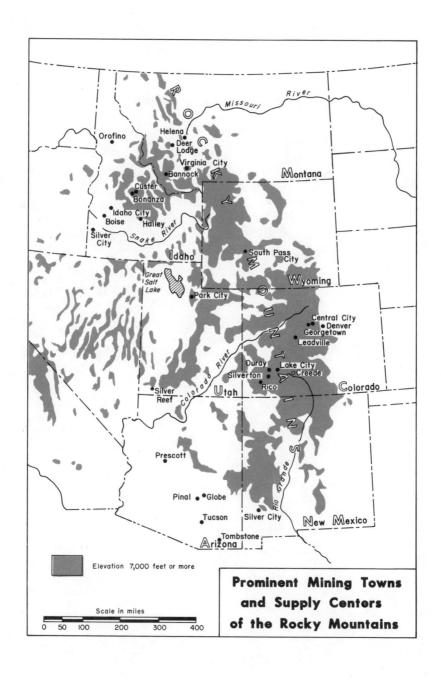

Elevation 7,000 feet or more

Scale in miles

0   50   100   200   300   400

**Prominent Mining Towns
and Supply Centers
of the Rocky Mountains**

1

The Sacramental Glass of Whiskey

THE stage that left Virginia City, Montana, in 1865 followed a long, looping route to the south and west before arriving in Boise, Idaho, after a journey of nine days. Along the way its passengers, among them the Kansas journalist Albert D. Richardson, could gaze in wonder at some of the most rugged and spectacular scenery in the mountain West—lofty peaks, the deep and narrow Port Neuf canyon, the churning cataracts of the Snake River, towering columns of basalt, and the desolate wastes of Idaho's lava beds. White men had barely begun to make their mark upon this region, and except for the isolated stage stations where they took their rest, the passengers saw no signs of humanity. None, that is, until three objects appeared suddenly in the road ahead of the coach. Here was evidence, Richardson noted, of the sure arrival of civilization: a newspaper, a matchbox, and an empty whiskey bottle.[1]

Richardson's wry observation was similar to many others of his day. In fact, the American public traditionally has seen the mining frontier as a place virtually saturated in alcohol. Contemporary reports commented upon the impressive drinking habits of the region. Early novels and short stories told of the miners' whiskey-guzzling, an image perpetuated by the first motion pictures. Indeed, the earliest film on a Western subject was not, as many believe, Edwin S. Porter's *The Great Train Robbery* (1903) but the Edison Company's *Cripple Creek Bar-room* (1892). In the twentieth century both scholars and creators of popular culture generally have continued to pay homage to this view.[2]

1

Was drinking and drunkenness in fact as common in these camps as tradition would have it? A closer look at this question can help the reader both to appreciate the popular demand that nurtured the saloon and to understand the social setting that forms the backdrop for the chapters that follow.

An investigator of the drinking practices of the towns of the Rockies naturally should begin by asking those on the scene. "We have never lived in any country where the use of intoxicating drinks was so prevalent. We do not know of over a dozen men in the Territory who abstain from their use altogether," a Colorado editor observed. One of Denver's founding fathers, William H. H. Larimer, viewed the situation somewhat more emotionally. "Oh, how they drink!" he wrote his wife of his first days on Cherry Creek. "You cannot conceive of anything as bad as they carry on here." Reminiscences of old-timers later would concur. "It may be said that the entire fabric of the Territory was constructed on liquor," recalled an early Arizona settler. "The pioneers were most of them whiskey fiends."[3]

Diaries and scattered records of stores and taverns indicate that many mountain dwellers, and not only the hell-raisers, allowed themselves a ration of between a quart and a gallon of whiskey as part of their weekly regimen. The respectable Montana tin merchant, Thomas Conrad, wrote shocked letters home to his wife and priest denouncing the libertinism he saw all around him on the streets of Virginia City, but at the same time he observed, "I have played no billiards or cards yet—but my whiskey keg is getting very low," and, scarcely two months later, "My keg is nearly empty again—and it takes 18 dollars in gold to fill it." Though the saloon was a predominantly male institution, alcohol was not monopolized by one sex. Sallie Herndon, a young and proper schoolmistress of Virginia City, usually averted her gaze from the wilder side of life in her town, and her diary is filled with accounts of teas and prayer meetings. Suddenly one Sunday she blurted out:

I have just witnessed a most shocking sight—a woman so intoxicated that she couldn't walk without assistance. She was taken into a house just opposite and as she stepped in the door she fell sprawling to the floor beastly drunk. Alas! alas! . . . how humiliating to a true woman to know that any of her sex can become so vile.[4]

This kind of indulgence was so common that one writer saw the need for a new definition of sobriety. No man should be considered drunk in the mountains, it was suggested, as long as he could make a noise.[5]

Names given to the land itself—the many whiskey hills and brewery gulches—sometimes suggest that liquor was not far from the minds of the first arrivals. In Colorado, Jimtown, near Creede, was called Gintown until soberer heads decided to improve the moral image of their camp, and miners in another settlement dubbed a nearby stream Fortification Creek in honor of the location of the region's first saloon on its banks. As with the land, so with its inhabitants. Among the nicknames of Montana pioneers catalogued by an early historian are not only Dog Eating Jack and Fred the Ratter but also Sour Mash Charlie and the particularly descriptive Old Tomato Nose.[6]

Jokes and anecdotes dealt frequently with themes of drinking and the humorous side of overindulgence. In the songs and ballads that illuminate aspects of the everyday life of the miners can be heard references to alcohol:

> I drink my beer among the boys
> I sit down with them to play
> And sometimes I got it blind
> For a whole night and a day
> I look a rough old specimen
> And I've had a rough career
> Trying to make the riffle
> For more than twenty year.[7]

Others indicate that immigrants brought their thirsts with them. These lines, composed by a passenger on a stage to Leadville, were meant to be sung to the melody of the First Lord's song from *H.M.S. Pinafore*:

> When I was a youth and to college went
> I spent all the money that my father sent;
> Fitting up my mind for societee
> By filling up my bowels with bad whiskee;
> And I fitted up myself so splendidlee,
> That now I am always on a D. B. D. [damn big drunk].[8]

To be sure, those on the mining frontier were not universally besotted. Some visitors saw less drunkenness than they expected, and temperance societies found converts among the diggings. "In this country where every body drinks, I don't taste a drop," one teetotaler assured his mother. But as with this letter, these immigrants usually admitted, with a touch of self-righteousness, that they were part of a tiny minority. Most would have agreed with Myron Eells, a Boise minister, who noted glumly that no more than a dozen families of his community avoided altogether the kiss of King Alcohol.[9]

There is plenty of evidence of heavy drinking on the mining frontier. Dwellers in the camps, like the rider on the stage to Leadville, may have been fond of "filling up their bowels with bad whiskee," but that fact alone does not add much to our understanding of life in the Rockies. Specifically, what conditions encouraged those in the mountains to turn to drink, and what were the social consequences when they did? The first question, at least, can be approached somewhat systematically. If their everyday lives lead persons to look for liquor, if they find plenty of it near at hand, and if they encounter many chances to indulge, the result will be a society of high alcoholic consumption. The mining towns of the Rocky Mountains were characterized by all of these factors.

Of the three parts of the equation, the first is the most difficult to evaluate. What social conditions encouraged individuals to drink alcoholic beverages in large amounts? The imposing body of medical, sociological, and anthropological literature that addresses this question can provide some helpful suggestions that shed light on conditions of the mining frontier. In highly competitive societies that stress individual success, liquor can alleviate for a while the frustration of unfulfilled hopes. Gatherings of competitive, extremely mobile individuals are by their nature highly unstable, and in them group drinking can provide a feeling of association and a sense of belonging. Two sociologists recently described drinking under these circumstances as a "timeout," a temporary easing of the demands and a momentary escape from the conditions created by prevailing values of society. Yet the same competition, mobility, and instability that encourage mass drinking also leave these societies without the deeply rooted moral consensus, backed by family and church, that in the past has effectively controlled the disorder that often follows when liquor is consumed in large amounts. The same conditions that encourage excessive drinking make it more difficult to cope with its undesirable results. Thus heavy drinking is promoted, and its problems exaggerated, among groups of competitive men on the move who are free of traditional restraints—exactly the kind of society to be found in the new mining towns of the Rockies.[10]

The collection of humanity drawn to the isolated urban frontier of the Rockies was a richly cosmopolitan one, but there were limits to its diversity. The populace was overwhelmingly white, and most of the European-born came from northwestern Europe. The substantial numbers of Chinese who made their way to the northern Rockies and Arizona were systematically excluded from the mainstream of society. But within these limits a polyglot mixture of men of varied origins sought their fortunes in the gold fields. "The streets are thronged with robust miners, hailing from all climes and countries," a correspondent wrote from Bear Gulch, Montana:

Old England's sons mingling with those from the "Green Isle of the Sea," Italy and Spain's "suavite" and French "naivete," with the muddled tongue and stern purpose of Germany, South Carolina's cotton planter joining labor with Massachusetts weavers in bringing forth the precious metals from the virgin earth of our virgin Territory.[11]

Federal census reports confirm this journalist's impressions. Of a sample of just under three thousand adults living in fifteen mining towns of the Rockies, a little more than half (55.6 percent) were born in the United States. Of the rest, a quarter (25.6 percent) came originally from England, Ireland, or Germany, and the remainder looked back to homelands in Italy, France, Poland, Switzerland, Hungary, Scandinavia, South America, China, and many other parts of the world.[12]

Only a minority (33.7 percent) were miners, with about a tenth more (9.4 percent) working as common laborers. The rest came to "mine the miners," providing goods and services or seeking profit in the frenzy of speculation over claims and town lots. A typical cross section of a camp, one editor wrote, showed "thirty active miners, ten merchants and saloon keepers, five mechanics, fifty loafers, gamblers and fancy men. Lousy with lawyers, pettifoggers and scrub doctors."[13]

It was a young man's society that gathered at the diggings. The median age of the adults in this sample was just over thirty-three years, and almost eight of ten persons were men (78.8 percent). This sexual imbalance was even greater during the early life of a camp. An informal census of Owyhee County, Idaho, in 1864 revealed only fifty females over the age of eighteen out of a population of 1,425—less than 4 percent. Many who lived in such a place must have sympathized with the author of this scrap of miners's doggerel:

> When weary I are
> I smokes my cigar:
> And when the smoke rises
> Up into my eyeses,
> I thinks of my true love,
> And, O, how I sighses.[14]

The law of supply and demand naturally enhanced the social value of women, but, ironically, this exaggerated respect may have actually weakened the institution of the family on the mining frontier. Where her charms—and labor—were in such demand, a woman not infrequently was tempted to exchange her husband for a companion more to her liking. Critics of the day, however, showed less concern over any decline of feminine morality than with the erosion of social values due to the scarcity of women and settled home life. "Left by themselves, men degenerate rapidly and become rough, harsh, slovenly—almost brutish," the Reverend William Goode observed after visiting Colorado's Clear Creek mines. Frank Hall, Colorado editor and historian of early Central City, went even farther and concluded that a collection of many men and few women simply cannot maintain any system of civil order.[15]

Hall's sweeping judgment nonetheless neglected probably the most important of all the barriers facing those trying to establish traditional moral guidelines: the restless, ever-moving nature of mining camp society. This instability grew inevitably from the economic and emotional underpinnings of the early-day towns. Those who came to the Rockies from California or across the plains, whether prospectors or others bound to capitalize on the needs of the gold seekers, all were united by a speculative and optimistic view of life. They were held in one spot only by the anticipation of quick profits, and when another place boded better, they were gone. What a clover field was to a steer, and a mudhole to a hog, the *Portland Oregonian* suggested somewhat indelicately, such were new diggings to these men. This attitude produced some of the most transitory gatherings in the history of the nation. A study of two California gold camps during the early 1850s demonstrates that only six years after the birth of these towns fully 95 percent of the original inhabitants had left, and there is no reason to believe that the experience in the Rocky Mountains was much different. Men tried to establish a semblance of common identity by living with others from their place of origin and by forming clubs, lodges, and political organizations. Leadville in 1880, for example, had Texas, Omaha, Pacific Coast, Michigan, and New England societies, clusters of men using past regional ties to provide moorings in the chaotic present.[16] But these groupings proved as impermanent as all other social contacts during the initial stages of the mining frontier.

Such a restless gathering seemed less a community than a swarm. Where some saw "an air of life and bustle which is pleasing to witness," others found "a fierce and turbulent cauldron" of "excitable, nomadic, reckless, unmanageable" multitudes. This impression of turbulence was present in all towns and almost overpowering in the most prosperous, especially Leadville. Visitors compared the eager, milling crowds on the main streets of the largest camp in the Rockies to a perpetual Fourth of July and circus day, and "a Monaco gambling room emptied into a Colorado spruce clearing."[17] These conditions, if sometimes exciting, could repel those who valued close and lasting ties of friends and family. After her stay in Leadville, the Victorian novelist Mary Hallock Foote wrote of the terrible spiritual toll exacted from those adrift in "that senseless, rootless place."[18]

In this quicksilver society, any attempt to create a compelling community consensus would be hindered by yet another factor—the predominance of materialistic values. Mining towns were among the supreme expressions of an age of economic individualism. The first arrivals in particular journeyed to the mountains with a get-it-and-get-out philosophy. Even those who came out of simple curiosity found themselves caught up in the bonanza spirit. "It is almost impossible not to partake of the general enthusiasm," wrote Demas Barnes of the Colorado fields:

You hear the turning of the water wheels, the puffing of the engines, the pounding of the stamps, the clatter of the pans—you see the steam of the retort and assay—you hold the pure golden nuggets in your hands, your eyes dilate, your mouth waters . . . . Dear reader, it is hard to break the charm.[19]

Unfortunately, infatuated gold seekers soon discovered a yawning gap between their expectations and reality. Only an infinitesimal minority stumbled on a true bonanza, and most found that backbreaking, monotonous labor was required to provide the barest necessities in a market with prices bloated by scarcity and high transportation costs. The most promising claims were quickly controlled by wealthy investors who had the capital to tap their true potential. Some disappointed fortune seekers remained as wage workers for the larger companies. Many others, however, fit the description of one observer—a "class who prefer uncertain chances while working for themselves, to a certain income to be derived from the receipts from daily labor from others."[20] Most of these left, in the phrase of the day, with eyes dry, pockets ditto, and returned to the East or wandered on to the next strike.

Where even ministers and doctors "make extreme love with the pickax and shovel," scant attention was given to ethical concerns that did not involve individual enterprise. Those immigrants trying to preserve other moral principles, like Lafayette Bristow, a merchant of Idaho's Salmon River mines, discovered they were a minority amid "a rough unsympathyseing Society, who are all Scrambling for gold." Even this gentleman may have been speaking with the bitterness of dashed hopes, for he had come to the mines sure of making a fortune selling socks to miners, only to discover that someone had already covered the market. Now as he looked at the men around him he found that "all the finer feelings of ones nature . . . become Dedened or roughly seared by coming in contact with them."[21] Given this prevailing attitude, residents of mining towns proved largely indifferent to anything as ephemeral as moral stewardship and public rectitude.

"If 'Labor is worship' this is a most worshipful community," wrote a young wife from Montana's first gold strike, "but of any other kind . . . there is no public manifestation whatever."[22] Despite this complaint, ministers did arrive in many camps soon after the first strikes were made, and the argonauts greeted them with reasonable respect. Yet in retrospect it appears that those who attended these first services may have been more interested in entertainment than in salvation. Certainly the clergymen themselves complained often enough of the irreligion they faced among their new flocks. "Alas! deary, the men seem to be *all* demoralized," the young Episcopal minister Daniel Tuttle wrote to his wife of what he found in Montana in 1867. "The longer I live here . . . the more *deeply* bad . . . do I find the entire community to be."[23] Occasional sermons by a few itinerant ministers probably had a limited effect on men engaged in a frantic search for fortune far away from home and family.

One more fact of life of the mining camp should be noted. Despite an appearance of frenzied activity and vitality, the diggings could also be terribly boring and lonely places. Travelers and writers who gave their attention to the more prosperous camps overlooked the rather dismal existence in the many smaller settlements of the Rockies. The monotony of labor, the absence of entertainment, and isolation from friends and relations all tested even the strongest personality. "It is curious to notice the perfect forlornness of the mountain settlements," one tourist wrote of the bleak communities he passed through in southern Colorado. "It is a distinctly higher order of miserableness than any other regions can afford."[24] In all towns, large or small, life slowed considerably during the long winters. Confined indoors by the weather, residents who remained were hard-pressed for any sort of diversion. An exasperated reporter summarized the situation:

1. With its cheats and gamblers, knife-wielding ruffians, tired fiddlers, and pathetic barefoot man wagering his pocket watch, this scene from early Denver was a moral essay in pen and ink. *Courtesy of the Colorado Historical Society*

No news. Cold weather. . . . Town too dull to raise an interesting poker game. Vigilantes won't hang anybody. Everybody is froze up or froze out or snowed under. What the devil am I going to do?[25]

These, then, were the prevalent characteristics of society on the mining frontier, and their general outline jibes closely with conditions that traditionally have encouraged men to drink excessively. In a land dominated by competition and materialistic values, amid a heterogeneous collection of young men of disparate backgrounds in almost continual movement from place to place, individuals might well have felt a powerful need to drink together to face disappointment and foster feelings of companionship and a sense of association. Here were societies of chance and change, life with few moorings, and many of the members could be expected to seek out the ready fellowship of the bottle.

Circumstances that encouraged the consumption of alcohol meant nothing if residents of mining towns had nothing to drink. All accounts, however, make clear that anyone in search of strong refreshment need not have looked far. Practically from the beginning, a ready supply of many kinds of intoxicants satisfied the second prerequisite of a hard-drinking society—availability.

"By all means take some whiskey." As this advice from a veteran of plains travel to a party setting out for Montana suggests, those who had acquired a taste for liquor did not hesitate to carry an ample supply with them westward, and there was plenty to be had in the grogshops and wholesale houses of the rough settlements of the Missouri Valley. All around them immigrants saw experienced hands drinking as part of the daily ritual of travel—a stage driver pulling on a bottle as he manipulated the reins, a mule packer reaching for a flask in a leather pouch slung over the saddle horn, and even the wagon train guide himself. One leader, in fact, threatened to take his charges into hostile Indian territory unless his rum ration was increased. Travelers packed whiskey jugs in their wagons and handcarts alongside stores of jerked beef, flour, pans, and picks. They drank to celebrate special occasions, but most of all simply to ease the strain of a long day of difficult labor. "If whiskey often and much is an element of success, we lack for nothing," wrote one traveler sarcastically, "for all from the head of the Command down . . . drink deep and long."[26]

Along the route west were isolated pockets of Anglo settlement, military posts, and an occasional roadhouse or "ranch," and there too wilderness merchants offered ardent spirits for sale to weary travelers. Accompanying the flood of fifty-niners to Colorado, Horace Greeley came upon a grocery by a creek crossing in far western Kansas, and he entered it eagerly in search of a fresh meal. The *Tribune* editor quickly discovered the limits of the proprietor's inventory.

"Have you any crackers?"
"Nary cracker."
"Any bread?"
"Any what?"
"Bread."
"No, *Sir*, (indignantly), "I don't keep a bakery."
"Any ham?"
"No."
"Well what *have* you?"

"Why I have sardines, pickled oysters, smoking tobacco, and stranger, I have got some of the best whiskey you ever seen since you was born!"[27]

Drinking, at least, was one tradition that made the passage to the frontier with remarkable ease. One early Denver saloonkeeper, in fact, complained that the freshest arrivals brought so much of the ardent with them that they never entered his doors except to ask for water. When these personal supplies were drained, however, the thirsty could draw upon deep local reservoirs sufficient to meet a hearty demand. In the far southern reaches of the mountains, miners could find mescal, made from maguey, and other indigenous drinks. A flourishing distilling operation in northern New Mexico that earlier had supplied fur traders with whiskey met the needs of the first Anglo miners in Arizona, and when word arrived of the strike on Cherry Creek, traders immediately set out to greet the first-comers to Colorado with wagonloads of "Taos Lightning," a distilled liquor of uncertain composition but well-documented, spectacular results when drunk by frontiersmen.[28]

Camps outside the reach of these southern sources of supply, however, were thrown upon their own devices. Although some persons made cider and a variety of wines from fruits and wild berries, most took a more direct approach to furnish their needs. Raw alcohol carried in from the states was doctored with chemicals and other ingredients at hand. One recipe, for example, instructed:

To one gallon of alcohol, five gallons of water, one pound of red pepper (to make it whizz as it runs down your throat) one pound of old government oravy tobacco to give it color and flavor, add two pounds of brown sugar and I'll guarantee it to distribute as much happiness as anything an Indian can get hold of.[29]

The colorful nicknames given this liquor—forty-rod (because it could kill from that distance), extract of scorpions, chain lightning, and San Juan paralyzer, to name a few—show that almost immediately its wretched quality became part of frontier folklore. Nonetheless, because of the demand for any strong refreshment in the early camps, residents adopted the caveat emptor philosophy expressed by a visitor to Idaho in 1861: "It is counted no murder to sell [whiskey] to a man if he survives long enough to get out of doors."[30]

Eventually Colorado and Idaho legislators imposed harsh penalties on anyone caught adulterating liquors. But although clandestine production of rotgut continued to supply the lowest deadfalls, intoxicants of a higher quality began to appear on the frontier remarkably early. Liquor was high in value in relation to its bulk. That basic economic fact, combined with excessive demand, made reasonably good whiskey an item of freighting as attractive as sturdy work boots and tempered ax heads. So only five months after the first wagonload of Taos Lightning arrived at the site of Colorado's initial gold strike, a participant wrote home that Kentucky bourbon was driving the raw New Mexican wheat whiskey from the market, and by the following Christmas, miners washed down their holiday dinners with an astonishing array of potables. In fact, once any mining town showed that it might well survive, its saloons soon began to advertise well-known brands of whiskey from Kentucky, Pennsylvania, and Ireland, gin from England, rum from the West Indies, and wines from California, Missouri, and abroad. Later rail connections only facilitated the trade that liquor merchants had carried on almost from the beginning.[31]

Contrary to the popular image of rough-hewn Westerners standing at the bar and tossing down jiggers of whiskey right from the bottle, miners often preferred elaborately mixed drinks. Some bartenders specialized in such things, and these "mixologists" were featured prominently in advertisements. While some of their concoctions were of Eastern origin, others, including the martini, were born of the fertile imaginations of saloonmen operating on the Pacific coast and in the Rockies. Regardless of the genealogy of these mixed drinks, mining camp topers embraced them as their own—iced creations in the summer, Tom and Jerrys and toddies in the winter, and juleps, smashes, cocktails, punches, cobblers, and sours all year long.[32]

After the Civil War, lager beer proved increasingly attractive to American tastes, and those on the mining frontier were not immune. Breweries on the last fringes of Eastern civilization offered cooling draughts of the foaming beverage to persons heading West, and those same immigrants likely would find more of the same waiting for them in the mountains. Unlike distilled liquors, beer could not be transported from east to west until late in the century because of problems of bulk and spoilage. Frontier brewers moved quickly to fill the need of miners, but in the absence of the usual equipment and ingredients, they often had to be quite innovative. The first beer marketed in Montana reportedly was made from wheat, sorghum, and the tops of spruce trees, and one of the territory's earliest breweries was a makeshift affair of whiskey barrels and sheet iron. Unshackled by traditional techniques, producers often would be selling their goods only a fortnight after construction had begun, and the Miner's Brewery of Idaho City reopened for business exactly one week after burning to the ground.[33]

The quality of the products from these places can only be imagined, but as with distilled liquors, a higher quality of beer soon was available in most towns. German brewers opened small mountain breweries in towns throughout the Rockies, and a few key points became major distribution centers. By the middle of the 1860s Denver was shipping beer to camps along the Front Range, and Helena, Boise, and Tucson later emerged as suppliers of growing regional markets. In the 1880s, the mammoth brewers of Saint Louis and Milwaukee took advantage of steadily improving transportation and innovations in sterilization and bottling to tap a vast Western market. Most mountain dwellers then enjoyed a choice of local and regional brew as well as Schlitz, Pabst, and "Anheuser's cough syrup."[34]

The men and women who came to the Rocky Mountain frontier thus had access at virtually all times to intoxicating beverages of many kinds and varying quality. Easy to make and profitable to carry, liquor was a product of some of the area's earliest manufacturing and a favorite burden of mountain freighters. The westering miner might have had to give up some indulgences of his past life, but drinking was one habit he could keep.

The third and final element of the equation remains to be discussed. Circumstances might incline men toward the bottle. Liquor might be found in abundance. But a truly hard-drinking society still had to bring together these first two factors, to unite the desire and the thing desired. In mining towns, in fact, a multitude of occasions and rituals provided almost continuous opportunities for men to drink. So closely entwined was drinking with the day-to-day social contacts of men on the mining frontier that all but the most steadfastly temperate were tempted to wet their whistles, sometimes to the point of oversaturation.

An elaborate body of folklore encouraged miners to drink, if for no other reason, because alcohol supposedly promoted good health. Near the end of the thirteenth century, Europeans heard the first defense of distilled liquor, aqua vitae, as a marvelous potion that extended the life of the drinker. Since then alcohol had been proposed as the cure for a whole catalogue of maladies from lung disorders to excessive gas. Miners carried all these beliefs with them and added a few of their own. Even those who frowned on social drinking acknowledged the medical uses of alcohol. "I had pretty serious times with my bowels for some hours," the Reverend Tuttle wrote his wife after a meal of pork and beans. "But endurance and Jamaica jinger [a patent medicine of high alcoholic content] . . . bro't me thro' well." Many believed liquor necessary to survive the demanding climate of the mountains and the air polluted by fumes from smelters. Others argued that the most abominable whiskey was safer to drink than water from streams fouled by sewage and muddied by placer mining, and indeed saloon sales declined noticeably in Leadville after sanitary hydrant water was introduced.[35]

Liquor had other practical uses as well. Mountaineers used it as a medium of exchange to pay for room and board and to buy lumber for sluices. Such a popular item made an obvious gift, as the proper young wife Mollie Sanford discovered in Gold Hill, Colorado, when an admiring Irish neighbor presented her with a flask for Christmas, saying, "It's thinkin' we did that ye might nade it in case of sickness, or snakebite, ye know." Charles Poston of Arizona put his whiskey to perhaps its most unusual use when he substituted it for holy water for the baptism of his workers' children.[36]

In most cases, however, men relied on intoxicants to enliven moments of social contact. Perhaps to help forge bonds of companionship among competitive men of diverse backgrounds, a bottle was

2. The Fourth of July was an occasion to celebrate with a drink. This saloon in Arizona, draped with flags and bunting, featured cloths to wipe mustaches clean of beer foam and a mesh mat for better traction on a floor wet with spilled liquor. *Courtesy of the Arizona Historical Society*

called forth on most public and many private occasions. Religious and patriotic observances especially encouraged much carousing. "Al [l] holidays are selibrated here by being or geting drunk," the sheriff of Neihart, Montana, wrote his mother wearily on New Year's Eve, 1884. "It would be a very common afair and dull time with out a shooting a fair for doxoligy."[37]

Coming almost exactly half a year apart, Christmas and Independence Day gave miners a chance to expel months of tension and frustration. Probably because of winter's boredom and the sentimental memories the season evoked, Yuletide especially filled saloons with men drinking cold-weather drinks like hot toddies and Tom and Jerrys as well as their usual fare. The Fourth of July provided an occasion to pause in the midst of the busiest season of the year. Considering the amounts of cool lager and iced drinks consumed, is it any wonder that references to drinking found their way into the rhetoric of the day?

Lovers of Liberty and beer,
We welcome you from far and near,
We welcome you around this rag,
To shout for freedom while we brag.

All honor to our brave Squedunks,
All honor to our brave dead-drunks!
Some are groveling in the gutter,
While some have gone home on a shutter.[38]

 Residents of early mining towns seemed to regard political campaigns as another kind of holiday during which they could escape their daily drudgery, and on these occasions too liquor played a prominent part. ''Oh Father above! In mercy guide and rule our rulers!'' prayed the Reverend Tuttle after attending a Democratic rally in Virginia City, Montana, addressed by politicians full of Irish whiskey. Candidates considered whiskey the standard coin of the realm with which to buy support, and intoxicants were not unknown to the supposedly more solemn judicial process—at least one Idaho judge had to admonish his grand jury for their free use of liquor during their deliberations.[39]

 Traditional rites of passage furnished opportunities for further indulging. Births and marriages, as affirmations of life's renewal in a society of transience and change, occasioned particularly joyous celebration, while death brought men together in alcoholic mourning. One group of Irish miners, in fact, emerged from a wake in a Montana saloon so bleary-eyed and head-sore that they managed to lose their friend's corpse on the way to its burial.[40]

 Those few who struck it rich traditionally treated friends, and occasionally the entire town, to a drinking spree. Almost any event—the arrival or departure of old companions, the opening of a mill or a business, the discussion of an issue of local concern—might be accompanied by social drinking that could range from a single round of beers to a full-blown ''Rocky Mountain hoodoo.'' No occasion was too unlikely. When the Episcopal bishop Ethelbert Talbot arrived at the remote Idaho camp of Clayton Gulch, a besotted miner assured him that the men of the town stood in dire need of preaching to correct their misbehavior, especially their drunkenness. When Talbot observed testily that his new acquaintance was guilty himself, the man readily agreed: "You are right . . . , but don't you see when the Bishop comes a feller just has to celebrate."[41]

In fact, little excuse was needed to pull a cork. Most social drinking took place in saloons and cramped cabins as part of informal gatherings, chance meetings, or the welcoming of a new arrival. "It amused me intensely to hear this sort of thing repeated from rosy morn to dewey eve," reported a Leadville correspondent of *Leslie's Illustrated*. " 'How is business?' a newcomer asks. 'Business is fine,' is the reply; 'Come and take a drink.' "[42] At the close of a day's labors, prospectors met to discuss their efforts and to share their experiences over a jigger of corn. "It is a custom of some of the b'hoys to 'irrigate' to a considerable extent, when they strike a big bonanza," a Colorado editor observed, then added with a wink, "Some of them strike one every day."[43]

Given the competitive, turbulent conditions of the mining frontier and the availability of liquor, the frequency of occasions when men might drink supplied the final of the three requisites of a hard-drinking society. The result was a way of life noted by the Frenchman Louis Simonin during his visit to Colorado in 1867. Not only in saloons but also in stores, hotels, and banks, he wrote, "one partakes freely, several times a day, of the sacramental glass of whiskey."[44]

The drinking habits of the mining frontiersmen were not, however, without their unfortunate effects. If the motives and causes of crime, violence, disorder, and personal suffering were varied, liquor certainly was associated with many problems of the mining towns of the Rockies.

Ironically, many of the same conditions that encouraged the widespread indulgence in alcohol also severely undermined the forces that traditionally controlled the excesses of social drinking. The perceptive traveler Julian Ralph observed of Montana:

Men without the restraint of law, indifferent to public opinion, and unburdened by families, drink whenever they feel like it, whenever they have the money to pay for it, and whenever there is nothing else to do. . . . Bad manners follow, profanity becomes a matter of course. . . . Excitability and nervousness brought on by rum help these tendencies along, and then to correct this state of things the pistol comes into play.[45]

Ralph seems to confirm the conclusions of modern researchers discussed earlier. If the maintenance of a community's ethical standards, in particular the comportment of its drinking members, relies on a moral matrix of church, family, long-standing personal relationships, and well-established and respected spokesmen who draw the line between right and wrong, it would be hard to imagine conditions less promising than those in the settlements of the Rockies.

The impact of this social environment is suggested by the delightful diary of James Knox Polk Miller. Shortly after his arrival in Virginia City, Montana, in 1865, the nineteen-year-old New Yorker solemnly resolved to live frugally and not to spend a penny on billiards, tobacco, or liquor. Two days later he bought five gallons of beer and shortly thereafter confessed to drinking thirteen Tom and Jerrys during a billiards match. Soon a contrite Miller renewed his vow of clean living, but again he fell to drinking beer and carousing. The battle between the young man's impulses and his conscience continued until he left for the East in 1867.[46] Like Miller, many coltish immigrants out to see the world surely were tempted to taste the exotic life of the frontier, but when inhibitions were relaxed on a mass scale, the results could be far from happy.

The extent of violence in general and of homicide in particular on the frontier almost certainly has been exaggerated. Much of the brawling and killing that did occur, however, was associated in some way with the drinking of alcohol. Creede, Colorado, provides a case in point. Although a Chicago journalist gravely described the camp as "a turbulent sea of conflicting vices violently lashing the shores of peace and order," no murders occurred among the few thousand men gathered there for the first several months after the rush began in the late fall of 1891. Then on April 1, 1892, one Billie Wall left Grayman's Saloon after several drinks, walked the street, and began vomiting in the gutter. A drunken man standing nearby laughed and taunted Wall: "Puke, you son of a bitch!" When Wall replied in kind, the other man pulled a pistol and murdered him.[47]

Many mining camp homicides fit this pattern—random, apparently unpremeditated, and implying irrational tempers aroused by

3. Playful patrons in this Arizona drinking spot mimicked the saloon's violent image already familiar to the public by the late nineteenth century. *Courtesy of the Arizona Historical Society*

prolonged drinking. Those who committed murder with some motive and forethought, furthermore, often acted under the influence of liquor. Between March and October of 1880, newspaper files show only fourteen murders among the fifteen or twenty thousand residents of Leadville. Economic disputes over claims or debts accounted for three of them, four involved jealousy or sexual conflict, and the other seven either arose from unknown causes or resulted from the same sort of purposeless rage that left Billie Wall dying in a Creede gutter. In at least half of these killings, one or both parties involved had been drinking heavily.[48] A close look at any mining town during its early days probably would reveal a similar story.

Serious assaults and brawls seem to have been even more closely associated with excessive drinking. While some tavern fights were mere shoving matches, others left combatants with cracked skulls and with noses, ears, or fingers bitten off. A two-man scrap could escalate into a pitched melee that destroyed buildings and turned a business street into a battlefield. Regardless of the immediate causes of these fracases, the participants in virtually all cases had been drinking heavily before the violence began.[49] Liquor frequently was associated with robberies, not because drunken men preyed upon others, but because footpads lifted money and valuables from men lying unconscious in alleys and backrooms after a long night's carousal.

Since the earliest residents usually regarded their surroundings not as a place to build a better life but as a resource to exploit and leave, they looked on lesser mayhem and disorder with the kind of amusement expressed by an editor who commented that no one should expect hard-working, hard-drinking men to have the habits of Quakers. As a result, peace officers had to deal with many minor violations of public order encouraged by this live-and-let-live attitude. And among these lesser crimes, an astonishing portion had to do with drinking and its unruly effects. Note, for example, the monthly report of the city marshal of Telluride, Colorado, in the spring of 1888:

April 20	John Hoffman	Arrested for Drunkenness	Turned Loose
April 23	James Murray	Found dead drunk	Locked up overnight
May 1	Charles _____	Drunk & disorderly	Fined $10
May 3	Andrew Golson	Drunk & disorderly	Fined $5
May 3	Mike Peterson	Drunk & resisting officer	Fined $5
May 3	Gus Robenson	Drunk & disorderly	Fined $5
May 12	Louis Graham	Drunk & disorderly	Fined $20
May 4	John Dewey	Drunk & sleeping on street	Discharged
May 6	John Quinn	Drunk & noisy	Discharged
May 9	Fritz Bursted	Drunk	Discharged

The police dockets of Georgetown and Silverton, Colorado, show that almost six out of ten persons arrested for misdemeanors during these towns' early years were charged with public drunkenness, while about four of every ten arrests during the first year after the incorporation of Virginia City were for the same crime.[50] So frequent were such arrests in Leadville that the town newspaper used the abbreviation "d. & d." for "drunk and disorderly" to save space and type in reporting each night's crimes.

The term "disorderly," however, concealed a multitude of sins. Particularly alarming were those who punctuated their evening's fun by shooting their handguns into the air. "There are times when it is really unsafe to go through the main street on the other side of the creek, the bullets whizz around so," a young woman wrote from Bannock, Montana, in 1862, and an Idaho merchant built a four-foot wall of flour bags around his bed each evening as protection from stray shots of drunken men. Occasionally this gunfire wounded or killed innocent bystanders. Almost as irritating and dangerous were intoxicated riders who spurred their horses crazily down a town's crowded streets and sidewalks.[51]

More common was drunken revelry that disturbed the serenity of the camp. A correspondent in Quartzburg, Idaho, told of his fruitless efforts to rest during a noisy drinking bout in a nearby saloon that culminated when a prostitute began singing raucously in a voice "as soothing as a steam whistle." Her performance ended when a male companion hit another whore on the head with a pick handle. The brawl that followed ended only with the intervention of the U.S. marshal. The next day, the saloon owner commented that the previous night had been the quietest in weeks, and he congratulated the town on its improving moral condition.[52] This experience was far from unique. Editorials and letters from readers complained frequently of rowdy men and women who spilled from saloons and dance halls, yelling obscenities, performing lewd dances in the streets, and rousing the sober from sleep with singing the writers compared to the braying of donkeys and the wailing of lost souls. As a final complication, law officers and firemen sometimes proved to be too fond of the bottle themselves to be of much use.[53]

The crime rate, however, measured only the most socially obnoxious results of drinking. Alcohol added to personal problems and tragedies as well. Newspaper editors frequently advised their readers on the pitfalls of drink, sometimes with editorials and on other occasions with Franklinesque aphorisms—"In drinking the 'good health'

of your friends, see that you don't swallow your own"—and somewhat maudlin poetry:

> Beware of liquor! Fifty deaths I died—
> Losing in turn hope energy and pride . . .
> I reached that goal of agony and sin—
> A drunkard's grave—and blindly staggered in.[54]

In one way, liquor could pose an immediate threat to the life of the
unwary miner. A veteran of the gold fields once advised newcomers
never to start a winter journey in the mountains with a supply of liquor,
for they might end up, quite literally, stiff. The myth that alcohol
warmed the body led many to nip frequently while hiking through the
snow-choked woods. Actually, liquor reduces the body temperature
and acts as a depressant, eventually producing a deep sleep when taken
in quantity. Frozen corpses provided journalists occasions to pontifi-
cate on the folly of drunkenness. Even in Leadville, police regularly
rescued from probable death intoxicated men who had passed out in
alleys during the most frigid months of the year.[55]

In addition, because of an ironic biological fact, strong drink
constituted a more gradual but far more common hazard to health.
Alcohol is a rich source of concentrated energy, but it contains no
vitamins or minerals and, unlike virtually all other foods, its energy
cannot be stored. To the hard-pressed miner, the caloric burst of a
glass of corn offered the illusion of cheap nourishment. Unable to
afford inflated food prices, the poorest laborers and vagabonds too
often "drank their meals" and thus starved their bodies and weakened
their resistance to disease. This habit contributed especially to the
great killer of the mountains, pneumonia, and increased the danger of
exposure. After months of living on liquor and little else, a man might
lie down in a hut or a barroom corner and simply never wake up. Such
alcohol-related deaths were attributed vaguely to "black tongue disease," congestion of the brain, general dissipation, unknown causes,
or "too much whiskey for this altitude."[56]

Others who drank heavily followed a path to slow degradation.
Residents of the camps saw a side of life often unrepresented in the
romanticized histories of the period. A close reading of the contem-

porary evidence reveals not only the good times of sports, dances, and harmless entertainments but also a seaminess that appalled even the more hardened observers—a widow, nearly seventy, found drunk and sobbing in the mud of a street; men who drank up a lifetime's savings in a few months; a cripple hobbling from mine to mine begging money for a binge; a haggard wife whose mind was continually muddled by liquor and morphine; and victims of delirium tremens wallowing in the sawdust of a saloon floor or trying to cut their own throats to escape imaginary demons. In the frustration and despair of broken dreams, some turned to the final escape of suicide, and in many of these cases, prolonged drinking apparently deepened the depression that ended in the ultimate act of hopelessness.[57]

Social conditions and the abundance of liquor not only allowed the custom of drinking to survive on the mining frontier; they also encouraged a level of drunkenness that probably exceeded significantly that of the East and Europe. Drinking helped meet genuine psychological needs, but it contributed as well to public disorder and personal suffering. Whatever their result, these facts established the saloon business. Men drank on the streets, in their tents and cabins, and within shops and stores, but the main arena of elbow-bending always was the barroom. There alcohol would perform its needed functions and work its mischief. As the scene of much of a town's drinking life and many of its social activities, the saloon first should be described.

2

The Conspicuous Feature
of the Streets

THE trio of miners stomped the snow and mud from their boots before
pushing their way through the door and into the Board of Trade
Saloon. Just inside was a counter displaying cigars for sale, but all
three went quickly to the long bar to their right and ordered shots of
whiskey. As they drank they could look at the magnificent back bar
and see reflected in the large diamond-dust mirror others of their
kind—hard-handed working men of Leadville relaxing and sipping
from jiggers and steins. At the tables opposite the bar, men laughed
and swore as they played cards, while through a door to the rear came
the music of a band and voices of others risking their wages in games
of faro and keno. The room was well lighted by several kerosene
lamps, and through a haze of tobacco smoke those at the bar scanned
an assortment of decorations—prints of muscular boxers, a stuffed
deer, drawings of a few demure young ladies in bonnets and two
nudes, and several chromos advertising familiar brands of whiskey
and beer. At dawn these men would head for the mines up Stray Horse
Gulch, but now it was only ten o'clock and the saloon was warm and
the talk and whiskey good. With the wind whistling out of the north
down Harrison Avenue outside, it was a good place to spend the
evening.

The scene and atmosphere in this prominent Leadville resort were
not much different from those in thousands of other places across the
nation. "The main difference between the drinking habits in America
and our own country is this," wrote the British traveler David Macrae
in the 1850s, "the Americans drink more at bars and less at home."[1]

25

Whether or not Macrae's generalization was accurate, by the middle of the nineteenth century the saloon had emerged as an important and almost unavoidable American social institution. The barrooms that appeared in great variety and abundance on the Rocky Mountain frontier were Western representatives of a national phenomenon that was itself the product of a long evolution. Nonetheless, if the saloon in Telluride or Orogrande shared some characteristics with its cousins in Boston or Chicago, its story also told something of the town and society that nurtured it. It is best understood as a product both of past developments and its contemporary setting.

A full institutional history of the American saloon would begin with the waning of the Middle Ages, those generations when a mercantilist, urban society began to emerge on the continent. With this change came a new pattern of public drinking. Before, all segments and classes of a community drank together publicly as part of a communal celebration of holidays and festivals. Now, reflecting the social fragmentation and occupational specialization, individuals gathered regularly in a chosen place to drink with others of similar backgrounds and situations. The new society demanded a new institution as the site of this group drinking: the inn. Gradually the inn evolved into several variations, reflecting Europe's cultural diversity—the wine shop of the Mediterranean coast, the German beer hall, the café and cabaret of France, and the English public house, or pub.[2]

The American variation of this phenomenon descended from the English. Called "ordinaries" during the early colonial period and "taverns" during the revolutionary and early national years, drinking houses fell into two categories. Those found in rural or small-town settings offered meals and lodging as well as a place for convivial tippling and conversation. As the frontier advanced first across the Appalachians and then beyond the Mississippi, the country tavern continued to serve as a welcome refuge for weary travelers in search of bed and board. In the early cities a new type of American drinking house flourished. "The tavern as a place of resort for all classes exceeded any other urban institution in importance," Carl Bridenbaugh has written of the city scene on the eve of the Revolution.

"There town life came to a focus." As other businesses provided food and lodging, the urban tavern became primarily a place of drinking, relaxation, and the bandying about of current gossip and public issues. Customers found little more in the way of furnishings than some sort of bar for the serving of refreshments and tables and chairs for lounging. Amid the proliferation of these places, new terms such as "groggery," "grogshop," and "doggery" described the less reputable, and alarmed moral leaders began to call for a limitation on their number and for regulation of their activities.[3]

The appellation "saloon" probably was designed to give a more respectable aura to the public house of the city at a time when it was drawing increasing criticism. Derived from the French *salon*, the term in both England and America of the eighteenth century described any large room for public meetings or entertainments, but in the New World it carried also a slightly aristocratic connotation. It smacked of gentility and restraint and quite proper behavior, not of drunken hod-carriers offending the public peace. Whatever the purpose behind its invention, two things can be said with certainty: "saloon" had entered the popular vocabulary to describe an urban drinking house at least as early as 1841, and by the end of the century this word in turn had come to conjure up visions of vice, filth, and slobbering drunkenness.[4]

The saloons that opened on the Rocky Mountain mining frontier between 1858 and 1900 naturally tended to resemble their Eastern contemporaries. Along prominent routes of travel, taverns offered drink, food, and a place to sleep. In the camps, miners drank in places similar to those in cities of the Atlantic coast and Ohio Valley. But if there was continuity East to West, so were there important and instructive distinctions.

In fact, if an observant and perceptive visitor had arrived at a mining camp during its early days and had remained to watch it prosper, he would have seen around him saloons that varied significantly in appearance, function, and degree of comfort. The physical evolution and diversification of the drinking house, that business which one visitor called "the conspicuous feature of the streets," paralleled the growth of the mining town and its search for a kind of order and maturity.[5] Whether building a town or a saloon, men strove to recreate patterns of an older, "settled" society, but they did so within the needs and limitations of an isolated frontier.

If a community survived, its drinking places underwent a three-stage transition that reflected the changes of the society they served. The first stage came during the several weeks after an initial strike was made. The resulting camp—it could hardly be called a town—had a chaotic, unfocused look that bespoke its rapid appearance. "This place impresses one as having gotten there before it was sent for," a visitor wrote of the gathering of miners at Rico in Colorado's San Juan region. Structures were built haphazardly, with little or no order. Prospectors located near their claims, and businessmen sought spots near the prospectors. As a result, there seemed no arrangement at all in a new settlement like Red Cliff, Colorado, described by a seasoned veteran in the winter of 1880 as a camp "in its most primitive mold, the streets being undefined, the business center uncertain, and the habitations of the crudest build."[6]

The "crudest build" referred to places constructed overnight of canvas, logs, or unseasoned lumber. Emphasis clearly was on speed of construction with investment kept to a minimum. The author Helen Hunt Jackson found the site of Leadville in 1879 still filled with the stumps of spruce trees, while the newly arrived miners lived in a motley collection of dwellings:

Tents; wigwams of boughs; wigwams of bare poles, with a blackened spot in front, where somebody slept last night, but will never sleep again; cabins wedged in between stumps; cabins with chimneys made of flowerpots or bits of stove pipe,—I am not sure but out of old hats; cabins half roofed; cabins with sail cloth-roofs; cabins with no roof at all,—this represented the architecture of the Leadville homes.[7]

Implied in such a picture was an element of doubt in the future, for all could be removed without much effort or abandoned with little loss.

These were the circumstances under which the first saloons opened. During a camp's first flush, drinking places differed little in their outward appearance from the dwellings and other businesses around them. In fact, a new arrival was likely to find a single enterprise combining the sale of liquor by the drink with several other lines

4. During a camp's first months, saloons often were combined with other businesses, such as bakeries, livery stables, and restaurants, as in this establishment in Thunder Mountain, Idaho. *Courtesy of the Idaho Historical Society*

of trade. With relatively few stores to serve a population that swelled daily, each retailer might take on a number of functions. Thus Jean and Jerry's Saloon in Globe, Arizona, advertised a barbershop and bathhouse available in the rear. A prospective customer must have been a bit wary of Fred Schwenk's Vinegar Factory and Saloon, but the Miner's Saloon and Bakery of early-day Denver was more inviting. The records of at least one livery stable include entries for the sale of whiskey shots and draughts of beer. In extreme cases, an all-purpose drinking place might provide for most of the material needs of the Rocky Mountaineer. Arriving in Gregory's Diggings, later Central City, one author found three tents joined together. A crude bar and two gambling tables dominated the interior. To one side was a tray of cakes, pies, and bread, and on the other a barber's chair, while at the entrance several pairs of boots, moccasins, and mittens hung for inspection. A sign over the front flap announced Milk for Sale. The owner, the author concluded, was undoubtedly "an enterprising Yankee."[8]

As this description also suggests, a town's first saloon usually had only the most rudimentary structure and facilities. In what might be considered the official opening of the Rocky Mountain mining frontier's liquor trade, Richens "Uncle Dick" Wootton, a veteran mountain man and trader, carried a load of Taos Lightning north from New Mexico to the miners along Cherry Creek in December, 1858. On a spot that would eventually become part of downtown Denver, he commenced the sale of intoxicants across a bar made from a row of barrels.[9] His timely arrival made for a lively Christmas celebration.

In these first saloons, the customer was concerned mainly with the availability of liquor and the social occasion of its consumption. The comfort of the surroundings and even the quality of the beverage, if not irrelevant, seemed less important. Charles F. Bennett of Arizona has left a rare firsthand view of how one of these early businesses was established. When he and a partner heard of a new strike at Gillette, Bennett immediately set out to open the camp's first drinking place. In Prescott he bought a ten-gallon keg of liquor—"it was wheat whiskey; it had something to it"—and upon arrival at the diggings he pitched a tent, set the keg on a rock, and began selling his wares at twenty-five cents a swallow.

Everybody wanted to know where that whiskey was—so I ordered some more—then I put up a shack and got some more liquor—they drank up everything but some extracts—and I buried them.[10]

A tent and a shack—obviously there was little to distinguish the facilities of men like Bennett from the crude dwellings his customers built of canvas and green wood. A tent was particularly practical, for the makings could be carried in with relative ease to avoid the delay and cost of constructing a cabin. When a rush to a camp was especially enthusiastic, the demand for building materials might push the price of lumber to $1.25 per foot, and a two-room cabin of sawed logs might cost $400. With canvas or heavy cloth, an owner with limited capital but with a determination to reach his market quickly could open a place like one described in Slaterville on Idaho's Clearwater River.

This community's only saloon featured a board with the name "Shawmut" on its front and "Whisky" written in charcoal on its sides.

This temple of Bacchus is about eight feet square, and is open at the side, giving a delightful coolness to the interior. The roof is composed of two red blankets and a blue one. We have here a patriotic combination of colors.[11]

If lumber were available and reasonably inexpensive, a rough shack could be built with only a bit more time and effort. In southern Arizona men could make do with four corner posts, perhaps five feet high, supporting a brush-covered latticework for a roof and without walls of any kind—literally a low overhead operation. Most of the mining frontier required greater protection from the elements. Nonetheless, if he were not overly concerned with the niceties of architecture, an owner could construct a low hut of logs or cheap lumber in a remarkably short time. One of the early saloons of Coeur d'Alene opened forty-eight hours after its proprietors began shoveling snow for its foundation. Typically, such places made do with packed earthen floors, cramped quarters, and poorly constructed, drafty walls. A variation took advantage of the landscape by extending walls and roof from the side of a hill or a cave. The Collar and Elbow saloon near Aspen, Colorado, for instance, had for its sides an exposed outcropping of quartz and a row of vertical logs topped by willow boughs, brush, and rye grass.[12]

Like the exteriors of these places, the furnishings were starkly utilitarian. A Boise journalist entered a tiny shack saloon in the new town of Eagle City to find only a sack of flour for a bar, a single bottle of "coffin varnish," a bucket of water, and two glasses, the larger of which a miner tried to grab before the barkeeper poured a drink in the smaller.[13] As the description indicates, some sort of bar where the liquor was poured and paid for seems to have been the one feature that was provided even when chairs and tables were not. A customer also could not expect much choice in "wet goods," for an owner either brought in whiskey and dipped it directly from the keg, or he mixed raw alcohol with various chemicals and sold his own concoction from a bottle on the bar. If the customer did not care for what was offered, he looked elsewhere or went home dry.

5. The bare essentials—a log cabin, bar of unfinished pine planks, a bench, and a few bottles of whiskey—satisfied these miners of North Park, Colorado. *Courtesy of the Amon Carter Museum, Fort Worth, Texas*

Soon enough, however, a prospering camp entered a second stage, wherein its residents had available better facilities for drinking and relaxation. If a settlement survived beyond its first weeks, both it and its watering spots began to take on a look of some permanence and pretentions. As an early hint of urban order, a system of streets and a distinct commercial district emerged. Whenever topography permitted, a grid of one to three principal business avenues and several cross streets was adopted. Otherwise streets branched off a stream running through the center of town, as in Silver Plume, Colorado, and Idaho's Ruby City, or they conformed to a winding gulch, as in Central City, Colorado.[14]

Along these thoroughfares more substantial structures gradually replaced the small tents and crude shacks, suggesting that a strike's promise had been fulfilled enough to justify a greater investment in the future. A builder might rely on the tested device of notched logs or the newer technique of nailing boards outside a simple "baloon" frame and covering the inside studding with cheap muslin. In either case, the greater size and more orderly arrangement of these places gave an impression that out of a rabble of fortune seekers a true town was being born.

Closer inspection, however, would reveal that the transformation was far from complete. A newcomer to Virginia City, Montana, in 1864 found the traditional symmetrical grid of streets, but the town itself was a "dreadful, dirty place." In such a settlement, the tents and hovels of fresh arrivals continued to cover the hillsides and flats away from the business district. If residents had formed a town government, it provided few if any urban services. Individual merchants, for example, were expected even to build their own sidewalks, which slanted and dipped so erratically that in Leadville one resident's evening stroll ended abruptly when he walked off the end of a darkened wooden walkway and fell a full four feet to the ground, breaking his arm. Water had to be hauled from nearby springs because streams were hopelessly polluted from refuse and sluicing.[15]

The streets, pounded continuously by feet, hooves, and the wheels of heavy ore wagons, became quagmires of oozing mud in which pack animals foundered and occasionally drowned. Into these thoroughfares residents threw dirt from cellars, garbage, manure, and even dead animals, which in turn attracted large numbers of swine as scavengers. Impressed by the resulting stench, the editor of the *Helena Herald* warned that summer would bring malaria and "atmospheric scrofuls" unless the public acted. Life here could be unpleasant. During the spring thaw, businessmen along Harrison Avenue in Leadville spent much of their afternoons shoveling out the sludge that flowed off the street into their stores, and women took to wearing wool-lined rubber boots while shopping. A carpenter in one of these towns used wood so green, observed the Reverend J. R. Fisher, that "the sap of the board and the sweat of his brow mingled in one common stream," and roofs began to sag and walls to buckle almost immediately. With much of the ground cover taken for building material, erosion so undermined the foundations of stores and homes that owners sometimes had to prop them up with stilts.[16]

Nevertheless, there was in these towns a vitality that could not be

6. Once a camp like Creede survived its first rush, more substantial drinking places appeared with sturdy walls, roofs of canvas stretched tautly over frames, and cleanly lettered signs. *Courtesy of the Colorado Historical Society*

ignored. "The Sound of the Hammer and Saw are makeing ceaseless echo's during the day," one miner wrote from Placerville, Idaho, in 1863, "while that of the drunken carousal, lasts through the greater part of the night."[17] Apparently some of the day's clamor came from the building of places for the night's amusements. Like the towns around them, saloons took on a larger and somewhat sturdier appearance while retaining some of the cruder characteristics of the past.

Some were simply elaborations upon the first primitive structure. Like the Denver House in 1859 or the smaller Creede saloon of "Doc" Watson, a drinking place might have rather substantial wooden walls and white sheeting stretched tautly across a frame roof. Larger, almost circus-sized tents could be put up in a few hours—and taken down just as quickly if a town's gilded future proved illusory. Supported by frameworks of scantlings, tents up to one hundred feet long had enough room to shelter a full-sized bar, gilt mirror, gambling facilities, musicians, and a dance floor. An agent for a Scottish syndicate sent to scout for mining investments in Maricopa, Arizona, found the town composed entirely of tents, fifteen of them saloons. One of these, reputedly the largest in the region, required three bartenders to accommodate the crowd.[18]

Typically, several variations of wood and canvas could be found. Hailey, Idaho, in May of 1881 boasted the dubious distinction of "the finest tent in the Territory," John Allen's establishment, but other saloons of hewn timber, unsplit logs, and frame stockade competed with "Coal Oil Johnnie" for the town's clientele. Under construction was a thirty-by-eighty-foot building to house a saloon and gambling hall. Requiring a full sixty days for completion, it promised a new level of stability and comfort.[19]

During this period of transition there appeared the kind of drinking house that would become a familiar sight in a mining town in its final stage of maturity. Usually owned by one or two men of modest means, this saloon more often than not was of frame construction. If hardly glamorous, it at least had glass windows and a wooden floor. Within its one room, the use of more permanent fixtures and the first attempts at decoration indicated that the proprietor, like the community at large, was already groping for a kind of elegance and style. Though the following passage describes drinking houses in the cattle town of Billings, Montana, it would have applied equally well to saloons in mining towns throughout the Rockies:

The saloon may be a single-roomed plank cabin, neatly papered. On the walls may hang pictures of Abraham Lincoln and General Garfield, with a few comic sporting prints. A bar runs part of the way up the room, and is spotlessly clean; behind this counter against the wall are a few shelves decorated with specimen-bottles of wine, spirits, etc.; underneath, sugar, lemons, and ice, if these luxuries are attainable; a stove, three or four chairs, a bucket of water with a dipper, complete the furniture.[20]

Also like their towns, however, these places often paid a price for inadequate and hasty construction. The largest tents could collapse during the fierce gales that swept through the mountains, while heavy snows and poor carpentry could combine to bring down the roof of frame saloons. Other miscellaneous dangers threatened the unwary. A new woman employee of Helena's Gayety Saloon, unaware that hydraulic mining had eaten away much of the land behind the business, stepped out the rear door for a breath of fresh air and fell ten feet into a stream. She was shaken but unharmed.[21]

Despite some building improvements and the more orderly appearance achieved by street systems, these young towns thus still seemed somehow impermanent. Just as most residents showed little concern for the development of long-term institutions and services, so the buildings themselves, virtually all of them wood and most of them cheaply constructed, implied a lack of commitment to the future. Here was a paradox. Even as a few emerging leaders, speculators, and boosters predicted glorious tomorrows and gave grand and confident names to their "cities," most dewllers in these mining towns gave every indication that they were ready to move on at an instant's notice.

The transition of a town from its second to its third stage of growth was gradual, and the line between the two was indistinct. As much as anything else, the change was one of emphasis and prevailing attitudes. Prosperity attracted men, often with families, who were committed to remaining in the town and promoting stability and sustained growth. Stamp mills, sawmills, light manufacturing plants, and perhaps a smelter opened to service the needs of the expanding community. Business leaders often organized a board of trade to promote their long-term economic interests and those of their town.

Government began to provide the essential urban services, such as the apprehension and trial of lawbreakers and protection against the fires that almost invariably occurred in mining camps. Town fathers tried to insure a basic level of sanitation and passed ordinances prohibiting public nuisances ranging from the reckless riding of horses to the dumping of offal inside the town limits. All this assumed a faith in the future that was also expressed in the physical appearance of the town. Stone construction began to replace that of wood. In the commercial section, substantial business blocks built by wealthy investors catered to the needs of the merchant and professional classes. Public buildings, churches, meeting halls, and, in the larger towns, that ultimate badge of civic respectability, the opera house, testified to an increasing interest in political and cultural life. Growing outward were the residential districts, streets of neat frame homes of businessmen and miners.[22]

Places of drinking and amusement began, like the town, to look more refined and permanent. Owners did what they could to improve the earlier shoddy construction. Braces were added to shore up sagging walls, and to provide a feeling of airiness and greater room, the ceiling might be raised two or three feet. Outside, some saloonmen put frame siding on their log buildings or added an exterior of adobe bricks if the climate permitted, while others went further and decorated the entrance with a street light or mock marble facade. On many saloons there appeared the false front that became a familiar sight in Western towns after its first use in California. Ironically, this most distinctive contribution of the West to American architecture was designed to make places of business look as much as possible like their counterparts in the East. Some false fronts gave the illusion of a second story by using sham windows to conceal the actual pitched roof behind. Most were topped by cornices of imaginative design and decoration. All, whether of wood, brick, or metal, gave the saloon a more substantial and "citified" appearance and provided space for bold and fanciful signs.[23]

Within these remodeled buildings owners wainscoted the lower portion of the walls and lined and papered the rest. Local ornamental painters brightened the interior. Sturdier tables and chairs appeared, and with them perhaps a billiard table, gambling apparatus, and piano. The bar was no longer a makeshift affair but a more elaborate fixture securely installed. It became part of the building itself, to be sold with the structure; thus certain buildings of a town were recognized as saloons whose owners might change frequently over a few years but whose function remained the same.[24]

Such changes were more of degree than of substance. If an owner chose to remain in his simple one-room log or frame saloon, he made these improvements over a year or two, usually during the winter months, when trade was slow. In the spring the local editor would announce that the cheerful host had "fixed up his place in first-rate style" and would be ready for the rush that came with warmer days. Some owners looked for larger, sturdier buildings and there installed fancier facilities. George Gans of Idaho City, for instance, moved into an abandoned planing mill to accommodate his growing trade. The

7. Surrounded by refuse and undermined by erosion, this log saloon in Unionville, Montana, took on an air of respectability when its owner added a porch and false front. Sing Kee's laundry is out back. *Courtesy of the Montana Historical Society*

owners of the Montezuma Saloon and the Prescott Exchange in Arizona's territorial capital demonstrated yet another possibility when they knocked out the wall between them and consolidated their businesses. Whatever the approach, these changes represented a growing commitment and a gradual increase in investment that reflected the greater economic and social maturity of the community at large.[25]

A larger mining town's liquor trade, however, had not "arrived" until a drinking place appeared whose size, construction, and elegance set it apart from the usual class of saloons.[26] Unlike owners who bought or built a rudimentary structure and gradually added the trappings of prosperity, the proprietor of this type of saloon began with a grand vision. From the start it was recognized that these establishments would be quite a cut above the ordinary, and newspapers often followed their construction as a major cultural development. The buildings typically occupied long and narrow lots from twenty-five to

8. The imposing Wedge Buffet, with its gaslight and second-floor meeting room, dominated the main street of Kendall, Montana, and stood in contrast to the barren winter landscape. *Courtesy of the Montana Historical Society*

thirty-five feet wide and as much as eighty feet deep. Frequently a second story was included. This additional floor itself reflected changes in the social environment, for it often served as a reading room or as a meeting hall for social clubs, debating societies, dancing classes, and, in at least one case, a temperance organization. One building, then, could offer facilities both for the drinking and gambling that had dominated the recreational life of the town from its inception and, a few feet above, for the activities that formed an important part of the new cultural life.

For material builders might choose California redwood or high quality pine, but more often they used brick or native stone, not only for their more imposing appearance but also as a defense against fire. Often a storage basement or rear fireproof cellar was included. One such building required 160,000 bricks, another more than 13,000 cubic feet of stone. Tall ceilings of from twelve to fifteen feet gave a feeling of roominess that contrasted with the cramped quarters of earlier groggeries.

The interior sometimes consisted of one large room, but more often space was divided according to the various activities of the saloon. Upon entering, a customer might find a small area, usually called an ''office,'' partitioned from the rest of the business. Here cigars were sold and newspapers laid out for inspection. Beyond was the drinking area proper. The bar ran along one wall, while opposite it tables and chairs offered a chance for lounging and conversation. This section in turn was separated by a wall and door from a rear room devoted to gambling and entertainment. Participants could circulate among several gaming tables as musicians performed on a stage usually set in a rear corner. If women were available, the center of the area was set aside for dancing. Especially in the context of the town outside their doors, these saloons seemed places of wondrous comfort and elegance. Even critics of the liquor trade wrote in awe of drinking palaces so ''gorgeously fitted up,'' yet surrounded by squalid streets and flimsy buildings.[27] The interior walls might be paneled but more often were wainscoted, with the upper portion covered with paper displaying abstract designs, gilt flowers, or such classical scenes as an allegorical treatment of the four seasons. A frieze, a stile, and corner pieces contributed to an ornate, neoclassical appearance. Paintings and French plate mirrors adorned the walls, while chandeliers lighted the tables and bar. No longer did patrons drink from dirty glasses of assorted sizes; now the shelves behind the bar glistened with jiggers and mugs of Eastern manufacture or imported stemware like that from which Tombstone's Crystal Palace took its name. The total effect was of magnificence, spaciousness, and style.

The proprietors of these establishments frequently made special provision for the economic elite of the town, its leading investors, engineers, mine managers, and owners, so that they might relax with their own kind. J. A. Kelly of Tombstone offered a place ''where gentlemen can call and be made comfortable . . . free from the noise and confusion of the streets.'' In these secluded rooms, sometimes accessible only by keys distributed to a carefully chosen few, com-

9. Inside the Wedge Buffet customers bought cigars from a glass case, drank beer cooled in an icebox to the left, or ordered whiskey in fine crystal served across a trim buffet-style bar. *Courtesy of the Montana Historical Society*

munity leaders could read Eastern newspapers and gamble apart from the unwashed masses in an atmosphere of carpeted silence, rich mahogany paneling, and free imported cigars. These havens were the mining frontier's equivalent of the English private club. Indeed, one rather prim British gentleman expressed surprise and relief when he found one such "very good refreshment room" upon his arrival in Leadville.[28]

No wonder, then, that residents praised such places as milestones in the physical and social maturity of their towns. The editor of the *Montana Post* hailed the Stonewall Saloon as a "proud monument of our talismanic progress" inconceivable in the obscure mountain village that had stood on the spot only a year earlier. The praise was generally unrestrained: the new accommodations were not merely impressive, but "models of such places," "a credit to any town," "one of the finest establishments . . . in the mountains," and "by all odds the best constructed, the most substantial, and most carefully built of any [building] in [the Territory]." Trumpeters of each town's glorious future pointed to these halls of drinking and gambling as clear evidence of their community's superiority.[29]

With the appearance of such refinements, a town's liquor trade arrived at its final stage. A customer then had access to a variety of drinking houses with different atmospheres and styles. Larger saloons emphasized magnificent facilities, lively music, dancing, and a selection of games of chance. Except in the quiet sanctuaries of the elite, the floor was crowded and the air filled with the noise of exuberant men in search of excitement. More modest, one-room businesses offered greater intimacy and relaxation. Owners advertised such places as "strictly a drinking saloon," a "cosy retreat," or "a quiet place of resort" and held out no promises of high times and hussies.[30] A man looking for a drink and companionship could sit with individuals of similar background and shared experience, men who would understand his victories and frustrations.

In the larger towns, a careful observer could have told by the location of liquor retailers something of their degree of refinement and the clientele they served. A large stone palace of drinking and gambling inevitably occupied a corner of a prominent business block, a site befitting a source of civic pride. On streets radiating from this district and near major mines, mills, and transportation depots, fairly substantial saloons competed with smaller, dingier places for the trade of miners and laborers, while on the outskirts of town, shack and log saloons, usually called contemptuously "beer booths" or "deadfalls," served the lowest economic caste.

In the more populous mining towns, these divisions could also have an ethnic quality. In Leadville, for instance, the names of the owners operating east of Harrison Avenue suggest strongly that they drew upon the trade of their fellow Irishmen, who made up a large part of the labor force in the mines of Stray Horse Gulch, while to the west, names like Stockdorf, Gulberg, and Strobe, and by the end of the 1880s, Popovich, Zobernick, and Miklic indicate that Germans and later Eastern Europeans congregated here to wet their whistles. Because there were few blacks in most camps, only the most populous centers could support a saloon segregated for their use, like that of Leadville's W. H. Jones.

These drinking places could exhibit the worst chracteristics of the retail liquor trade. In some of the larger saloons and gambling halls, sharpers and toughs preyed upon the more naive greenhorns and miners with rigged games and drugged liquor. The cheaper dives ranged from the unsightly to the repugnant, and all were almost surely breeding grounds for disease. No French plate windows admitted light. What little sun filtered through small, dirty panes of glass lit the interior only dimly. Photographs reveal graphically that even when spittoons were provided, customers showed either a casual indifference or remarkably poor aim, for the floor in front of the bar typically was stained dark by tobacco juice. Visitors remarked often on the stale air in the poorly ventilated barrooms, a "stifling atmosphere of stove-heat, unwashed humanity, whisky-fumes, and a cloud of tobacco smoke." At best the more respectable small taverns had "a strong sickening smell," while the worst "steamed with . . . odors from empty beer kegs around [the] entrance and obnoxious receptacles [urinals] just to the rear."[31] For all the genuine social value of the saloons, there was good reason for the disgust of later temperance reformers.

In short, as a mining camp grew into a true community, its collection of saloons gradually came to resemble those of most American cities. After an initial period when all the drinking places looked alike and all were scattered among a jumble of temporary buildings thrown up overnight, different categories of drinking spots that catered to the diverse needs of the townspeople and reflected the economic, social, and even ethnic components of the town began to appear.

Yet within this diversity was a certain unity. A customer entering any saloon—gilded barroom or deadfall—could expect to encounter certain familiar sights and furnishings. While these common elements might have had practical purposes, they also formed together the peculiar environment of the saloon, and in the popular mind they came to symbolize such places. Most obvious was the bar itself. From the earliest days, when owners sold drinks across pine planks and sacks of flour, it had been the defining feature of the retail liquor business. With prosperity there appeared ever more elaborate facilities. Before the arrival of the railroad, a prospective owner could hire local craftsmen to build a bar or he could pay to have one carried in by wagon.[32] In either case, costs limited the size. Rarely did the length exceed ten feet, though a delicate curving of the counter, or front bar, and the use of contrasting strips of dark and light wood made up in attractiveness what might be lost in expanse.

Rail connections allowed the wealthy proprietor to indulge his most extravagant tastes. Some bars were imported from Europe, but most came from California or the Mississippi or Ohio valleys. Particularly in Colorado, owners often relied on the same Brunswick works in Cincinnati that provided many of the billiard tables throughout the West. Measuring up to twenty feet long, Brunswick creations featured dark wood carved in intricate curling patterns and magnificent back bars dominated by large mirrors that were often flanked by small columns topped by an ornate cornice.

Turning from the bar, a customer might well see another object common to many saloons—a billiard table. Since at least the early eighteenth century, public houses and taverns had offered patrons facilities for a relaxing game, but the opening of the Rocky Mountain frontier coincided with a period of rapid change and growth in the billiard industry. The popularity of the game had increased greatly after the development by the New Yorker Michael Phelan and his son-in-law H. W. Collender of composition cushions that assured great accuracy and uniformity. During the last three decades of the century, when a series of championship tournaments further encouraged popular interest, many Eastern saloons furnished a table for the amusement of the customers.[33]

If anything, Westerners were even more enthusiastic about the game than their compatriots back in the states. In New England, a Montanan told one tourist, the first thought in a new community was of a church and schoolhouse, while in the mining regions the first public institutions were a piano and a billiard table.[34] Local artisans occasionally produced "pigeonhole" tables, but because of the high level of craftsmanship required, owners usually looked to established firms. Far and away the most popular was that formed when Phelan and Collender merged in 1878 with the Cincinnati company founded by the Swiss immigrant John W. Brunswick. Thereafter Brunswick tables dominated the national market, including the West.

The arrival of the first table in town was an event of some moment, moving one editor to claim solemnly that his community had taken another step along the path of civilization. Indeed, nothing speaks more for the tenacity and initiative of frontier entrepreneurship than the remarkably early arrival of these heavy and bulky tables at the remotest camps. Trudging along the trail to the Silver Bow mines in Montana, a correspondent was astonished to see "some *sanguine* individual" laboriously maneuvering a billiard table among the throng of immigrants. In time marble-bed tables of all styles—carom as well as four- and six-pocket—made their way to the mountains by rail, river, and wagon.[35] An ordinary tavern often had at least one, while a billiard saloon often featured several types. Though such a purchase represented a substantial investment, the competitive pressure of the game's popularity apparently was hard to resist. Thus the billiard table, which provided customers an opportunity for friendly social contact and an exhibition of individual skill, became an expected part of a saloon's furnishings.

On the walls, above the bar mirror, and hanging from the ceiling were examples of a distinctive kind of art that also helped define the peculiar environment of the saloon. Upon the death of the Idaho City saloonkeeper William Baird, the county sold his business and all its furnishings to settle the estate. Among the items listed in the probate records were one large and seven smaller oil pictures, six "horse pictures," one portrait of George Washington and his family, and eleven other unidentified illustrations. Baird's holdings suggest both the amount and diversity of art found in many drinking places. Community artists sometimes provided mountain landscapes, but paintings and lithographs appealing to a masculine view of life were far more common. "Sporting prints" occupied a prominent place on the walls of most barrooms. Paintings of thoroughbred horses spoke not only of the customers' interest in racing but also of their debt to Kentucky, the heartland of bourbon. Most sporting prints depicted that prominent

10. The open floorspace, tables for cards or billiards, and the languorous nude all contributed to the relaxed, masculine mood of this saloon in Van Wyck, Idaho. *Courtesy of the Idaho Historical Society*

hero of the American common man, the prizefighter, particularly John L. Sullivan. Bare-chested and with fists clenched and raised, the subjects struck heroic poses at once virile and dignified.[36]

Critics of the saloon charged that the prominent display of portraits of naked women inflamed the sexual desires of men already aroused by demon rum. Many drinking houses did indeed feature prints of voluptuous damsels languorously posed in various stages of undress. Yet these erotic pictures also placed their subjects somehow at an unattainable distance from the common drinking man. Typically they reflected the Victorian fascination with anything classical. Chubby cherubim waited upon beautiful goddesses who reclined amid luxurious foliage, the whole scene viewed through a gauze-like mist, as if in a dream. The women themselves rarely were shown looking directly toward the viewer and appeared not so much inviting as detached. On balance, the effect of these portraits was less lascivious than idealized.

In addition to the themes of athletic virility and femininity disrobed, the decor of the saloon often reflected an unblushing nationalism. Increasingly popular by the latter years of the century, this theme paralleled the emergence of a spirit of national self-confidence that replaced the divisions of the Civil War and fostered a fresh outburst of expressions of manifest destiny, culminating in war with Spain in 1898. Such trappings also might have provided a way for an immigrant saloon owner to show he could wave the flag as vigorously as the next man. Expressions of patriotism took many forms. A proprietor might hang distinguished portraits of founding fathers, historical demigods, and reigning presidents. By the time of the Spanish-American War flags and red, white, and blue bunting were being draped from the walls and ceilings.

This nationalism, coupled with the sporting prints' emphasis on the heroic individual, helps explain the phenomenal popularity of the most widely distributed of all saloon pictures, F. Otto Becker's *Custer's Last Fight*. Copied from an original by Cassely Adams, it portrayed a longhaired and buckskin-clad George Armstrong Custer standing with upraised sword as he awaited death at the hands of a horde of savages at Little Big Horn. In 1896 the Anheuser-Busch Brewing Company began distributing prints of Becker's work as advertisements. Eventually more than 150,000 copies were given away, and *Custer's Last Fight* became a standard feature of saloons West and East.[37]

Taken together, these illustrations and decorations made up *genre* best described as Victorian *macho*. They spoke of women to be lusted after but still kept on a pedestal and of an admiration for muscle-flexing heroics. The men who leaned on the bar and stared idly at such things shared with the world outside a secure confidence in America's destiny, but in this masculine environment they expressed their beliefs in an exaggerated vernacular of virility and bravado. How natural that representatives of Young America should raise their steins to John L. Sullivan and George Custer, for the Boston Strong Boy and the blonde Boy General were the perfect icons of the male subculture that flowered in the saloon.

There was a human dimension as well to the setting, a cast of characters any regular customer would recognize. Gamblers operated in most larger saloons and in some smaller ones. If run properly, the popular game of faro required two or three persons—a dealer; a "lookout," who sat beside the dealer to oversee the action; and a "case keeper," or "hearse driver," who sat across the table with an abacuslike device that showed which cards had been played. At the door might stand a "steerer" inviting customers with a chant of "Faro! Faro! Faro tonight!" A shill sometimes was employed in games of faro and keno and was particularly important in con artists' specialties like three-card monte and the thimble-rig game. Usually called "cappers," or, in Arizona, "sons of rest," these men used the siphon principle to encourage the flow of action, posing as greenhorns and hooting for joy when the gambler conveniently allowed them to win. Others quickly moved in to take advantage of a sure thing, and just as promptly they lost. A variety of other menials and free-lancers circulated on the periphery of the action—"moppers," who performed chores for free drinks, bootblacks, and vendors selling food to the late-night crowds.[38]

Although the saloon was a predominantly male institution, a woman was a powerful lure among men longing for feminine companionship. When word circulated around Georgia Gulch, Colorado, that a waitress was serving customers in a nearby drinking place, miners flocked from the surrounding hills to stare at her like "boys who go to see a monkey." Some Tombstone saloon owners advertised in Los Angeles newspapers for women to perform as singers and to serve as hostesses. Their job was to greet customers and encourage them to patronize the bar, and for their efforts they received 20 percent of all money spent by their clients.[39]

Larger saloons often offered their customers a chance to dance with tired and haggard women, who usually were paid by the number of dances they endured. Typically, a man paid from twenty-five cents to a dollar for the privilege of a Virginia reel or quadrille, and he was expected or required to follow up by buying drinks for himself and his partner for as much as a dollar a shot. Dance halls, or "hurdy-gurdies," relied on dancing fees for a large part of their income, but some saloons apparently used a band and a few women mainly to attract customers into their doors.[40]

Despite the questionable reputation of these women, those who worked in saloons as hostesses, performers, or dancers did not always practice prostitution. Some were young, unmarried immigrants, often from Germany, trying to support themselves, and others were wives of poor miners supplementing the family income. But some undoubtedly did work also as prostitutes. The distinction between a brothel and a barroom, like that between a dance hall and a saloon, could be a fine one. Certainly any whorehouse sold liquor, but the proprietor depended on the sexual commerce of the boarders as his main source of revenue. Some saloonmen, on the other hand, seem to have employed a few hardened hussies to supplement the income of the bar. A saloon might have one-room cribs behind or to the side, or simply a back room, to which women took their customers. Prostitutes usually were expected to encourage their men to drink before concluding the transaction, and some of them performed other services as well. The St. Elmo Saloon of Globe, Arizona, featured women acrobats and singers who doubled as whores between acts.[41]

One final character, the "bummer," was all too familiar to the saloonkeeper and his customers. Unable or unwilling to find work, vagrants lived on the fringes of camp life, spending their days and nights looking for free shelter and enough nourishment to stay alive. Who were they? Probably veterans, the unskilled Eastern poor who somehow had made their way West, "a variety of pretenders and adventurers who have no knowledge and never will acquire it," wrote a visitor to Wyoming's South Pass rush, "[men] who are drifting along this particular current because they happened to drift into it."[42] This most anonymous segment of mining town society was regarded with derision by those who believed, rightly or not, that any man willing to bend his back could support himself on the frontier. An Idaho editor's parody of Hamlet, a "bummer's soliloquy" for such a man debating whether to move on to the next rush, illustrates this general public contempt.

To go or stay (and bum as usual)—that's (hic) question? Whether it's more high-toned to suffer the slings and dregs of outrageous whisky, or to take somebody's six-shooter and blankets and by leaving town in the night, get a clear track for Blackfoot? . . . No—that pup won't suck. Rather bum on the friends I have than fly to others I know not of. Thus bumming does make cowards of us all.[43]

Its long hours and warmth made the saloon an alluring refuge for "stove-sharks" who hoped to take advantage of the tavern's characteristic spirit of generosity. "Had a fearful lot of bums around all day," the barkeeper George Hand recorded in his diary, and on another occasion, "Closed with six sleepers." Caretakers of the public weal might complain of those who spent their days lounging in groggeries, preying on honest citizens, and "shoveling sunshine," but the number of bummers was apparently so great and the saloon such a natural gathering place that they remained an unavoidable part of a town's drinking life.[44]

A description of these saloons tells something of both the special conditions of the mining frontier and the persistence of older traditions of the United States and Europe. Because the great number of saloons and the rapid turnover among their proprietors encouraged a greater variety and adaptation than in any other type of enterprise, the evolution of a town's barrooms mirrored its physical maturity and its search for refinement and respectability. As part of this development, saloons took on features and fixtures common to most drinking houses throughout the mountains and the nation. The structure and furnishings helped define the saloon not simply as a business but as a social experience celebrating companionship and a masculine, hairy-chested approach to life. Among men who recognized these sights, the surroundings must have encouraged social contact and triggered familiar rituals. There remains to be discussed, however, the centerpiece of the setting, the most crucial influence on the barroom's atmosphere and its chances of success—the saloonman himself.

3

The
Natural-Born Saloonman

IN 1863 James D. Agnew arrived in Boise, Idaho Territory, already a
veteran of the frontier. Like most of those around him, the Virginian
was a young white man, only thirty-one, but he had worked as a
freighter in Utah, a court reporter in California, and a county sheriff in
Walla Walla, Washington. He knew Westerners and Western ways.
When word came to Walla Walla of Idaho's first gold strike on the
Clearwater River, he was off again, this time to try his hand at mining.
He found no fortune at Pierce City or Centerville, so he came with the
first settlers to Boise, helped survey the town, and turned to yet
another occupation. With H. C. Riggs as a partner, he opened a
saloon. Their adobe building at the corner of Main and Seventh streets
was one of the settlement's first, and as a barkeeper and later a livery
stable operator, Agnew prospered. His fellows respected him and
elected him coroner and county sheriff, and they seem to have liked his
whiskey. Above all, Agnew was good company—one of "Boise's
chief funmakers," a contemporary recalled. An accomplished practical joker and storyteller, he and a group of friends paraded through
Boise every Fourth of July as the "Hornique Brindles," dressed
grotesquely and babbling in strange tongues. Even his Newfoundland
dog, Tige, was a town favorite. Jim Agnew was a good man with
whom to sit, drink, and swap lies.[1]

A barkeeper like Agnew often was one of the best-known members of a mining camp's business class. The saloonman was an
important part of the social life of the town and an all-but-inescapable
sight on its streets. Although the bare facts of the lives of Agnew and a
few others can be sketched, however, it is impossible to know in much

detail what the typical saloon owner of the Rockies was really like. He remains something of a mystery.

Who was he? Something must be said of the saloonkeeper and his characteristics, but unfortunately most barkeepers are of little help. They were on the mining frontier by the hundreds, and they sometimes stood out as colorful characters, but they offer few answers to questions asked of them. Considering the great number of drinking places that operated in the Rockies, remarkably few diaries and letters of saloonmen have survived, and these documents have little to say about the lives of saloon owners.

More information can be drawn from federal census records, early histories, reminiscences, and newspapers, and from the comments of literary tourists. None of these records can give a clear picture of the life of a particular saloonkeeper, but taken together to show patterns of background, behavior, and attitude, they contribute to a composite view of this familiar but somewhat enigmatic figure of the mining frontier.

Manuscript censuses show that saloonmen were little different from the other members of the society around them. Census returns for 1870 and 1880 from fifteen towns in Arizona, Colorado, Montana, and Idaho listed 466 saloonkeepers. I compared information about them with data on a sample of 2,963 individuals, about 10 percent of the adult population.[2] If the sample of the general population was predominantly Caucasian (91 percent) and male (78.8 percent), the saloon owners were even more so (99.8 percent and 98.7 percent, respectively). Similarly, the median age of barroom proprietors (34.2) and that of the adult men and women of the camps (33.2) were about the same. It is hardly surprising that the saloon, run by relatively young white men, fit well within the social environment of the mining frontier.

In marital status and place of birth, saloonmen differed more from the society at large. Owners were more likely to be single than those persons in the general sample (56.5 percent to 48.3 percent). This difference takes on added interest, moreover, when the general population is broken down by occupation. About six out of ten miners and unskilled workers were unmarried, but among the skilled workers, merchants, and professionals, about half were married. To the extent that saloonmen were bachelors, therefore, they resembled more the lower economic order of common workmen than they did those nearer the top of the occupational ladder.

At first glance, barkeepers seem almost identical with the society at large in place of origin. Among both groups, a little more than half (54.3 percent and 55.9 percent) were native born, and in both cases, most of those individuals born in the United States originated in the Middle Atlantic and Ohio Valley states. But these generalizations should be qualified in two ways. First, foreign-born saloonmen were far more likely to be German or Irish. Of all owners, 30 percent were of one or the other of those ethnic groups. The popular cliché of the Teutonic "mine host" and the smiling son of Erin serving up foaming mugs of lager and jiggers of Irish whiskey thus was certainly well founded. Second, saloon owners resembled the working class in their place of birth, just as they did in their bachelorhood. Many among the miners and unskilled workers in these towns had been born abroad (52.5 percent), far more so than in the ranks of skilled labor (26.9 percent) and professionals (22.6 percent). The upper occupational ranks were dominated by native-born Americans; those farther down, by a more varied mixture of immigrants and persons born in this country. Of the two groups, saloonmen were much more like the second than the first.

Like most of those who walked the streets outside his doors, the typical saloon owner thus was a white man in his early or middle thirties. He was more likely to be single than married. He might well have been born away from American shores, and if so, he probably looked back to Germany or Ireland. These demographic facts reveal no glaring differences between him and the society in which he lived, but insofar as distinctions can be made, the saloonman probably identified with the young, foreign-born bachelors who worked the mines and did the heaviest manual labor of the camp. And in turn, they probably saw him as one of their own.

The census taker, however, caught his subjects at one frozen moment in time, and he asked them only what his government told him to. Although this information suggests some generalizations about saloonmen as a group, the resulting picture is rather flat and lifeless. Such statistics do not tell why and when these men came West, and they say nothing of their experience once they arrived. Neither do they hint about those personal traits that suited them for their chosen business.

Although most barkeepers remain almost totally anonymous, some biographical facts about a few have survived in early state histories, newspaper stories, and scattered reminiscences of contemporaries. Based on these sources, a collection of 101 sketches of saloonmen has been assembled.[3] A profile drawn from these biographical sketches will be slanted in favor of the survivors in a highly competitive business; the individual who wandered back East or drifted from one boom town to the next is not represented. This group biography, however, can suggest something of the background of the more successful practitioners of the trade and so can contribute to a better understanding of the retail liquor business on the mining frontier.

The ethnic profile of these men is little different from that shown in the census. Of the 101, place of birth can be determined for 80, of whom 57 percent were native born, while about four out of ten had come to the United States from elsewhere. Here is another indication that immigrants found the liquor trade inviting. And again most of these alien keepers of the bars were German (20 percent) or Irish (7 percent).

These men probably received public school training of the kind available to most Americans of that day. For a majority there is no educational information, but most of these went to work around the age of sixteen or seventeen, so their schooling presumably stopped about that time. In only two cases is there any mention of higher education. One Bozeman, Montana, barkeeper had enrolled for a while in Wabash College before embarking on what his biographer discreetly called a ''checkered life'' that included filibustering in Central America with William Walker. Another was graduated from Yale and later studied law until the Civil War intervened; twenty years after Appomattox he stood behind a bar in Montana. This much, at

least, seems clear: Most saloonkeepers had little in common with the
elite of lawyers, doctors, and engineers in the larger camps, who could
look back on years at the universities of the East and Europe.[4]

A look at the occupational background of these men reinforces
such an impression. Eight briefly occupied what could be called
"professional" positions before moving on to less exalted jobs. Eight
others, including a Nebraskan who had opened his first saloon in
Omaha at sixteen, had worked in some aspect of the business in the
states or on the continent and apparently came West planning from the
start to open a drinking house.

By far the greatest number, however, came to the saloon business
only after trying other ways of making a living on the mining frontier.
Forty-five had owned some other kind of mercantile business, and
most of these enterprises emphasized services over goods—hotels,
livery stables, and restaurants, for example. Twenty-five had operated
farms or ranches in neighboring areas that supplied the mining centers.
Not surprisingly, 41 of the 101 had worked as miners at some time
during their years in the mountains, while 11 others had been
employed as unskilled workers and 6 more as skilled laborers.

If we shift the focus for a moment from this sampling of owners
from throughout the Rockies to another group concentrated in one
city, a similar pattern emerges. Out of the many grogshops and liquor
palaces that operated in Leadville between 1878 and 1890, 656 owners
can be identified in city directories. For 154 of these, the individual's
occupation immediately prior to opening his saloon can be determined. Of the 154, two had been engineers and nine had been government workers. About a fourth of the owners had entered the trade
after working at some other aspect of the liquor business. (Typically a
bartender would serve an apprenticeship for a few years in an established bar and then strike out on his own.) Another fourth had owned
or worked as a clerk in another kind of business, usually a hotel,
restaurant, or other enterprise providing a service to its customers.
Finally, about four out of ten of these men had been workers, most of
them miners (25 percent), but also skilled and unskilled laborers (11
percent and 8 percent). Perhaps they were sick of the numbing toil and
sought to enter the more prestigious merchant class through one of its

least expensive portals. At any rate, they knew firsthand the way of life and the needs of the working man.

What this tallying and categorization fails to reveal is the frequency with which these men moved from job to job and place to place. Considering the group biography of the 101 saloon owners, a few might be considered classic frontier speculators. For sheer diversity of enterprise, for example, the career of Jim Wardner is a genuine source of wonder. Before making a fortune investing in strikes in the Coeur d'Alene region and having towns named after him in both Idaho and British Columbia, Wardner plunged into mining schemes in California, Arizona, and the Dakotas, ran a store, supplied food to miners in the Yukon, and claimed to have cornered the Deadwood egg market, organized and promoted the walking championship of the Black Hills, and founded one of the most bizarre businesses of the West, the Consolidated Black Cat Company, Ltd., a firm that sold as material for gloves the skins of cats he kept and slaughtered on his own island off the coast of Washington. Periodically in the course of this remarkable odyssey he also ran several saloons in Idaho and Deadwood.[5]

Most, however, were not plungers and speculators so much as ordinary working men ready to try their hand at whatever jobs were available. The Irishman Michael Burns, for instance, came with his family from County Clare to Iowa at the age of seven, and by the time he was twelve he was working for a railroad. His arrival in Idaho in 1864 began several years of frenzied movement in Utah, Montana, and Canada, during which he prospected, drove a stage, ran a threshing machine, packed lumber, worked for a water company, and finally set to work tending bar in Helena. Soon he bought his own saloon and settled down. Charles F. Bennett of Casa Grande, Arizona, farmed, read law, sold horses, and scouted for the army, while John Cady of the same territory ran a bakery and butcher shop, raised sweet potatoes, and worked as a chef, assessor, stage driver, and restaurateur. Although he put in time as a ferryman, packer, and government agent, William Mellon concentrated on mining in Oro Fino, Elk Creek, Deer Lodge, Virginia City, Boulder Creek, Little Blackfoot, Pioneer Gulch, and the Black Hills.[6]

When the facts of these biographies are combined with those from the federal census, a pattern emerges. Both sources suggest that saloonmen had little in common with the well-educated engineers, geologists, lawyers, doctors, and investors whose command of Eastern capital placed them in the uppermost stratum of mining camp society. In origins, schooling, marital status, and background, barkeepers seem to have been closer to the workers and, to an extent, to others of the merchant class. Compared with skilled workers and professionals, saloonmen, miners, and laborers were more likely to be single and of foreign origin. That bar proprietors resembled the working class in these ways is not surprising, because many of them had themselves been employed as laborers and prospectors, ranch hands and millworkers, clerks and hostlers.

Perhaps of equal importance is the fact that saloonmen usually had worked at a multitude of jobs as they moved at a rapid, sometimes dizzying, pace from one mountain town to another—a tendency that might be called the "footloose factor." Most of these relatively successful bar owners obviously did not come West in a single-minded search for wealth. Instead they showed a marked flexibility of enterprise. They appear to have been ready to seize whatever opportunity arose to make money, and the saloon business, which demanded only a relatively small investment and promised a quick turnover of goods, must have seemed an alluring possibility to them.

When they did open for business, moreover, their experiences probably were of great help in their new trade. For they surely knew their customers. They might have met their kind on the placers of Boise Basin or in the mines of Washoe; they had freighted in their goods and dealt with them in livery stables and restaurants. Given their origins, upbringings, and lives, these barkeepers must have thoroughly understood the young, ethnically rich collection of unmarried men who stood facing them across the bar. The saloonmen's travels would have provided them with a fund of tales and encouraged the development of the kind of personality so important to the atmosphere of the barroom. The result might have been a "natural born saloon man" like one Peter Martin, described by a veteran of the northern gold fields. "This early day westerner was a living, walking

11. The owner of this tent saloon stood confidently with his customers, a collection of youthful newcomers and grizzled veterans near Creede, Colorado. *Courtesy of the Colorado Historical Society*

story," his acquaintance recalled. "He had seen it and lived it to the fullest extent."[7]

Yet in the end, the saloonman can be understood better in terms of his personality than of his age, nativity, and occupational experiences. Beyond the spare outline of his biography, what characteristics distinguished the barkeeper from others in his community? With few exceptions, the owners themselves did not record their thoughts and feelings in diaries and letters. Some, however, did speak of themselves in other ways. Like other businessmen, for instance, the liquor dealer sometimes advertised, and his appeals for trade can reveal something of the traits and abilities considered helpful in his line of work. Personal and public activities, as recorded by local journalists, can suggest other aspects of his character and image. In addition, the narratives and reminiscences of tourists and residents of mining camps sometimes included observations of local barkeepers, men they seemed to consider colorful individuals worth special mention. Throughout these varied accounts, the image of the saloonkeeper that emerges is consistent, suggesting that certain qualities of character and personality were perceived by both the public and the saloonkeepers themselves as essential to the trade.

One fact of life can help explain the importance of these traits: in most mining towns, there were more drinking places than any other type of retail business. Each time he stepped outside his saloon and looked down the street, a barkeeper faced the hard facts of competition. All bars, moreover, sold basically the same goods. How, then, was an owner to convince a customer that his place was preferable to a score of others? A saloonman had to appeal to the less tangible needs of the drinker—his search for human contact and for an amenable social atmosphere.

If contemporary descriptions are to be believed, virtually all successful saloon operators shared one characteristic—geniality. Over and over, observers remarked on the "inexhaustible good nature," the "wide-extended reputation for good fellowship," and the "good cheer and immense yarns" of the men they found behind the bars.[8] "I flatter myself that I can please everyone," one owner boasted in his local newspaper, and others gave similar assurances in their advertisements. In part such men simply were conforming to a Western preference for an open and outgoing personality. "Just the kind of man to succeed in this country," noted one writer of a local barkeeper, "affable, obliging, active, sharp, and good looking."[9] Joviality was expected even more from a saloon operator than from other men of trade because most customers entered his business seeking relaxation and companionship as much as liquor. There were troubles enough outside. Within the saloon a smiling face and ready hand were anticipated, and if they were not in evidence, they were sought elsewhere. An ability to mix easily and well with a variety of individuals thus became a critical asset. When he came to Montana as a young boy, an acquaintance recalled, barkeeper-to-be George Shoutz quickly developed two talents that would serve him well in his future career—he learned to play poker and to get along with people.[10]

Whether such friendliness was affected or genuine is unknowable and largely irrelevant, but in their more private moments saloonkeepers gave an occasional hint. "We have lots of fun here," a Montana operator wrote to his sister, and added with a superior tone, "you do not no [sic] how to live back East and have fun." The page from George Hand's diary for Saint Patrick's Day, 1875, also suggests a spontaneous enjoyment of a good (if rambunctious) time: "Treated all the boys. Everyone drunk. No fights. Made some egg drunks [sic] for the girls in the corral [prostitutes]. Got tight myself. Shot at a dog and missed him. Kept full all day. Went to bed early."[11]

It was not surprising to find the saloonman taking part in the public celebrations and "jollifications" of his community. Holiday festivals, balls, and special benefits granted participants the same sort of temporary reprieve from a grueling life that they found in a visit to a tavern. Similar talents were required of the men in charge of either type of activity. So the owner of the Parlor Saloon, resplendent in a white, starched apron, dispensed candy and lemonade with a smile at a Hailey, Idaho, Sunday school picnic. Others founded baseball clubs and sponsored and helped organize dances and entertainments, particularly during the months of winter boredom. In the grand burlesque held in his Custer, Idaho, saloon, Larry Donnelly sang in the opening chorus of "O, Bury Your Dog in the Garden," took part in a sparring exhibition with another barkeeper, and delivered an oration on "The Comforts of Old Rye."[12]

George Hand's description of his Saint Patrick's Day activities indicates that proprietors might be expected to join their customers in drink as well as in conversation. Hand himself sometimes began drinking as early as eight in the morning, at least partly to stimulate the flow of trade. "Buck Ryan came in and got drunk in fifteen minutes," he once wrote, then explained, "I was obliged to get drunk myself to make him spend his money." Again, the ethic of good fellowship seemed to demand the owner's participation. If a convivial host offered to set up glasses of the agreeable for himself and regulars along the bar, a customer was bound to accept, and to buy a round himself. The man who could sustain a steady pace of drinking stood to profit from his endurance. When Tombstone's M. E. Joyce opened his Oriental Saloon at ten each morning, he would join his first patrons in a free round. He then would proceed to tell the first of an apparently endless series of stories and jokes. At the end of each, someone along the bar usually would volunteer to treat him and the crowd, and when the liquor had been downed and the mustaches wiped clean, the ritual would begin anew. Although this cycle continued for an astonishing sixteen hours, until the Oriental closed two hours past midnight, Joyce reportedly never showed any effects from the liquor.[13]

The heroes of such gargantuan drinking feats perhaps were employing a familiar deception by drawing upon a bottle of colored water. Others, however, used the genuine article, and the results were not always happy. Years of daily doses could finally produce a tragic case, like that of the Tucson saloonman who drank his business into bankruptcy and killed himself soon afterwards. At the very least, some seemed to view the world through an alcoholic haze. One hot morning in July 1876, George Hand confided cheerily to his diary, "Feel tip-top for one who has been drunk for six years."[14]

Yet in all this the saloonkeeper faced a dilemma. It was in his interest to encourage among his patrons a spontaneity and an easing of inhibitions. The saloon's atmosphere of freedom from social restraints recommended it as much as its beer and whiskey. At some point, however, an overly boisterous drinker became obnoxious or threatening to those around him. Under such circumstances, the better-behaved majority expected the barkeeper to provide a minimum of protection. A proprietor talented in peace keeping thereby gained an important edge over his competitors.[15]

Some promised in their advertisements to keep a proper balance between entertainment and security. C. J. Coles of Fairplay's Red Light dance hall and saloon pledged the public a "quiet and lively time; everything necessary to secure good order will be done and every attraction to draw a crowd will be furnished." He was only one of many who assured all of an atmosphere of decency and gentility in which no improper characters would be tolerated.[16] In general, the rougher the image of the town, the more an owner would attempt to cultivate his reputation for decorum amid revelry.

To make good these assurances, a saloonman required some ability in the manly arts. Certainly well-known pugilists who ran drinking spots—Billy Dwyer of Creede and Con Orem of Virginia City, for instance—guaranteed by their presence alone a degree of order. Just as necessary was the instinct to sense when a calming word and free drink would pacify a troublemaker and when persuasion should give way to force. While visiting Denver in 1859, Albert Richardson encountered a bartender who learned a practical lesson in what was needed. This man's guests sometimes amused themselves by firing their pistols near the host to make him jump.

At first he bore it laughingly, but one day a shot grazed his ear, whereupon, remarking that there was such a thing as carrying a joke too far and that *this* was "about played out," he buckled on two revolvers and swore that he would kill the next man who took aim at him. He was not troubled afterward.[17]

Typically, an owner would use gradually escalating force on the belligerent—first a harsh word, then a firm hand on the shoulder, and finally a toss into the street, perhaps with the aid of a pistol butt. The barkeeper who overreacted by handling too roughly a loud but relatively harmless drunk could face a harsh public rebuke. Such cases underscored what was expected of the saloonman. He had to be a benevolent despot, a bare-knuckled glad-hander who defined the line between acceptable and forbidden liberties and then reacted reasonably but firmly against those who crossed over.

This characteristic helps explain why saloon owners frequently served as law officers. Certainly most saloonmen were not lawmen, nor did most lawmen own drinking houses, but to the extent that barkeepers did perform as public officials, they did so more frequently as law officers than in any other capacity. During the first two decades after formation of Ada County, Idaho, for instance, four of its sheriffs, Dave Updyke, James Agnew, Lute B. Lindsey, and Joe Oldham, and at least one in neighboring Boise County, James I. Crutcher, were men who also ran saloons at some other time in their careers. Both Martin Duggan and P. A. Kelley divided their time between keeping the peace and keeping their bars during Leadville's early years. Many other examples might be cited—among them Jerome J. "Sandy" Donahue of Flagstaff, Tom Iliff of Kalispell, Montana, and John S. Ramey of Lemhi County, Idaho—of men who operated drinking places either during, before, or after their tenure as county sheriff or county or federal marshals, and even more liquor dealers served as constables, deputies, or undersheriffs.[18]

The explanation is simple enough. A prominent saloonman surely would have known more about the people of his community than practically any other businessman. More important, the abilities a barkeeper used to keep order in his place of business could be applied in the world outside. Both jobs required an understanding of violence and disorder, both petty and major, and of how to cope with them (in fact, the most common crime in the mining towns was not murder or robbery but simple drunkenness). As one-time saloonman W. R. Sellew of Montana explained to his mother when he was chosen deputy sheriff and later constable and had to deal with tough individuals, "I am very stout or scienced in handling them."[19]

Open, gregarious, a man not above drinking with his friends, a fine fellow but hard when he had to be—to all these qualities observers added others that distinguished the best and most successful saloonmen. "There never lived a more honest and worthy man than Jerry," a pioneer merchant and the first mayor of Kalispell, Montana, recalled about Jerry Phillips, owner of the town's most prominent resort. "He was a better man and more charitable than all the preachers I have ever known. . . . He made lots of money but gave it all away to unfortunate men and died a poor man himself."[20]

The themes of generosity and honesty, often expressed in similarly romanticized and maudlin tones, reappear frequently in these descriptions. Even as they criticized the social evils of his business, guardians of traditional morality still could recognize these traits in a saloonkeeper. After a long acquaintance with Joe Oldham, the popular proprietor of a Hailey, Idaho, saloon and gambling hall, the Episcopal bishop of Idaho, Ethelbert Talbot, saw in Oldham a "certain title of nobility." He "was a generous soul, warm hearted and loyal to his friends. His kindliness to the widow and the orphan, to the man hurt in the mines, to all in trouble, made him greatly loved."[21]

Whether or not a particular owner's character truly deserved such tribute cannot be determined. What seems clear is that such individuals recognized the prevailing ethic that applauded the virtues of openhandedness and loyalty and identified them as distinctively Western. "Old miners, prospectors and mountain men are, as a rule, a big hearted people," as one editor put it. "They make money and spend the same freely.'' By contrast, newcomers from the East were considered tightfisted and niggardly. Successful saloonmen appear to have played upon this article of faith. The wealthier of them might support generously the expansion of urban services by donating land for a schoolhouse or subscribing to fire companies and road construction. They could be counted upon to organize or participate in fundraising community benefits and to contribute to local charitable causes.[22]

Jack Pape, the host of the Grizzly Saloon in Park City, Utah, provides a vivid example of this sort of activity. During a period of only two months, the barkeeper helped sponsor a grand ball to raise money for a new firehouse and then personally persuaded local carpenters to contribute their time free, canvassed other businessmen for funds to hire a night watchman, and led a campaign to expand and improve the town cemetery. He also managed a benefit for the orphaned children of a local resident and organized a charity raffle for the family of a laborer who had fallen gravely ill. For public weal and private need, he energetically used his talent for entertainment and his ability to get along with many individuals. And he became very popular.[23]

A saloonman's generosity did not always stop with community projects and individuals down on their luck. He might keep a table laden with food free to all comers during holidays or open the spring mining season with a ''hoodoo'' featuring whiskey on the house. P. B. Cheyney, early resident and once mayor of Golden, Colorado, extended the occasional treating of his friends into a community ritual. Three times each day he took a tin horn down from its place above the bar and sounded it blaringly outside the door of his Chicago Saloon as an invitation to all for free drinks.[24]

Descriptions of saloon owners emphasized personal integrity less often then geniality and generosity, but they did so frequently enough to imply that honesty was a trait of some importance. Customers obviously would respect honesty in any businessman, but such a virtue perhaps was even more appealing in a tavern operator, who encountered his clientele during their most vulnerable moments. The man whose business relied on money swindled from customers in their cups was said to have "built his saloon on barrels of whiskey."[25] Conversely, the person known for his trustworthiness was singled out for special praise. One saloon—Tombstone's Crystal Palace, for example—might be commonly known as a place where one could expect fairer treatment than in others, such as the Oriental, across Fifth Street. Stories circulated about barkeepers who retrieved and saved valuables lost by patrons during heavy drinking bouts, and as one measure of trust, some customers left their cash in the saloon safe as protection against robbery and their own profligacy. In the long run, this kind of reputation could only help the proprietor.[26]

The qualities of personality and character mentioned thus far appealed to certain needs and expectations of patrons—fellowship, companionship, relaxation, protection from the belligerent and from the cheat. Through their actions and self-descriptions, saloonmen seemed to cultivate a public profile that conformed to the somewhat romanticized contemporary portrait of the liquor seller, an image that emphasized gregariousness, strength, open generosity, and a reasonable degree of honesty. Other actions and characteristics seem to have had a slightly different, though related, purpose. Saloon owners often did what they could to keep before the public eye. Their devices did not so much communicate specific virtues as acquaint the drinking public with the proprietor and show him to be in some way distinctive and memorable. These efforts helped give the saloonman the final quality he needed: visibility.

His own nickname could testify to a saloon owner's public image and sense of showmanship. A sobriquet might hint of a special talent, like those of "Banjo Bill" Dyer of Flagstaff and the otherwise anonymous "Jewsharp Jack" of Boise, or it might describe persons like "Peg-leg" Fenn of Bonanza, Idaho, or "Fattie" Weeks of Rico, Colorado. Most revealing of all, however, was the fact that the owner would be addressed in such terms at all, for a nickname implied that a man had been accepted by the public as one of its own. Like "Pap" Wyman of Leadville and Idaho City's "Pony" McConnell, most simply showed that the customers regarded such men with informal affection.

The name a saloonman chose for his business also could reveal something of him and his imagination. Certain standards—the Miner's Rest or the Pioneer—appeared again and again throughout the region. Others were merely monuments to the proprietary ego— Hyman's (Leadville) and Grayman's (William Gray and Robert Mann of Creede)—or, like the Big Tent Saloon of Gunnison, they might simply describe the facilities.

Most, however, showed greater originality. Names like the Alhambra and Oriental of Tombstone conjured up exotic visions. Another category reflected the economic environment that spawned and supported them. The Quartz Rock (Prescott), Bed Rock (Phillipsburg, Montana), and innumerable Nuggets and Gems reminded all of the glittering vision that had brought them there. The Little Pittsburg Saloon (Leadville), Holy Moses (Creede), Bobtail (Central City), Atlantic Cable (Cable City, Montana), and Yankee Girl (Red Mountain, Colorado) all took their names from the mines that had sparked the local boom and had set the communities pulsing with life. Still others recalled the cultural life around them. When two actors quit the Central City stage and opened a bar, they called their new enterprise, naturally enough, the Shakespeare. Similarly, the St. Elmo Saloon of Globe, Arizona, copied the title of a best-selling novel of the day.

Perhaps the most common were names that appealed to the rich sense of humor to be found on the mining frontier. The lowly pun was not forgotten, as with the Dew Drop Inn of Gunnison. Others struck a theme of good-natured pomposity—the House of Lords (Bonanza, Idaho), Board of Trade, and Chamber of Commerce (both of Leadville). Revealing a penchant for irony and a fondness for poking fun at his moral critics, the owner of a Buena Vista, Colorado, grogshop placed a sign over his door inviting the passerby to enter the Road to Hell. Should a customer hunger for salvation, he could travel thirty miles north to Leadville for a drink at the Little Church Saloon, which admitted its patrons through a mock arching chapel front that overlooked the crowd of whores, gamblers, and miners congregated at the intersection of Harrison Avenue and Chesnut Street. The painted signs identifying many other drinking houses—the Elevator Parlor, Blue Wing, and St. Anne's Rest, for example—probably referred to forgotten events or expressions of local significance.

12. The thirsty in Leadville could walk past street rubble and curbside loungers to enter the Little Church Saloon through a mock chapel front. *Courtesy of the Colorado Historical Society*

While these names were interesting enough in themselves, even more striking was the colorful variety of them all. They seemed to speak of scores of owners, each trying to place the stamp of individuality upon his particular operation. With a bit of imagination, a proprietor might make himself and his business just different enough that a worker would remember him and choose his bar as the place for a friendly drink.

This striving for distinctiveness did not stop with the naming of the saloon. There were other ways an owner could set himself apart from others of his trade. Some resorted to personal idiosyncrasies. An eccentric style of dress, a tendency toward abnormal bluster, or a well-publicized habit of reciting poetry or bursting unexpectedly into song—such were the makings of characters who attracted patrons willing to pay to see them in action.

An occasional barkeeper crossed the line between the unusual and the bizarre. Charles E. "Pap" Wyman ran a saloon, gambling hall, and theater on the strategic Leadville corner of Harrison Avenue and Second (or State) Street from 1881 to 1886. His floor shows, large rooms, and passable liquor seem to have kept his customers satisfied, but in these he was no different from many competitors. Yet while he was on the scene, Wyman was undoubtedly the most famous owner in town, and tourists in search of Leadville's livelier side usually were steered to Pap's Theater. Inside, an open Bible sat on a slanting mahogany shelf on the bar. Behind the bartenders towered a large clock emblazoned with the words, Please Do Not Swear. Elsewhere another sign invited all customers to stop before leaving to visit with Pap himself, for he was as crucial to the decor as the crystal chandeliers and the garish wallpaper. Short, powerful, and florid-faced, Wyman stood ready to engage in casual conversation on a variety of topics or to lay a heavy hand upon anyone unduly disturbing the peace. Local legend had it that he carried his change in a purse made from a human scrotum. No wonder journalists and literary tourists described Wyman's Place to their readers more frequently than any other Leadville resort.[27]

The mountains harbored few men like Wyman, but he represented an exaggeration of the common impulse among saloon operators to keep themselves in the light of popular attention as much as possible. A reputation, however, depended mainly upon relatively haphazard word-of-mouth communication. The mining camp newspaper offered a more efficient medium for the kind of exposure the owner sought. Not surprisingly, saloon owners sometimes showed that they knew how to exploit the local journal's role as entertainer and interpreter.

The relationship between a barkeeper and an editor could be an adversary one. The latter often sought to promote a degree of respectability among his readers that would attract the "proper" kind of immigrant, and so he would naturally condemn the rowdier consequences of the liquor trade. More often, however, the two figures came to a symbiotic understanding. Most journalists recognized the necessity of the saloon and counted the owners of the better ones among the community's leading citizens. Besides, barkeepers made good copy. To the saloonman, the newspaper offered a way to establish a public presence.

Between a respected liquor dealer and his local editor, a kind of ritual courtship often occurred. In an effort to make the bewildering life of the town a bit more comprehensible, newspapers occasionally recommended various merchants and described their wares, noting such matters as the recent arrival of a shipment of hardware or flour. Here was just the sort of recognition sought by a tavern owner on the make, and from his point of view, the surest guarantee of a kind comment in the local paper was a gift of liquor.

Some members of the fourth estate, in fact, openly solicited donations. ''If anybody has any fluid they want sampled,'' offered Mark Musgrove, editor of the Bonanza, Idaho, *Yankee Fork Herald*, ''we are prepared here to tell to a dot what it will assay to the pint, how old it is, what are its principal component parts, and whether it is safe to take inwardly.'' Even the slightly prim former schoolteacher, Thomas Dimsdale, accepted such donations on behalf of the working press of Virginia City's *Montana Post*. As many entries in the area's newspapers show, the custom was well established. A dozen bottles of beer or ale, a basket of champagne, or a pitcher of cocktails insured a brief item in a ''local jottings'' column advising the reader to patronize the donor.[28]

This indirect purchase of publicity could be formalized by buying space in the columns of a local journal. Enough barkeepers did so to justify in some papers a separate category of saloon advertisements, some of them allowing insights into the owner's method of appealing to his public. The late nineteenth century witnessed the appearance of many modern advertising techniques, and in the West as elsewhere businessmen chose the style or device that best displayed what they had to offer. General merchandisers usually used long columns and imaginative spacing and type size to emphasize the wide variety of goods on their shelves. By tradition, attorneys and physicians published brief, formal notices implying a somber respectability.

The buying public, however, certainly knew what the saloonman sold. Unlike the artisan, he could not boast of his craftsmanship, for if he did make his own product, he was not willing to admit it. Instead, except for a general promise of the choicest liquors, he created colorful copy emphasizing his good humor, ebullient personality, and the order and safety of his house. One such host bragged of himself: "He has laughed and grown fat, and can teach the art to others. Lessons every day and night." A Jewish proprietor put his ethnic background to good use, luring the reader deep into the advertisement before closing the trap:

FACT
It was not the golden calf that brought the children of Israel out of bondage, but the power which accompanied the rod of Moses, and had it not been for the prayers of that great and righteous man, who boldly threw himself into the breach, that nation would have been consumed in a moment for their outrageous and sinful idolatry. But as the matter now stands Berstein is on hand with a full cargo of Sour Mash whisky, St. Louis beer and Havana cigars. Drop in and see the ancient "Yahooder."[29]

Some played ironically upon the supposed vice and wickedness of their profession. Early in 1886, as Boise, Idaho, was experiencing one of its periodic temperance crusades, James N. Lawrence of the Naked Truth Saloon published this "Advertisement of an Honest Rum Seller as it SHOULD BE."

Friends and neighbors: Having just opened a commodious shop for the sale of Liquid Fire, I embrace this opportunity to inform you that I have commenced the business of making
                    Drunkards, Paupers and Beggars,
for the sober, industrious and respectable portion of the community to support. I shall deal in Family Spirits, which will excite men to deeds of riot, robbery and blood, and by doing so diminish the comfort, augment the expenses, and endanger the welfare of the community.[30]

For several inches of closely set type, Lawrence continued to confess his determination to grow rich by sending good citizens to poor farms and the gallows.

Obviously these ads were not designed to provide specific information at all, save the spare facts of name and location. Like the colorful and unusual names, such notices were meant to establish the distinctiveness of the saloonman and his place of business. They conveyed those same qualities of personality noted by travelers and

13. The brick columns of Lawrence and Smith's Spider Web Saloon in Boise, Idaho, provided space for a common style of advertising. Madison Smith, one of the owners, stands at the center in shirtsleeves, as if he had just come from behind the bar. *Courtesy of the Idaho Historical Society*

contemporaries—a kind of calculated bombast, expansiveness, and a broad sense of humor.

If the saloonman stood apart from other merchants and professionals of his community, it was not because of any one characteristic but rather a combination of traits and the emphasis placed upon them. Faced with withering competition and selling essentially the same product, saloon owners appealed mainly on the basis of themselves. The best barkeepers sold not just whiskey but also an atmosphere, a feeling a customer got when he walked through the door. No other businessmen went to such lengths to establish their public personalities. The saloonmen's popular image conformed to the values of young Western working men—generosity, friendliness, loyalty, and a salty, overstated humor. Alone among retailers, they sold goods that could change the behavior of the consumer quickly, drastically, and for the worse, so the saloonkeeper had to appear as protector as well as friend. More than anything else, it was his recognition of these roles and his highly visible playing of them that defined the saloonman as a character of the mining towns. These demands placed a premium on the saloonman's understanding of his clientele, and it is not surprising to find that in their backgrounds and experiences the more successful saloonkeepers closely resembled those whom they served.

Together the man and the place, the saloonkeeper and the barroom, formed the institution of the drinking house. This institution was the site of many activities in the young and changing camp—so many, in fact, that the social functions of the saloon deserve a more detailed investigation.

4

The Social Heart-Centre
of the Camp

THE role of the saloon on the mining frontier can be understood only in the context of the social conditions of the mining towns. Just as the barroom's physical changes followed those of the camp and its owner's image told something of the attitudes of his customers, so the activities in the saloon met some of the demands of those gatherings of prospectors, merchants, and soldiers of fortune who flocked to a new strike.

In a mining camp large numbers of persons, most of them young or older ones who had left their families behind, came together quickly in search of wealth on a spot that never had supported a gathering of such a size. In addition to the immediate problems of housing and provisions, these fortune hunters needed what might be called points of social contact. Residents looked for a forum for the workings of the first governments, for grappling with unavoidable urban problems, and for religious services when a minister was available. Other requirements were equally important. "Amusements and companionships the miner had to have," one early historian of the region has written, "and, in reaction from the hard labor on the claim he generally sought eagerly those forms of amusement offered to him in the towns." In organizing one of the first mining towns of the Rockies, the promoters of the Auraria Town Company appreciated this need. One of their first actions was to offer four free lots on land that later would become part of Denver to the man who would build some "house of entertainment"; two months passed before they made a similar proposal for construction of a church.[1]

The saloon helped to relieve some of the problems of the new camp. Because a great number of barrooms appeared early on, some of them assumed the functions of other institutions not yet on the scene. They provided a place where residents could deal with the practical demands of building a fledgling community. If the town survived and matured, the saloon would continue to meet the emotional needs of men looking for amusement and relaxation, a contribution the drinking house had always made in American urban life. Together its traditional role and the unique conditions of the mining town made the saloon, as the author of an early piece of fiction called it, "the social heart-centre of the camp."[2]

Of the host of problems spawned by the rush of humanity to the urban frontier, one of the most immediate was a chronic housing shortage. The situation was most acute in the most accessible towns. Traveling by railroad to Denver and marching over relatively good roads, between 100 and 200 persons a day fed a population of about 15,000 in Leadville during the mining seasons of 1879 and 1880. But even a remote mountain gulch could attract enterprising hordes during its first ambitious weeks. The better-prepared carried tents to pitch among the green stumps on the eroded hillsides, and in time many built crude shanties as shelter from the elements. The rest scrambled for a place in hotels, boardinghouses, and huge tents called "mammoth lodgers," but although men might crowd five to a bed, this often was not enough. The streets of a town like Hailey, Idaho, where a single hotel owner turned away fifty potential lodgers a night, were thronged with exhausted immigrants looking for a spot to sleep.[3]

The alert saloonkeeper was not blind to such a market. Upon arrival men without lodging gravitated to drinking houses, and as the evening progressed liquor only deepened their weariness. Finally, wrote an Eastern visitor, "a floor of a billiard room becomes an object of interest, while the table itself rises to the dignity of a luxury." For a fee ranging from a dime to a half-dollar, a bartender would allow a customer to snatch a few hours of sleep wherever he might find the room. Some simply slouched in chairs. Others sprawled across idle poker and billiard tables and bowling alleys. Most curled up on the floor, placed their belongings under their heads, and slumbered as best they could.[4]

14. Exhausted immigrants found a few hours of sleep on the floor of a Leadville saloon, the only resting place for many newcomers. *Courtesy of the Denver Public Library*

Some owners formalized the procedure a bit, handing out blankets or tossing hay into a corner to provide bedding and to absorb the odor of unwashed bodies. The proprietor of Tombstone's Diana Saloon dismissed his hired band and filled his dance hall with beds available for fifty cents a night, but he kept his well-equipped bar in full operation. These places came to resemble the traditional rural inn, but with a frontier touch. Newcomers seeking lodging in Ole Mack's Saloon in Fairplay, Colorado, were given a playing card which corresponded to another tacked above the door of one of several cramped rooms provided with mattresses of pine boughs. Others simply hung canvas from the ceiling to form tiny makeshift rooms and advertised as a "hotel and saloon."[5]

Attempts at privacy, however, were more symbolic than real. The rows of what one contemptuous editor called "recumbent bipeds" enjoyed nothing close to comfort. When cold winds were not whistling through open doors and poorly built walls, the air was filled with stale tobacco smoke, the sooty fumes of oil lamps, and the stench of spilled whiskey. The dull roar of barroom conversation and the murmuring and singsong chants of gamblers continued most of the night and made sleep all the more elusive. Yet even at their crudest, these accommodations filled an important need. Without the saloon floor, a newcomer might be left with only an alley or the side of a muddy street as a sleeping place.

New settlements also faced problems of communication. The turbulent, ever-moving population made the dissemination of news especially difficult. Most of the camps that seemed likely to survive could boast of at least one newspaper, and sometimes more. Only the largest towns could support a daily journal, but these did not usually appear until a year or more after the initial rush. More often, only a weekly paper was available.

As a gathering place for the male population, the saloon provided a clearinghouse for more up-to-date communication. Rumors of new ledges were passed by word of mouth. An experienced bartender was adept at receiving and filing away pertinent information, both mineral and social, to be dispensed at the proper cue. Saloons frequently featured cabinets displaying samples of ore from nearby mines. Some added a map of the area and a register summarizing the history, depth, and output of the more successful enterprises. This arrangement not only provided a useful service for hopeful miners, but also promoted a kind of community boosterism that could only help business.[6]

For those wanting a more detailed account of news from the states than that offered in the local newspaper's excerpts, some owners laid out the latest available papers and periodicals. European immigrants eager for word from the old country sometimes could browse through issues of the continental press. Here, also, word could be left for friends or relatives who might wander through. Entrepreneurs without a formal place of business, such as carpenters, painters, and musicians, often made contact with potential customers at a local drinking establishment. In all these ways the saloon acted as a sort of institutional newspaper, facilitating the flow of information, maintaining contact with the larger society outside the mountains, and boasting of the camp's wondrous resources and splendid future.[7]

Among mining camp businesses, the bank often was one of the

last to arrive. General economic uncertainty discouraged banking houses from risking the substantial investment needed to locate in a mountain community. The opening of a bank symbolized a degree of financial stability, just as an opera house signaled that a camp had "arrived" culturally. While saloons and merchandising firms could not deal in drafts on outside banking houses, exchange foreign currency, or assume other more complex functions, they could perform certain services on a limited scale.

Because the volume of its retail trade was generally the greatest in town, the saloon was often one of the first firms to require a safe, and customers hoping to protect their valuables or large amounts of cash or dust sought out the barkeeper to deposit their treasures. As much as $35,000 might be found in the safes of the more prominent and trustworthy saloonmen. Owners apparently provided this favor free to friends and regular customers, and some felt duty bound to reimburse any losses by theft, even if they had to borrow funds to do so.[8]

Limited, short-term loans might be given by saloonkeepers to clients looking for a grubstake or money for day-to-day expenses. The daybook of a Cripple Creek, Colorado, saloon, for instance, reveals that the owners extended numerous cash loans of from five to thirty dollars, particularly at the end of each month. Again, the proprietor was not acting purely out of philanthropic motives, for a man who deposited or borrowed money in a drinking house could be expected to spend part of it there as well. Finally, saloonmen often cashed the paychecks of wage laborers when no bank was available. Some sought a quick profit by discounting checks by up to 12 percent. Others, however, realized an even better return by offering this service without charge. When an owner in Mineral Park, Arizona, generously agreed to such an arrangement, the local editor reported that "the boys blew in their wealth in splendid style to this same gentleman who had the spondulicks [resources] to accommodate them."[9]

No two institutions were more naturally antagonistic than the saloon and the church, but in the early days of a camp, the minister and barkeeper might form a temporary alliance. Some men of the cloth were repelled by the crudities of life and by the loosened morality, but others, like the Reverend Ethelbert Talbot of Idaho, understood the need to conform somewhat to local mores: "To do men good they must be met on their own ground. It is not a loss of dignity, but the truest dignity, to identify one's self with the sorrows, anxieties and even with the joys of those whom it is an honor to serve just because they are men."[10]

And what better ground could there be for this work than the drinking house? Practical-minded ministers realized that the saloon, dance hall, and billiard room had one important advantage—they usually were filled with people. Thus, successful mountain ministers like Thomas Uzell and the "snow-shoe itinerant" John L. Dyer in Colorado, A. M. Hough in Montana, and Talbot in Idaho often used the facilities of cooperative barkeepers for their services. The ecumenically minded of California Gulch, Colorado, in the spring of 1860 could attend a Campbellite sermon at Haldeman's saloon on Sunday morning and a Universalist meeting at the recorder's office in the afternoon. The service might be a full-blown one, complete with prayers, hymns, and lengthy sermon, like the meeting in a Signal, Arizona, saloon that featured an armed choir to keep order.[11] More often, a minister simply delivered a brief message and passed the hat during a temporary halt in the gambling and drinking. Then the bar reopened, and calls of "first ball 41" and "keno!" were heard again.

While he might be moved by genuine religious feeling, the saloon owner also had more mundane reasons for opening his doors to the men of God. An impromptu sermon effected a peculiar combination of nostalgic power and entertainment that owners were quick to recognize. In short, it was a good show, and that was good business. Sam Danner of Tombstone, in fact, did not wait for a minister but performed the honors himself in his tent saloon, and afterwards the crowd celebrated with a round of drinks. These performances apparently paid. Touring the West in 1892, Richard Harding Davis asked the owner of Creede's largest gambling saloon how much he had lost when a preacher interrupted a busy night's wagering to deliver a sermon from atop a table. "Nothing," came the reply. "I got it all back at the bar."[12]

Nevertheless, ministers found other quarters as soon as possible, and the arrival of families encouraged a more sedate form of worship.

In time preachers of all denominations would join their Eastern brothers in campaigns against the barroom. In the initial stages of a camp's growth, however, the more aggressive clergymen found the saloon a convenient forum for carrying the Word to those who seemed to need it the most.

At least equally significant was the part played by the saloon in the early development of urban services. Because they usually hoped to acquire as much wealth as they could as quickly as possible before moving on, dwellers in mining camps at boom time generally showed little concern over the need for government and facilities that would encourage steady, long-term growth. Some problems, however, could not be ignored. The registration and protection of claims posed the most immediate need. Typically, prospectors in a given district would hold a mass outdoor meeting to organize a miners' association, set up basic rules, and settle disputed cases. When weather forced the crowd indoors, a saloon was often the popular choice of location. Watrous and Bannigan's barroom and gambling hall probably offered the only building in Creede large enough to hold the five hundred men who came in from the February cold in 1892 to form a miners' and claim-holders' protective association.[13]

Early residents came together in drinking places to solve other common problems. The merchants of Hailey, Idaho, met in Faylor's Saloon to discuss hiring a night watchman until the town or county could provide such protection. More alarming than footpads, however, were the devastating fires that swept at least once through almost every town of the Rockies. The haphazard crowding together of flimsy shacks and log cabins, the lack of regulations, and the fierce winds whipping through the mountains all combined to heighten the chances of a holocaust. Contemporary descriptions suggest that saloons were particularly vulnerable to such blazes. Fires that virtually destroyed the business district of Idaho City in 1865 and 1867, for example, both began in barrooms. Thus it was only natural that saloonkeepers of that town took the lead in providing minimal fire protection. Late in 1864, the proprietors of Idaho City's Gem Saloon paid to repair the town's outmoded fire-fighting equipment and called a meeting at their place of business to form a volunteer hook-and-ladder company. Less than two years later, a meeting at Taylor's Exchange reorganized the company and appointed an inspection committee that included two of the community's leading saloonmen. Six months later, another assembly in another saloon went through the procedure yet again. On other occasions, owners served as officers in fire crews, helped pay for iron buckets and Babcock fire extinguishers, and placed them strategically in their businesses for easy access by fire brigades. Still others played upon the fraternal bond of the fire company by sponsoring parades and races of hook-and-ladder teams and by providing free drinks after the festivities.[14]

If a mining camp survived, agencies of formal government eventually appeared, but the public functions of the drinking house did not end completely. As a convenient stopping place for miners, for instance, the saloon was an ideal location for a post office. The owner of a Helena resort posted a sign encouraging communication with the world outside: "Don't forget to write home to your dear old mother. She is thinking of you. We furnish paper and envelopes free, and have the best whiskey in town." Saloons frequently served as midwives at the birth of the first governments. Throughout the late winter and spring of 1892, the drinking houses of the Creede region were filled with crowds debating the virtues of incorporation and laying the boundaries of the cluster of towns in the district. Prior to the construction of public buildings, peace officers and town and county officials took up residence in popular drinking spots that guaranteed easy access by local townsfolk. Even courts might convene in an available barroom, perhaps with the bartender himself wearing the ermine. What was probably the first trial in the region eventually organized as Montana Territory was held during the spring of 1862 in Bolt's Saloon in the town of Hell Gate. Finally, the tavern served as a general gathering ground for the young camp's day-to-day activities— organization of public ceremonies and celebrations, collection of money for the relief of the poor, discussion of public nuisances, recruitment of volunteers for the army or for expeditions against Indians, the raising of scalp bounties, formation of clubs and benevolent societies, and the naming of the town itself.[15]

With the appearance of a formal structure of government, the mining town entered a new stage in its political life. Some citizens, at least, chose to participate in the scramble for offices, and although most continued to concentrate on the mundane pursuit of riches, they still took time out to observe the action. Elections often were close and bitterly contested, with all sides portraying each race—from police judge to the presidency—in life-or-death terms. "Politics in this country are much like the whiskey," wrote a resident of Central City in 1860, "plenty and most villainously mixed."[16]

The comparison was especially apt, for the saloon and its wares held a prominent place in the political events of the mining frontier. In this, the mountain West was certainly not unique. Since colonial times, men of all classes had met in the public houses to discuss issues of the day, voice common grievances, and organize to turn resolutions into results. In the tavern, John Adams wrote of Boston in 1760, "diseases, vicious habits, bastards, and legislators, are frequently begotten."[17] This tradition survived elsewhere in Gilded-Age America. City bosses and their lieutenants in the East and Midwest used saloons as channels of communication with supporters and as staging grounds for squads of voters on election day.

On the mining frontier, however, two considerations made the importance of the drinking house proportionately greater. First, in the absence of other facilities, it was simply the most convenient place to carry on the activities necessary to the pursuit and distribution of power. The second factor was somewhat more subtle but equally important. The editor of the Silver City, Idaho, *Owyhee Avalanche* hinted at it when he complained that in his camp the "political mill is grinding harshly."

Locally, there are seldom any principles involved in elections—though rectitude and ability should be. The best evidence that principle is entirely ignored, is found in the individual wrangling so common in bar-rooms, saloons, streets—everywhere. The whole issue seems to be individual—with little regard to capability.[18]

In short, the style of politics emphasized image over issues. The typical voter assumed, for better or for worse, that he would be moving on before long, and he considered issues of long-term development irrelevant. Instead, he looked upon politics as entertainment and as a form of personal, momentary service on the part of the office seeker. The ideal arena for this style of politics was not the meeting hall but the saloon.

Those who did take time to organize in pursuit of public office met in bars to form Democratic, Republican, and, in the 1890s, Free Silver clubs. Some businesses gained a reputation for their party allegiance or as supporters of union or "sesesh" or as Fenian sympathizers. In barrooms or in the halls added to the more prosperous establishments, political groups held caucuses and chose delegates to county and territorial conventions. Come election day, saloons sometimes were used as polling places, but usually other businesses or private homes were preferred. Even at the highest levels the saloon played its part. The first territorial legislature of Arizona met in Charles O. Brown's Tucson drinking house, Congress Hall, while that of the short-lived Jefferson Territory assembled in Libeus Barney's Apollo Hall in Denver before the creation of Colorado Territory.[19]

For his part, the politician recognized the saloon for what it was—a place where crowds of voters were ready to be gathered in. The constituency here was in a sense passive; rather than contributing to the political dialogue they waited to be won over. The politician who understood this found the drinking house well suited for forging this patronage of good fellowship. His tools were his personality and his purse, and his techniques were the pressing of flesh, the telling of jokes, and, above all, the buying of drinks. When he threw cash on the counter and set up the house, the candidate was offering more than an outright bribe. It was a symbolic act of good will and deference, a democratic gesture by which the office seeker admitted that for all his ambitions, he was no loftier than the grimiest sourdough or the laziest stove-shark.

The evidence of the early days strongly suggests that many, if not most, politicans performed this time-honored ceremony of treating. "Nowadays when we see a man 'setting them up,' " observed one journalist, "we involuntarily ask, 'What is he running for?' " At the local level such electioneering went on almost continuously. Nor was the process always more refined at the higher levels. In the spring of 1866, Montana's acting governor, Thomas Francis Meagher, called the territorial legislature into session. During the tumultuous weeks that followed, Meagher apparently spent much time in a Virginia City tavern, for he ran up a bill there for $619.75. While part of this sum went for meals for himself and his friends, his bar bill alone came to $332.25. His purchases of individual drinks, pitchers of beer, tumblers of cocktails, and baskets of wine indicate that during the controversial session "the Acting One" was keeping his political fields well irrigated. From top to bottom, alcohol apparently was a familiar part of the quest for power.[20]

The practical effect of such customs is not difficult to imagine. When free-flowing liquor combined with the atmosphere of the tavern and the audience's desire for entertainment, the result was more theater than political forum. One contemporary recalled an evening in a Logan City, Arizona, liquor shop when a legislative candidate appealed for support from atop a table:

He scraped and bowed, and scraped and bowed and then he said, "Ladies and gentlemen, Well I'm here. I came from Tucson and I'm going to stay until I go. Or I may be here day after tomorrow—but I'm going to stay until I go. Gentlemen, name your p'ison." And he threw four twenty-dollar gold pieces on the bar. He got most of the votes.[21]

At their worst, rallies degenerated into brawls and shooting scrapes. As a campaign neared its end, barkeepers closed early to conserve their stock, and those in the more remote towns imported large shipments to insure an adequate supply for the occasion. Given such a prelude, election day in some camps proved remarkably calm, but in others office seekers reserved cases of champagne for later celebration and hired wagons with barrels of liquor to circulate from poll to poll, leaving the electorate a "drunken, howling mass" by nightfall. Some local officials openly declared a one-day moratorium on public drunkenness and arrested only the most violent offenders. In the final act of the drama, participants filled the public houses, the winners to crow victory, the vanquished to soothe their pain.[22]

The saloon was not alone in performing these services. Politicians glad-handed voters in hardware stores and smithies. Miners slept in livery stables, deposited their dust in Wells, Fargo and Company safes, and heard sermons in general stores. But when floor space was needed, the abundance of barrooms and their long hours made them the most accessible source. The saloon's atmosphere and the rapid flow through it of a broad sampling of the population made it better suited than any other place to the needs of the flamboyant preacher, the politician, and the man in search of information.

The saloon, however, was first and foremost a place of entertainment and relaxation, and any successful operator understood that all its other roles were secondary. Unmarried bucks and husbands temporarily "batching it" had no families to fill their hours after a day of backbreaking, often frustrating, labor. Tired, restless, and lonely, these men were in search of escape by nighttime. "The people are eager for some decent place and means of recreation," commented an Idaho editor. "Frequently a man needs a good square laugh worse than a 'square meal' or dose of pills."[23]

The need for diversion was felt from Coeur d'Alene to Tombstone, but it was particularly strong during the long winters of the central and northern Rockies. Storms swept into the region from the north and west, and frigid temperatures froze the streams and brought work in the diggings to a halt. One winter resident wrote: "Everything is dead here. . . . You cannot imagine the ennui I endure." The gray skies and bitter winds rasped the nerves of those who stayed, and time seemed to flow as slowly as cold-thickened syrup. Men held parties and balls and formed reading groups, sledding societies, and exercise clubs. They convened mock trials and sponsored lying contests, but not even these could fill the void. "And now," one editor wrote, "genius is taxed to provide amusement to pass the long winter evenings, and many are the devices to drive dull care away."[24]

The business that met this need was as important in its way as a lodging house or merchandising firm. In responding to the demand, the saloonkeeper showed his greatest imagination and his understanding of the public's attitudes and tastes. The saloonman's efforts illustrated both his own entrepreneurial talents and the desires of the people he served.

"The American miner is a gambler *pur sang*," observed one tourist in the Rockies.[25] Indeed, whatever his place of origin, the typical resident of the mining towns shared with his fellows the conviction that fortune had singled him out for favor. The act of emigration itself implied such a faith. This popular belief explains the great popularity of the saloon-sponsored lottery. As many owners seemed to understand, anyone who had staked his savings on the chance of finding a rich vein somewhere among a chain of remote mountains would usually be willing to risk a dollar or two on a raffle.

Some were brief and spontaneous affairs. A miner down on his luck might toss a gun or other personal article on the floor before the bar, and the customers would roll dice at a dollar a throw for it. Other lotteries treated the town to weeks of delicious suspense, carefully heightened by editors hungry for a story, before a drawing determined the lucky winner of a horse and saddle, gold watch, sewing machine, musical instrument, rifle, or garish example of Victorian domestic art. Sometimes lotteries virtually monopolized a community's attention. During the summer of 1865, saloon raffles were all the rage in Idaho City. As competition among the owners escalated, so did the value of the reward—jewelry, watches, a fireman's trumpet of solid silver, $1,000 in gold coin, then $5,500. The peak was reached when one proprietor offered his saloon, complete with fixtures and lot, to the fortunate holder of the right two-dollar ticket. In all cases, however, the prize seemed less attractive than the process. A bet on a raffle was an act of faith in the ultimate success of the bettor's pursuit of the main chance.[26]

Besides lotteries and the games of chance that ran continuously in many saloons, owners seized every opportunity to play upon—and profit by—their customers' wagering instincts. Close contests of ten pins, or "pin pool," and high-stakes poker games drew large crowds who added to the excitement with vigorous side-betting. A Virginia City barkeeper constructed raised seats so the audience could see better a billiard match between two local favorites for a $500 prize. Others sponsored marathon checker games, marksmanship and shuffleboard contests, and walking matches. One provided facilities for cockfighting in his bar and hung out a new sign rechristening his business the Chicken Debating Club.[27]

Another type of saloon entertainment, prizefighting, offered both an opportunity for betting and a display of abilities that were much admired by a young and virile clientele. The discovery of precious metals in the Far West coincided with the emergence of prizefighting as a popular national sport. Here again the barkeeper put his promotional talents to work. He might advertise his place as a source of opinion and general long-windedness: "THE GREAT NATIONAL PRIZE FIGHT BETWEEN HEENAN AND KING—Who will win? Ask any person connected with Nuttal's Concert Room, under the Charter Oak Saloon."[28] More frequently, he would be involved in setting up fights in his own town. The process usually began with anonymous "talk" proposing a bout between two local stalwarts or between a well-known outsider and a local favorite. After one of the participants issued an official challenge, there often followed an exchange of statements in the press replete with veiled insults and hints of cowardice, then, finally, a date was set. Such ballyhoo fanned popular enthusiasm and encouraged much argument—and drinking—in local bars; thus it was not by coincidence that saloon owners usually sponsored these exhibitions and provided space for the fight.

One of the most famous prizefights on the Rocky Mountain frontier pitted John Con Orem, himself a Virginia City saloonkeeper, against the hulking Hugh O'Neil. So great was the public's interest that the promoter, A. J. Nelson, erected a log building behind his tavern especially for the occasion. With Nelson as referee and another saloonman as timekeeper, Orem fought his heavier opponent to a draw after 185 grueling rounds. For each such extravaganza, many other lesser bouts took place. They might be held in drinking houses, public halls, or outdoor rings, but in most of them a saloonkeeper was involved in some capacity. The financial inducements were substantial. While the fighters received prize money put up by each side before the battle and any "ring money" tossed at them at the conclusion of the bout, organizers profited from admission fees, side bets, and extra traffic at the bar. Inevitably, such an opportunity lured unscrupulous promoters. In later fights in Helena against O'Neil and Billy Dwyer, Orem was accused of taking dives, and other contests were condemned as lackluster waltzing exhibitions. Yet as long as there was action, audiences seemed satisfied by the spectacle, whether it offered genuine skill or an hour of controlled brawling. In the last years of the mining frontier, another dimension was added to this tradition when saloons installed special telegraph connections that brought reports of eastern prizefights to barroom sportsmen.[29]

More decorous activities, however, were not neglected. To satisfy their inhabitants' musical interests, camps often organized amateur orchestras or bands, though the quality was not always the highest. The upbeat selections of the brass band of Ketchum, Idaho, sounded to a local journalist like "a regiment of tom-cats with their tails tied together and strung on a clothes-line," while its more somber numbers recalled "the last groan of a dying calf." Nonetheless, any amusement was appreciated. Here again, saloonmen did their part by giving their facilities over for organizational meetings, hosting balls to raise money for instruments, and featuring professional itinerant musicians when they came through town.[30]

Few forms of entertainment captured the interest and enthusiasm of mining town dwellers as much as dancing. A fancy dress ball lent a touch of elegance to the rough society, allowed an outlet for pent-up energies, and provided a chance for young men and women to meet and court under proper chaperonage. These advantages, and the general demand for diversion, broke down whatever moral doubts some may have had. "Were you to venture to suggest here . . . that it is wrong to dance," the Reverend Daniel Tuttle wrote his wife from Virginia City, "people would look upon you with mingled feelings of amazement and pity."[31] Particularly during the winter doldrums, social clubs and fraternal orders sponsored hops, flings, and masked balls. For those untutored in the intricacies of the waltz, schottische, varsovienne, and Virginia reel, dancing academies provided instruction as well as advice in the subtleties of etiquette.

Despite an absolute lack of women, the miners of Sawtooth, Idaho, were so determined to hold a masquerade ball in the winter of 1882 that four of their number arrived at Joe Pierceson's saloon dressed as "a Chinawoman, negro wench, Irish market woman and Eastern esthete." The festivities proceeded. Fortunately, women were available in most cases, and whenever possible more respectable facilities were used. Proper ladies found the masculine atmosphere of

15. Properly dressed miners in Cripple Creek, Colorado, could find both a glass of beer and feminine companionship at Crapper Jack's Dance Hall and Saloon. *From the Special Collections, Tutt Library, The Colorado College, Colorado Springs, Colorado*

the saloon uncomfortable, yet in the absence of other alternatives, organizers of dances often looked to the drinking house, though they felt the need to issue assurances. "No bummers or ladies of doubtful fame" were admitted to the fancy dress ball in the Shades Saloon of Virginia City in 1864, and its owner promised the strictest propriety would be maintained. With further growth and maturity came meeting halls and other buildings with more room and more suitable surroundings for the refined rituals of the dance. Even then, however, saloonkeepers responded to the need by constructing halls adjacent to their businesses. Thus they sought to add to their income by adjusting to the town's social evolution and its changing demands.[32]

In sponsoring lotteries, prizefights, and dances, the saloon owner demonstrated his understanding of the diversity of camp society—its speculative spirit, masculinity, and pretensions to respectability. In many other ways this entrepreneur tried to occupy his customers' idle hours. He might feature displays of local oddities. A bored miner could waste time gawking at a captured bear—invariably "the largest

16. In Idaho City, men leaned on the bar of the Shanahan and Haggerty saloon beneath a fine set of stuffed animals. Joe Shanahan, with his hand in his pocket, is on the left of the old-timer with the white beard; Red Haggerty, his coproprietor, is the man in the white shirt two places further to Shanahan's left. *Courtesy of the Idaho Historical Society*

ever seen in the Rockies''—an eagle, a stuffed snake, strange, glittering rocks, or some accident of nature, such as a petrified mushroom. Jack Kiausch's place in Park City, Utah, was a mini-museum with a live monkey (''Darwin's missing link''), newborn chicks stuffed by the local taxidermist, various notions and novelties, and some otherwise unidentified ''toilet adornments.''[33]

Occasionally itinerant troupes came through to provide more formal entertainment. In smaller camps not yet blessed with a theater or opera house, these groups turned to the saloon. The veteran Western actor John McGuire recalled performing on billiard tables against a painted backdrop of scenes suspended from the ceiling. Minstrel groups presented dancing, farces, and ''negro extravaganzas.'' More often, however, an owner was left to his own devices, but many were equal to the challenge. Anything, in fact, offering action and a bit of broad humor could draw a crowd. A casual tour of drinking spots might turn up shows ranging from a mock trial to bearbaiting to a pie-eating contest. Competition for the attention of the drinking populace produced some strange sights. In the winter of 1865 Virginia City's Shebang Saloon hosted the plank-walking championship of Montana, a spectacle featuring two contestants pacing elevated pieces of lumber for forty-eight consecutive hours. The exhibition testified to both the participants' endurance and the sponsor's imagination.[34]

The minstrels, dancers, prizefighters, and other special events concocted by the saloonmen however, should not obscure the saloon's most common purpose. The barroom periodically offered colorful entertainments, but during all its open hours, men entered its doors for another reason. They were looking for a bit of conversation and companionship. Theirs was a highly competitive society and a hard-working one, and the saloon provided a temporary refuge. In it a few drinks could lessen frustrations and lighten the heart as well as the head and a sense of a common bond with others could be fostered.

Much has been made of the democracy of the saloon, and though the term usually remains ill defined, it traditionally has implied that men of all backgrounds, social ranks, and economic levels met and drank on the common ground of the barroom. The saloon as melting pot, however, had its limits. As noted above, the larger saloons in the more prosperous towns often had clubrooms where the economic and social elite assembled, away from the crowd. Other evidence indicates that men sometimes tried to be selective in their choice of drinking companions. The names of some saloons—the California Concert Hall, Pennsylvania Headquarters, the Washoe, the New York, Joplin Headquarters, and Texas House—suggest that in a transient society men from these places may have sought the contact and friendship of others of similar origin; and in the Fenian Headquarters and Free Silver Saloon, advocates of those political causes met to drink and relax with men of the same persuasion. Some barrooms had reputations as ethnic gathering spots. The credit records of Peterson and Anderson's Pioneer Saloon of Cripple Creek are filled with such Scandinavian names as Erikson, Carlson, Strom, Skoglund, and Christenson.[35] Still others catered to certain occupational groups—miners, smelter workers, or railroad employees.

In towns with larger populations and a greater variety of saloons, such businesses might become specialized gathering places in which a common background, belief, job, or economic status could provide a sense of association. Rather than encouraging economic leveling and indiscriminate social mixing, these places allowed a society to sort itself out into its various parts.

However, most moderate-sized towns did not support such a variety of drinking spots. Although each saloon probably had its "regulars," the customers in this highly mobile society presumably would have had little in common with each other except in their ways of working and living, in the act of drinking itself, and in experiences in other barrooms across the country. These would be the basis for human contact and for whatever conviviality developed. Because companionship and relaxation were part of the saloon's appeal, its structure, the personality of its host, its customs, and even its language all played their part.

Just as the floor plan of any merchant's shop must conform to the needs of the business, so has the physical arrangement of the drinking house traditionally been designed with an eye to its social purpose. In Europe and in the United States, different types of layouts have encouraged varying styles of behavior. The open space and round tables of the Mediterranean wine shop provide a setting for conversation among small groups, while in the larger German beer halls, with their long, parallel tables, more of a communal spirit prevails. In the modern, middle-class cocktail lounge, the dim lighting, high-backed booths, and small tables fragment the crowd and promote intimacy.[36]

The owner of a frontier saloon built his facilities so he could sell liquor efficiently, but the physical setting also furthered the barroom's social function—the marketing of talk and conviviality. Along one wall ran the bar, and opposite it were tables seating four to six persons each and perhaps facilities for a game of billiards. In the larger businesses, this area was separated by a wall and door from the main gambling and entertainment room to the rear. This arrangement allowed for different types of personal interaction. When it first appeared in England, the bar was designed to accommodate large numbers of men quickly, as when workers leaving a factory crowded into a public house to cool their throats, and in the West it served a similar purpose. In quieter hours, however, a drinker could stand alone with his boot on the bar rail, talk with the bartender and those immediately to his right or left, or lean with his back on the bar and survey activities before him. The side-by-side arrangement along the bar discouraged conversation and allowed the man seeking a moment of solitude to sip his beer with few interruptions. At the small round tables, the billiard table, or the area around the stove, however, those in search of companionship and banter were likely to find others with a similar intent. Anyone could move from place to place to observe the action and to seek out the people or talk best suited to his mood. Only in later years were secluded wine booths added, usually enclosed by doors or curtains, where men might dally with prostitutes or drink with friends in great privacy. The artistic representations of prizefighters and scantily clad women also provided topics of talk and generally complemented the masculine atmosphere of the place.

The layout, in short, emphasized relaxed contact but still allowed a measure of privacy for whoever wished it. Emphasis was clearly on the group. The room was open and usually well lighted, and the ready visibility and easy movement made anonymity elusive. But the individual was not forgotten. Among the small parties seated at tables a man could make himself heard, or if he preferred, he could find a time of relative solitude at the bar.

The barkeeper contributed to the convivial mood and easy personal contact encouraged by the arrangement of his facilities. He did his best to live up to his well-publicized reputation for gregariousness and geniality. As a teller of tales, he loosened reserve among his patrons. As the one individual with whom they all dealt, he could work to establish a common bond among the group. The owner's personality and his surroundings thus worked to the same end.

Like any institution that emphasizes relations among men, the barroom developed its own rituals and customs. Of its ceremonies, the most common was "treating," the purchase by an individual of drinks for a group or for all the customers in the house. An owner naturally encouraged this practice, for it could increase his trade substantially. Five men drinking alone might buy one shot apiece and then leave.

17. An unknown photographer in Helena, Montana, received a toast from this saloon's clientele—including a plaster bulldog balancing a tiny beer stein on its snout. *Courtesy of the Montana Historical Society*

Should one treat the others to a glass, however, each of the rest would be expected to reciprocate, and the total liquor purchased would increase fivefold. When a bartender set up a free round, then, he usually did so partly out of good humor and partly to set in motion a profitable process.

For the patron, treating was evidence of his generosity and a symbolic recognition of his membership in the group. The man who thus obliged his fellows became "one of the boys," "a good fellow who spends his money freely," and "a man to trade with." Anyone who accepted a drink and then refused to buy in his turn was branded a skinflint, while the man who turned down a free shot risked physical retaliation. The roots of the custom can be traced as far back as the wassail bowl and loving cup of the fifth-century Saxons, and beyond them to practices of the Egyptians and Assyrians.[37] By the nineteenth century, treating had evolved into its familiar form in the pubs of England and the saloons of urban America. Except for variations in vernacular, the procedure on the mining frontier differed little from that of eastern cities. The solemn ritual began with an expansive customer's offer to buy a round. A contemporary observer described what followed:

And now they stand in a row at the bar; the barkeeper is mixing the long and the short drinks. Each man waits, says nothing, and eyes every motion of the bartender. The silence is impressive. All is ready. Each glass is grasped and raised, and then from each to each, and more than all, from all to the drink donor, there is a nod, that incantatory phrase is uttered, "Well, here's luck," and the poison is down. As it rasps, they call "Ahem!" with varied degrees of modulation.[38]

The ceremony was repeated until each member of the party had treated the others and in turn had received his nodding salute.

Treating was the most formalized of the saloon's customs, but when it combined with alcohol's relaxing of inhibitions, it encouraged other group activities, games of billiards, poker, and freeze-out or animated discussions of current political and social topics or of certain favorite questions, such as "Does lager beer intoxicate?"[39] There were tales, tall and taller, of individual prowess and a large body of jokes and anecdotes concerning drinking and its effects.

The conversation on these occasions was enlivened by the men's use of a distinctive vocabulary. Not just in the barroom but on the mining frontier in general an outsider would have found some of the vernacular incomprehensible. A few words and phrases of the mountain West gradually gained acceptance in the East—"square meal," "you bet," and "that let's me out," for example—but many others remained confined largely to the Pacific coast and the Rockies. A young fop good at dancing but little else was a "Johnny boy" and his female equivalent, an "Evangeline." A deceased miner had "passed over the ridge" or "ascended the golden clothes pole." Something disapproved of was "gummy" or "toppy," while an acceptable person, object, or experience was "balmy," "gulitive," or "catouche," and anything first-rate was "skoocum." After a hard day's work, a miner might announce that he was "on it" (ready to eat, gamble, or fight), then proceed to a restaurant for "muk-a-muk" (food and refreshment) and a "torch" (smoke) before he "went under the blinks" (slept).[40]

Some of the most elaborate slang of the time, however, was to be found in the lexicon of the saloon. Western drinking terms showed the influence of both Eastern and local inventions. Many contemporary usages had first appeared during the period between the Revolution and the Civil War, years when Americans expanded their own language even as they built and tested their social and political institutions. One scholar has concluded that in the growing glossary of Americanisms there were more slang terms related to drinking than to any other human activity, including copulation. A few of these creations survive today—"fizz" and "cocktail" (in use by 1810), "eye-opener" (1818), "jigger" (1836), "on a bender" (1846), "set-'em-up" (1851), and "straight" (1862). Others have fallen from popular use, perhaps because they were often vulgar, though always imaginative and rich in descriptive humor. A few of the day's synonyms for liquor provide examples: "panther-sweat," "tonsil-paint," "stagger-soup," "phlegm-cutter," and "milk of the wild cow."[41]

As the mining frontier expanded throughout the Rockies during the years after 1865, Easterners were devising more decorous but less colorful words, such as "highball" and "Tom Collins," but the vigorous and unpolished society of the mountains seemed more comfortable with earlier, cruder creations, and there some of the older vernacular survived. For example, three favorite words for the region's cheapest and most powerful whiskey—"forty-rod," "tanglefoot," and "bust-skull"—often were assumed to be frontier creations, but in fact they had their origins in the East. Dwellers of the mountains, however, were not entirely imitative. They devised special labels for whiskey from a certain locality. "Taos Lightning" referred to spirits distilled in northern New Mexico and freighted to Colorado, though in time the phrase was applied to any inexpensive liquor of poor quality sold in the central and southern Rockies. A customer in the camps of Idaho and Montana who bought "valley tan" whiskey, on the other hand, knew his pleasure had come from the area around Salt Lake City. To describe the habits of the barroom, mining terms were adapted, so a man who had overindulged was said to be "smeared with a tellurium stain." Any drink of whiskey was a "wash," one bought on credit was "jawbone," while the traditional free round provided by the owner when he first opened his doors was a "morning's morning." Some "break-of-day places," however, never closed. "Needle-gun," "scald punch," and "flashes of lightning" referred to especially strong liquor that would leave its imbiber "swipsey" if he did not use caution in "swallowing the tods" or "throwing a drop down his neck."[42]

Together the older Eastern terms and these newer Western inventions composed an institutional language that not only described the activities of the saloon but also helped establish common ground among its patrons. The ritual of treating, the games and contests, the tradition of relaxed conversation, and the drinking vernacular formed something like a fraternal order of habit and phrase that could unite, if only temporarily, strangers from all parts of the states and the mountains. Men could meet with other men, sheltered for the moment from the demands and loneliness of the world outside.

Considering the many activities that took place within its doors, it does not seem too much to say that the saloon was the mining camp's most versatile social institution, particularly in the early days. With its roominess, availability, and large crowds, the barroom filled many practical needs and provided space for public gatherings. In time other institutions arrived to provide the services the saloon had handled by default, but it would never lose the one traditional social role it had played from the start. As a place where men could find a momentary easing of inhibitions in the camaraderie of the bottle and stein, the saloon was unique. In a turbulent, almost atomized society, this was its most common and important function. The saloon owner did not, however, provide his services out of altruism; he acted on a hallowed assumption of the frontier, that the retail liquor trade offered an easy and certain chance for riches. The reality of that assumption requires a closer look.

5

The Revenue
Flows Freely

We Would Be Happy
To see the snow disappear.
Fifty of our mines shipping ore.
A thousand more men at work in our camp.
A man who does not think he can make a
    fortune running a saloon.

THIS irritated editorial comment expressed a common article of faith
among residents of the Rocky Mountain camps.[1] Briefly stated, this
belief held that any aspiring entrepreneur with "wet goods" and a
place to sell them could parlay a modest grubstake into a life of ease
and economic plenty. It was one of many such dreams in an optimistic
society perpetually in pursuit of the main chance.

Many who came to the mountains learned quickly that digging for
gold was about the most difficult way to acquire it. The ambitious
immigrant could often fare far better by supplying the many needs of
those around him, and a casual look about the town would suggest one
of the more obvious possibilities. To an Eastern visitor to Idaho City,
the evidence was ever-present: "The principal corners of the streets
here are occupied by *saloons*, from whence issue everybody, usually
wiping their mouth and tying up a money bag—indications that while
filling up the first, they had partially emptied the latter—another
lesson in 'Cause and Effect.' "[2]

The presence of masses of men looking for a drink and a place of
companionship seemed to offer sure and ample profits to those who
could provide these things. There were enough examples of individual

97

success, like that of Daniel Floweree (or Fleury), to encourage this impression. Floweree arrived in Montana from Missouri in 1864 and, after prospecting briefly and unsuccessfully, opened a saloon and gambling hall in Helena. The enterprise prospered with the town, and within a year he was investing his profits in ranching. Eventually he sold his drinking establishment, and by his later years Floweree had become one of the state's leading cattlemen, a dabbler in Florida grapefruit properties, and a figure of some social stature. When city fathers in the state capital named a street after the former saloonman, they were acknowledging a genuine frontier success story.[3]

The few such spectacular cases, however, tended to obscure the many others whose outcomes were not so happy. The small mining town of Emery, Montana, for example, attracted three saloon owners soon after its founding. The first died of pneumonia, the second deserted his wife, who then poisoned herself, and the third hanged himself. "It's plane [sic] to be seen," a resident wrote later, "the first saloon men in Emery didn't do too good."[4]

Where is the truth? Definitive answers are elusive, for among the few available financial records, there is not one surviving example of barroom bookkeeping that details costs, income, and profits of a single saloon owner over even a short span of time. Any investigator must rely heavily on contemporary comments and circumstantial evidence. Even so, the hopes of these businessmen can be examined in light of the conditions they faced in the camps—overhead, competition, and other factors indigenous to the mining frontier economy. On the basis of these facts, some suggestions can be made about the waking realities of a familiar frontier dream.

The Expectation

A veteran of the Arizona camps stated clearly the appeal of the saloon business. Both a mine and a barroom could turn a tidy profit, he reasoned, but

there is this marked difference . . . in the getting started. Frequently the miner invests a fortune before he receives a farthing in return. On the other hand, ten dollars will establish a saloon. And not unlikely, the first day after the screen is adjusted inside the front door, revenue from the modest stock of mingled water, chemicals, and alcohol begins to flow freely.[5]

Here were summarized the most alluring aspects of the trade. A low initial investment could set up a hopeful businessman. Implied was a second inducement, easy access to the product sold, the "mingled water, chemicals, and alcohol" passed across the bar. And on this the merchant could expect a rapid and substantial return.

The first point—that only a small amount of money was needed to open a saloon—depended upon the kind of barroom in question. Descriptions of mining towns seem to show three classes of drinking establishments. Some of the most useful insights into this economic division come from the lists of buildings destroyed and their values published by newspapers in the wake of fires that swept periodically through the mining towns. Such lists typically include one or two drinking and gambling houses worth substantially more than the rest, a second category valued at between $1,000 and $2,000 each, and a third group inventoried at around $500 to $700 apiece.[6]

Surviving firsthand accounts indicate that a prospective saloon-man could indeed enter the trade with relative ease, provided he did so at the lowest level. Two examples serve as illustrations. Charles Bennett of Arizona started his first whiskey business when he carried ten gallons of liquor from Prescott to Gillette and sold it from a rock beside a river. Eventually he took the profits and built a crude shack. Far to the north in Montana, one George Schoutz did likewise. He apparently could not face working all his days for the local mining company, and the prospect of the liquor trade attracted him. Unfortunately, he had practically no money, but as a friend later recalled, "George didn't let a little thing like being short of funds stop him if he took a notion to do something." He secured a cabin so cramped that a six-foot customer could stand only in the center.

In these humble quarters George took two rough boards about 8 feet long and ten inches wide and laid them side by side on jack legs. That was the bar. Against the wall he fastened another board that was the back bar on which rested a few whiskey glasses and beer mugs. There was no plate glass mirror for the boys to admire themselves in. . . . George was dressed up in his best six-year twenty-dollar suit, beaming with good nature and cracking jollie and laughing long and loud at all of [the customers]. The remaining furniture consisted of one card table, two decks of cards, some poker chips, and stove and for chairs a few empty 50-pound powder boxes. His stock of liquor consisted of one gallon of whisky and a case of beer.[7]

These descriptions suggest that men of slim means could scrape together the modest stake needed to open a saloon, as long as their standards of comfort were not too lofty. Bennett's ten gallons of whiskey would have cost between fifty and seventy-five dollars in Prescott or in most supply centers in the mountains. When transportation and miscellaneous expenses are considered, the total cost of establishing his crude business almost certainly did not exceed twice that amount. And even if George Schoutz bought rather than rented his one-room cabin, he probably paid no more than a few hundred dollars for it and its primitive furnishings.

Here were the tents and shacks of logs and rough-hewn timber that sprang up overnight in a newborn camp and continued to operate on the periphery of the business district after better facilities had appeared. Starting these businesses was especially easy during a camp's beginnings, when a man could carry in a keg or two of crude liquor and find many ready takers, or in smaller camps, like the one where Schoutz settled, which could not support better-heeled competitors. But even in larger towns, an aspiring barkeeper could open a marginal drinking spot on the fringes of the town's trade. The literature of the mining frontier contains chance references to others who financed liquor businesses on a shoestring—the Montanan who traded his horse for four gallons of alcohol and set up shop, or the disgruntled mill hand who lost his job but still had the capital needed to buy out a local groggery. [8]

The middle, somewhat costlier, class of saloons included those available for two to five times the price of the lowest order. Occasional deeds of sale and lists of fire losses suggest that a buyer probably could have purchased a well-established drinking house and all its furnishings for between $1,500 and $3,000 in most mining towns of the Rockies. Sometime after his experiences in Gillette, Charles Bennett was working as a miner in Pinal. Tiring of that occupation, he approached a local businessman for help.

So I went to Jack Ryan; Jack, says I, I want $500. So he took a sack down from off the wall with three or four thousand dollars in it; I said I was going to buy old Jim Foley out—he had a big saloon. I paid him [Foley] $500 down and took it over. . . . When the boys came in from the shift I said we had two kinds of drinks—beer and gin. Well do you know there was six weeks I never saw a bed; just slept on the billiard tables; I kept right by the saloon and never closed it night or day. I made $20,000.[9]

These places, fairly roomy structures located along the main business streets and having facilities for lounging and often gaming, obviously were less accessible to the man with an impulse to enter the trade but little cash with which to do it. Yet men of ordinary means could use two methods to break into the business at this level. Like Bennett, a hopeful barkeeper might borrow funds on the gamble that future profits would eventually give him full title. Informal loans were preferable—a friend like Jack Ryan, who simply pulled a bag from a shelf and handed out what was needed, or someone like the Charleston, Arizona, rancher who advanced an acquaintance $600 to open a saloon and charged as interest all the whiskey he could drink plus a pint to take home at night. When formal banking facilities were available, rates of interest varied widely, but as on most frontiers they were typically high, sometimes as much as 10 to 25 percent per month.[10]

The prospective liquor merchant who either could not or would not borrow the money he needed might pool his resources with like-minded colleagues. In fact, partnerships often were the rule, for they not only provided more capital but also divided up the burden of the long working hours essential to the trade. William Nuttal of the Charter Oak Saloon in Central City, Colorado, must have thought so when he advertised for an ambitious partner with a small amount of money looking for ''a rare chance'' for a lucrative investment.

An agreement recorded in Idaho City reveals how such an arrangement might be drawn up. Of the two partners of the Challenge Saloon, J. R. Totman and W. W. Boardwell, the second wanted out, and two new investors, H. B. Smith and H. S. Wolf, agreed to buy his interest. Under the new arrangement, Totman would remain as manager, while Smith and Wolf promised to renovate the saloon at their own expense and to provide a melodeon for entertainment. Accounts were to be settled and profits divided weekly.[11] Thus Totman contributed his earlier investment, his experience, and his name, and Smith and Wolf the working capital needed for improvements. The

18. In Arcadia Hall, one of Denver's largest gambling saloons, a collection of businessmen, speculators, soldiers, and mountain veterans courted the favors of Dame Chance. *Courtesy of the Colorado Historical Society*

result was a revamped and revitalized business that perhaps no one of the individuals involved could have established alone.

The elite of the liquor trade operated out of magnificent establishments in the more prosperous mining towns. Businesses in this final category might be purchased for as little as $5,000 or as much as $20,000, but most of them ranged in price from $7,000 to $10,000. These large halls, outfitted with elaborate and costly facilities, almost always offered gambling and dancing as well as a place at the bar, and they were as much general entertainment centers as simple saloons. Invariably located on a prominent and costly corner of the business district, these places stood out as the most active centers of a town's retail trade.[12]

In many cases local proprietors of more modest bars took the plunge and converted merely adequate saloons into palaces of carousal. After running his business on Main Street for a year, for instance, John Cody of Idaho City spent much of one winter totally renovating the structure and its interior in time for the spring rush. Men like Cody probably financed their ventures with a combination of previous profits and credit, but given the costs of construction and conversion and the expenses of upkeep, it was not an investment to be taken lightly.

Outside investors sometimes built or bought and expanded a saloon in an especially promising location. This practice seems to have been limited almost entirely to the most prosperous of the mining towns, Leadville and Tombstone in particular. By 1880, with the Tombstone boom at its peak, California interests were buying some of the town's plusher drinking places, just as others from the Pacific coast were investing in the region's mines and smelters. In Leadville, the popular Board of Trade Saloon apparently was controlled by Chicago interests, and others, like that of Phil Golding, were backed by investors or successful practitioners of the trade in Denver.[13]

Regardless of how these businesses were financed, they were obviously beyond the reach of the great majority of those trying to enter the trade. Too great a pool of capital was needed. Of local owners, apparently only those who gathered in substantial profits and could command the necessary credit entered the ranks of the elite. The popular wisdom that any man with a modest roll of bills or bag of dust could open a saloon, therefore, was close to the truth at the lower levels of the business, particularly in younger and smaller camps, and in the middle range, especially if an owner was willing to take on a partner or borrow what was needed. At least in the starting of the saloon, there seems to have been room for the aspiring barkeeper so long as his sights were not set too high.

The second of the three assumptions concerned the easy availability of sources of supply. Here again, there was an element of truth. Alcohol was both popular and relatively easy to carry, and with few exceptions frontier freighters were able to bring in large quantities of it over the most challenging terrain in the mountains.

By definition, frontiers are relatively isolated places, but some parts of the Rocky Mountains posed much greater problems of access than others. Of all the mining regions, Colorado was the easiest for the businessman to supply, while the settlements of Arizona and those of the northern Rockies were not so fortunate. To carry goods over great distances merchants relied on a variety of means. When all else failed, unemployed miners or willing Indians could pack in some material over snow-choked trails in loads of up to 100 pounds apiece. Whenever possible, however, mules and horses were preferred. Particularly in the northern mountains, freighters depended on burros fitted with Spanish packsaddles, or *aparejos*, to supply towns beyond the reach of wagons. Between 1863 and 1869, muleteers led thousands of animals from towns on the Snake River to Florence and the Boise basin in Idaho and to Helena, Virginia City, and Kootenai in Montana.

In time, all major mining regions were served by roads that accommodated wagons able to carry large amounts of supplies. Freighters developed these routes quickly after the first strikes along Colorado's Front Range and in the area around Prescott in Arizona. The burro trails from the Snake River to the Idaho and Montana camps were improved for use by wagons, and an alternative route developed from northern California to southern Idaho. After 1865, caravans of wagons began carrying Eastern goods from Fort Benton on the Missouri River to Helena and the southern Montana camps. The ultimate achievement in transportation, the railroad, usually served directly only those camps that proved both easily accessible and particularly rich. By the middle of the 1880s, major rail lines had reached regional supply centers from which wagons could transport material to other markets. Denver furnished the most spectacular example of a city that flourished as a distribution center, but there were several others, among them Boise, Helena, Tucson, Corinne, and Durango.[14]

Freight rates varied greatly according to terrain, distance, weather, and competition. Unless direct rail connections were available however, rates rarely fell below five cents per pound, and except during brief periods of climatic disaster or Indian depredations, they rarely exceeded twenty cents. In most Rocky Mountain mining towns, merchants paid freighters between eight and fifteen cents per pound to bring in their goods.[15]

Like all merchants of the region, liquor sellers used this transportation network. Only rarely did the most isolated parts of Colorado and the northern Rockies, whose lines of supply were sometimes totally disrupted by weather or the threat of Indian attack, run short of whiskey. Even then, when the price of flour tripled and men weakened from malnutrition and scurvy, barkeepers could postpone the crisis with a raw concoction of drugs, alcohol, and snow water. As an owner in Fairplay, Colorado, assured his customers, "Don't be uneasy. Ole Mack will churn tonight, and there will be plenty tomorrow." In a few cases, this device was not enough. Near the end of the bitter winter of 1861–62, a correspondent from Florence, Idaho, wrote to his readers:

Yes Sir! The alarming fact has transpired that there is no whisky in camp. We made it go as far as we could. When but a few gallons could be found we lengthened them out by the usual appliances, but there is an end to the elongation of most things, and we come to the point where disguised water is unable to make drunk come, and then we must perforce suspend.[16]

Nonetheless, a crisis like this was highly unusual, for as frontiersmen from the whiskey rebels to the far western fur traders already had discovered, alcohol had two important characteristics to recommend it as an item of freight. First, it could be packed and carried in a variety of ways with relative ease. And second—and more significant—its price upon arrival was high in relation to its weight. To elaborate: a hundredweight of flour typically sold in mining towns for twenty to thirty dollars. The same weight of whiskey, brought in with the same effort and at the same cost, would bring between two and three hundred dollars when retailed by the drink. With such a return, high freight rates were of relatively little concern.

No wonder, then, that alcohol ordinarily was one of the first products to appear in a town and one of the last to be depleted. Depending upon the circumstances, merchants relied upon all available means of transportation to make sure their clientele had plenty to drink. With small casks strapped to their backs, men plodded on snowshoes over lonely trails to the remote camps of Idaho. When poured into casks, each holding about twenty-eight gallons, enough alcohol could be loaded onto a single burro to fill one large barrel; thus liquor furnished a substantial proportion of the tonnage carried by the long lines of "Mexican mules" that preceded and supplemented wagon traffic.[17]

19. Horse-drawn carts shuttled daily between wholesalers and saloons to supply the needs of the drinking men of Boise, Idaho. *Courtesy of the Idaho Historical Society*

Most liquor arriving in the camps, however, came by wagon or by a combination of rail and wagon transportation. Because of the harsh winters from Colorado northward, most wagon traffic began in April and ceased by mid-November. During this freighting season, the amount of alcohol passing through major distribution centers on its way to other markets was indeed prodigious. During four weeks of the late spring of 1871, for instance, one Helena wholesaler received more than 20,000 pounds of liquor from Corinne, Utah, the nearest depot of the Union Pacific. As winter approached, merchants increased their orders to insure that their customers would not go thirsty during the months ahead. On the last day of November, 1864, an eighty-wagon train, devoted entirely to liquor, arrived in Denver with 1,600 barrels of whiskey and 2,700 cases of champagne. The *Rocky Mountain News* commented with awe: "That's a train what is a train."[18]

Trade slowed somewhat during the months between but still remained substantial. The *Saguache Chronicle* estimated that wagons passing through town on their way to nearby camps contained a gallon of whiskey for every pound of flour. This editor surely exaggerated, but newspaper items from elsewhere in the Rockies noted a whiskey shipment of 5,000 pounds to one saloon owner, of twenty-seven barrels to another, and enough to fill seven prairie schooners to yet another. Throughout the summer and fall, burly teamsters unloaded barrels of bourbon, Scotch, gin, brandy, California wines, and Irish whiskey and cases of champagne, ale, and porter before wholesale and retail houses throughout the region.[19]

This extensive trade supported large wholesale liquor houses in all the area distribution centers and in most of the more substantial mining towns. In some cases agents of distillers in the states came directly to the Rockies to solicit orders from individual saloons. But usually barkeepers bought from middlemen in their own town or in the nearest market. By 1861 large firms had appeared in Denver, notably that of Bernard Slavin, to receive and forward a wide variety of intoxicants to the blossoming mountain settlements. Others, merchants such as Jacob Schloss and Adolph Hirsch of Leadville and R. F. Hafford of Tombstone, kept in stock up to several hundred barrels of whiskey worth as much as $40,000. In many places general commission merchants included immense amounts of wholesale liquor in their inventories and devoted much of their newspaper advertising to a description of its variety and quality. One such listing boasted of 147 barrels of goods ranging from ''Mon'gehala whiskey'' to St. Croix rum and cherry bounce.[20]

Local production played an important role in supplying the miners' demand for beer. Distilled liquor could be carried overland cheaply and efficiently, and wine has to be imported because it could be produced only where soil and climate allowed. Mountain brewers, however, could import raw materials and turn out a product of reasonably high quality. As a result, Germans trained in the craft established businesses in many mining towns quite early and carried on a busy trade. The Virginia Brewery of Virginia City marketed a little less than two thousand gallons of beer at two dollars per gallon in November, 1864, less than a year and a half after the first discovery of gold in Alder Gulch. Its output thereafter actually dropped, probably because of competition, but a few years later it still was selling almost

20. Liquor wholesalers, operating out of warehouses holding thousands of gallons in goods, were major businesses in a distribution center like Boise, Idaho. *Courtesy of the Idaho Historical Society*

twelve thousand gallons annually. The popular brewery of Nicholas Kessler in Helena was supplying its customers with more than six hundred barrels of lager annually four years after it opened in 1865. All such records clearly reveal the seasonal appeal of the brew. Sales in the hottest summer months typically soared to four times those during January and February. These establishments and others in distribution centers like Denver, Tucson, and Boise, as well as smaller breweries of limited output, probably provided most of the beer for the mining camps during their first years.[21]

The last two decades of the century witnessed a phenomenal increase in national beer consumption. During these same years improved transportation and technical breakthroughs in bottling and pasteurization allowed for the first time the marketing of beer on a national scale. Agents for large brewers in California, Missouri, and Wisconsin fanned out through the mountains, and drinkers could cool their throats with the best that Schlitz, Pabst, Blatz, and Budweiser could offer. After the arrival of the railroad in Helena, one distributor sold more than 1,600 kegs of Schlitz alone between April and July. By late 1879, the Leadville agent for Anheuser Busch and Company had contracted with the railroad to keep at his disposal his own crew and train of seven cars so his warehouse would never be empty. Saloons began to advertise as exclusive outlets for the better-known brands available in bottles that "a child can open . . . with all ease."[22]

Contemporary evidence thus indicates that the teamsters and muleteers who made their way over the web of roads and trails carried with them enough liquor to satisfy a thirsty market. Popularity with consumers and relative ease of transport virtually guaranteed alcohol a place in many shipments of provisions. Mountain breweries and, later, national suppliers provided large quantities of beer for those who preferred it. Consequently, in all but the most extreme cases abundant intoxicants were on hand. "Whisky and provisions of every description are plenty," wrote a correspondent from Alturas, Idaho, at the end of the freighting season, "but the former prevails."[23] The second of the three elements of the saloonman's dream—the ready availability of liquor—was well founded in fact, provided the barkeeper could pay the prevailing price.

What of the third part of the conventional belief, that a quick and handsome return would follow this initial investment in a saloon and liquor? Its accuracy depended upon conditions and circumstances. There were many tales of saloon operators grabbing fistfuls of greenbacks and pouches of gold dust from parched prospectors clamoring for liquor. An early resident of Colorado reportedly sold the contents of two barrels of whiskey for $2,700, while another saloonman was said to have made $4,000 in three weeks during the salad days of Caldwell, Idaho. Having opened "a little store with a little Valley Tan Whisky" during the rush to Bevens Gulch, Montana, Z. E. Thomas claimed to do between $500 and $800 a week in trade.[24]

Contemporary reports and reminiscences may well have been exaggerated, but the facts of the liquor trade of early mining camps suggest that the potential for substantial profits was indeed there. For the barkeeper aggressive and fortunate enough to reach a mining camp soon after the first strike, conditions were close to ideal, for both costs and competition were at a minimum. Smaller operators had not yet arrived in great numbers, and larger entrepreneurs would not consider coming until the place had proved itself financially. The first arrivals at the diggings did not insist on a high quality of merchandise nor on the other accouterments of the trade found in better-established communities.

In short, the saloon business was reduced to its most lucrative fundamentals. On one side of the bar was a thirsty miner, none too choosy about what he drank, and on the other a man with the goods to sell. No other factors complicated this profitable economic equation.

Specifically, an owner's margin of profit under these circumstances depended upon four factors: the wholesale price of liquor, transportation costs, the number of drinks he sold per gallon, and the price he charged across the counter. Depending upon the interplay of these factors, his income could range from modest to astronomical.

A barkeeper could buy whiskey from the nearest supply center for between two and ten dollars per gallon, the variation in price depending upon availability and demand as well as quality.[25] As mentioned above, the cost of transportation depended upon geography, season, and available service. Freight rates might range from five to twenty cents per pound but usually were between eight and fifteen cents. A gallon of whiskey weighed about eight pounds, but to this must be added the weight of the cask or barrel in which it was carried. In these calculations, the weight of the whiskey alone will be increased by one-fourth to account for its container. Thus it will be assumed, for example, that ten gallons of bourbon in a cask totaled about a hundred pounds and that the saloonman paid accordingly to have it brought to him by mule or wagon.

One gallon contains 128 ounces, and drinks sold in saloons varied in volume from an ounce to an ounce and a half. Depending upon spillage, accidents, and his own generosity, a saloonkeeper could sell between 80 and 120 drinks of whiskey from each gallon. Of all four factors, the retail price is the easiest to establish. Although a few outraged observers claimed to have paid up to two dollars for a shot of bellywash, barkeepers in newly founded camps almost universally charged their customers twenty-five cents per drink, and this price prevailed for at least several weeks. Eventually, improved lines of supply and a reduction in freight rates as well as the inevitable growth of competition resulted in announcements like the following:

A BIT SALOON!
French & Purviance
Have Just Opened On
Main Street, one door north of Wells, Fargo
& Co.'s Express Office
Hailey.
A saloon, where first class wines, liquors, and
cigars are served at
ONE BIT! ONE BIT! ONE BIT!
Go and see them.[26]

A few owners might cling to the older, higher price, but the "bit price" of 12½ cents for a shot of hard liquor or a mug of beer quickly became standard in the established town. The drop in the cost of a drink was eagerly anticipated by residents who had witnessed the procedure elsewhere. The colorful editor of Ouray, Colorado, David F. Day, parodied the popular feeling in the overblown romantic style of the day:

I may wander in sad and pensive thought upon the banks of flowing rivers; I may tread carpeted vales, or climb cloud-capped mountains, revelling amidst beauty, grandeur and simplicity, and yet find no repose—no rest for this restless mind—no peace for this troubled heart—no harbor for this sinful soul. Not a star above nor a flower below tells where to go—But ah! From yonder window beams a ray of hope; that comprehensive and sublime announcement: "Two beers for a quarter."[27]

Considering these factors, if a saloonkeeper bought the best liquor wholesale, paid the highest freight costs of twenty cents a pound, and doled it out straight at a generous swallow for 12½ cents, he might clear as little as four dollars on a gallon of goods bought for ten dollars, a 40 percent profit. At the other extreme, should he import the cheapest rotgut at the lowest transport costs and pour it scrupulously in one-ounce glasses at two bits a shot, he could clear as much as $27.50 on a $2.00 investment—a healthy return of almost 1,400 percent.

Obviously, the typical saloonman's actual margin of profit generally fell somewhere between these two extremes. But there is good reason to believe the second case prevailed more often than the first, particularly when the entrepreneur operated in a newly settled mining camp, where whiskey was sold at the higher price of twenty-five cents a shot. Observers agreed, moreover, that the liquid products marketed during a camp's earlier days were of the cheapest and most wretched sort. Given the economic temptation before them, most owners chose to maximize their profits at the expense of the customer's stomach. Such whiskey probably cost from four to six dollars a gallon and was borne by mule or wagon for between eight and sixteen cents a pound. Depending on how carefully a saloonkeeper rationed his whiskey, his profit after costs on each gallon would vary from about $12.50 to $25.00, or between 200 and 600 percent.

The common belief that the saloon was a sure way to wealth, therefore, seems to have had some basis in reality. The economic opportunities were especially great during the first months after men began to gather at a new gold or silver strike. The costs of setting up a simple tent or shack were small, and customers were willing to pay high prices for cheap goods that could be brought in by any method of transport available. The return on a gallon of liquor was substantial for the merchant fortunate enough to be on the right site at the proper time.

The Complications

Relatively quickly, however, this situation began to change. Although the advantages of the trade did not disappear, most owners soon faced expenses and problems that they had not encountered during the camp's early days. If a mining town survived, its expansion and maturity presented a growing number of challenges.

Customers did not remain content for long with the early primitive facilities. If nothing else, four fairly sturdy walls and a wooden floor were expected, with at least some rudimentary furnishings. A lot and a moderate-sized saloon might cost from a few hundred to a thousand dollars, and once local government was in operation and ownership of town lots well established, the man who chose to rent rather than buy might find rates extremely high. Particularly in rapidly growing camps where the speculative fever and the scramble for street-front space drove up all property values, a single month's rent might equal up to one-fifth of the total value of the structure itself. A saloon large enough for a bar, a few tables, and perhaps some gambling equipment might command several hundred dollars a month. The owner of a one-story wooden building, twenty-by-forty feet, on Helena's Main Street in 1867 demanded $6,000 per year in rent. Such amounts, condemned by the local editor as "unbearable and extortionate," bit deeply into the income of the most lucrative business.[28]

Furnishings and equipment required additional investment. The bar itself and tables, chairs, lamps, and an adequate stove were just the beginnings. The few surviving saloon inventories show that a well-appointed drinking house featured a large collection of glassware and other materials for serving its patrons—decanters, glasses, pitchers, tumblers, demijohns, jugs, goblets, and buckets. To cool the beer and to make the popular drinks of summer an owner needed ice. While he might gather and store his own and sell the excess to competitors, a saloonman usually bought from businessmen who cut up to 3,000 tons of ice from rivers in the winter and then kept it in large buildings insulated with sawdust.[29]

More expensive were the elaborations that appealed to the patron's love of gaming and elegance—diamond dust mirrors, fine tile floors, glittering lighting fixtures, and billiard tables. Imported mirrors, as large as six-by-eight feet, cost between $800 and $1,000, while, depending upon the style and freighting expenses, a billiard table could require as much as a $1,400 investment. These expenses were not limited to the largest saloons. The $400 billiard table in a Central City whiskey mill represented more than one-fourth of the value of the building, lot, and all furnishings. A large, richly endowed drinking house could easily require $3,000 for furnishings alone, while one of more moderate proportions might cost $1,000 to fix up.[30]

More money might be needed for an expanded labor force. A bartender's experience and reputation were important, and well-known "spiritualists" often were featured prominently in barroom advertisements. Larger saloons might reach out as far as New York City or San Francisco to hire someone to help behind the bar. Regardless of their background, bartenders commanded a higher salary than most other wage earners of a mining town. The 350 bartenders of

Leadville in 1879 each received the handsome sum of $100 a month. Where there was a shortage of their kind, bartenders could earn much more. Although he had never worked at such a job, N. H. Webster was offered $250 per month plus board and washing to tend bar in Bannack, Montana, in 1863. He declined the offer as morally unacceptable. To entice customers into their doors, some drinking spots employed musicians, and though some were of dubious quality, owners might pay up to $300 per month for their services.[31]

The maturing town inevitably brought yet another expense—the license. Collection of any sort of fees was understandably difficult during the first stages of a new camp, and barkeepers did not have to concern themselves with these regulations. But once government was established in a new region, the situation changed. Officials at all levels quickly showed great interest in taxing the liquor business. The first legal instrument recorded after the creation of Idaho Territory, for example, was a county license for Capps and Bolt's National Saloon in Orofino.[32] Territorial legislation provided for county fees, and upon incorporation of a town, its new council typically would include among its first ordinances a license requirement for all persons retailing liquor by the drink. The amount demanded varied by place and time from $25 to $250 every three months, though $150 was the most common amount. Governments often placed an additional tax on gaming equipment and musical instruments. Finally, a personal bond of up to $500 was required of an owner to insure both the payment of future fees and good order in his place of business.[33]

The appeal of the saloon license fee is easy enough to understand. From the start, saloon licenses were seen in part as a method of controlling the number of these potentially disruptive businesses, and in time this motive would grow in importance. But initially there was a simpler explanation: the tax on barrooms was a lucrative and relatively dependable source of public income. The collection of property taxes proved to be an extremely frustrating task, for the transient frontier population rarely stayed in one place long enough to pay the annual bill, and so expected income traditionally had shrunk alarmingly by the final reckoning. Consequently, governments often had to rely heavily upon licenses required of businesses. Because they were collected quarterly and in advance, these fees provided a far more dependable income. And of these licenses, those for public drinking houses were always substantially more costly, sometimes up to ten times greater, than those for other enterprises. One Colorado editor stated bluntly the reasoning behind this discrepancy: "[Saloons] are the cause of most of the crimes committed, and they should pay the greater share of the burdens of the local government."[34]

To be sure, the collection of saloon fees was far from an easy task. Official auditors complained loudly about the owners' reluctance to meet these obligations. Saloonmen sometimes adopted ingenious methods of resistance. Whenever George Hockderffer, Flagstaff's first city marshal, entered a saloon to ask for the owner's fee, he had to buy drinks for all the resident loungers, who were urged forward to the bar by the proprietor. By the end of his first year in office, Hockderffer had to take out a loan simply to survive. Nonetheless, saloon licenses were the most reliable tax available, and they often composed a fourth, and sometimes as much as two-thirds, of all money actually collected by county governments. In town governments, the story was the same. Between August 1879 and April 1880, saloon licenses accounted for two of every three dollars coming into Leadville's city coffers. This situation remained essentially unchanged throughout the decade. In Tombstone, this source of income provided about half of all city revenues in 1881, and in Silverton, Colorado, in 1878, about 90 percent.[35]

Saloon licenses thus contributed a crucial source of funds for local governments at a time when public expenses were great and finances uncertain. For officials, these fees must have been a boon, but for the barkeeper, they added still more to a growing number of expenses. The personal bond increased the cost of the owner's original investment. Even as rents, furnishings, and employee wages added to his overhead, the saloonman was asked to shoulder much of the burden of public finances as well. The promise of easy wealth was becoming much less certain.

Increasing expenses, however, were only part of the saloon owner's problem. Other factors in his day-to-day operations reduced his effective income. Like all frontiers, that of the Rockies suffered from a chronic lack of specie. In the absence of currency, gold dust was used in ordinary business transactions, but the medium of exchange posed significant difficulties. First of all, the value of the dust varied according to its origin. That of Orofino, Idaho, was worth sixteen dollars per ounce in the early 1860s, six dollars less than the product of Kootenai and four dollars more than that of Florence. All merchants, saloonmen included, had to be able to recognize various types of dust and quote their market values to avoid losses. Proprietors also had to look out for improperly refined or counterfeit dust. Furthermore, gold dust was naturally unwieldy. The host might adopt the casual approach by taking a pinch of about eight grains between the tips of two fingers as the price of a drink or cigar. More likely, in the lowest whiskey mill and plushest gambling hall, the customer probably would see a pair of jeweler's scales and a ''blower'' on the bar. The second item was a conical box; gold dust was poured sparingly into the larger end and gently blown out the smaller onto the scales. Even with such precautions, however, some of the tiny grains fell to the floor and into the cracks in the bar. Children and the poorest miners sometimes worked the dirt under the foundations of saloons, and the gold in their pans represented lost profits of the owner above them. Some barkeepers turned these problems to their advantage by using variations in the value of dust as an excuse to mark up the price of all goods, or, like ''Count'' Murat of Virginia City, by employing doctored weights on their scales to bilk customers.[36]

Far more serious than the irritation of dealing with gold dust was the problem of credit. If a customer were an independent placer miner, his income was highly uncertain; if he were a wage laborer, he might run short of funds prior to payday. In either case, these men might well plead with the local saloonman to dole out his liquor on credit, or ''jawbone.'' Some barkeepers steadfastly refused, posting signs prominently announcing a no-credit, cash-and-carry policy, but most found themselves caught in a perplexing dilemma. To compete they felt obliged to take the risk of selling goods on trust, though they might cut their losses by serving watered down ''jawbone whiskey.'' The diary of Tucson saloon owner George Hand mentions that many of his customers—including the local madame, Big Carmel—ran up bar bills of as much as seventy-five dollars, a substantial sum considering that Hand's rent was sixty dollars a month.[37]

Most surviving records, in fact, consist of page after page of notations of credit. In a single month of Virginia City's boom year, 1864, Peter Herbert extended credit for goods and services totaling $1,276, and of this $790 was for liquor. For the same period, Herbert took in only $865 in cash. Ledgers of four other saloons show whiskey and beer tabs averaging from $170 to $300 per month, although they do not indicate how much other liquor was paid for with dust or biting money.[38] If Herbert's experience was any indication, however, much of the operator's income may well have rested upon the promise of future payment.

Unfortunately, many among the highly mobile population proved quite casual in meeting these obligations. Newspapers frequently published notices of saloonmen threatening and pleading with reluctant clients to pay their bills. If persuasion failed, the owner could go to court. Apparently because too many Idaho saloonkeepers were crowding the dockets, the sixth territorial assembly passed a law specifically forbidding retail liquor merchants from suing for debts over ten dollars. Again, Hand's diary mentions lawsuits to force payment. Sometimes he was too late. "Edward Sampson died in the hospital owing me $20.00," he wrote in July 1877. "He settled his bill and left for a better world." More often, debtors simply disappeared into the ever-moving population and left the owners that much poorer.[39]

Nature itself sometimes seemed to conspire against the liquor seller. Particularly in the northern Rockies, virtually all mining stopped by the beginning of December, when water froze in the sluices and the bitter cold drove men indoors. A large part of the populace deserted the towns for more pleasant climes, fleeing, in the words of one veteran, "like blackbirds" and returning "poor as crows." Those who remained might have drunk more, man-for-man, out of sheer boredom, but the general exodus severely reduced the overall volume of trade. The cash received by a Rocky Bar, Idaho, barkeeper in the slowest months of winter was less than half that of the summer, and he took in more on the Fourth of July alone than during all of February.

Many owners gave up and followed their customers to lower and warmer places, then returned with the spring rush. In any case, most of them probably had to make their profits between March and November, or not at all.[40]

Contributing to all these problems was the growing competition. The lucky individual early on the scene did not have the field to himself for long. So many others were drawn by the same hopes that drinking places often outnumbered all other retail businesses. The general rush of merchants to a town heightened the demand for space and pushed rents ever upward. Competition pressured the owner to add expensive improvements. Customers at first seemed satisfied enough with the bare necessities—whiskey and a place in which to drink it. But once refinements began to appear, men began to seek out the place that offered something more—a billiard table, more comfortable furnishings, a touch of elegance. These additions could mean the difference between success and failure. Most obviously, the influx of barkeepers cut down the share of business available to each liquor seller. The same development thus reduced income even as it encouraged an increase in costs.

Time, growth, and political and social change therefore complicated the profitable simplicities of the saloon trade. Bonds, licenses, housing expenses, and expanding inventories all swelled both fixed and operating costs, and even as it cost more to open and operate a barroom, competitive pressures, problems with currency, demands for credit, and seasonal variations in trade all made income more uncertain. Given these circumstances, owners might well have discovered the sad truth that the possibility of quick and ample profits was not as sure as they had thought. Rather than striking a mercantile mother lode, many probably found themselves closer to the situation of George Hand, who on one occasion had to sell his watch and raffle off his favorite dog, Tinker, to pay the rent.[41]

The Case of Leadville

The points raised so far would have applied to most places throughout the Rockies. A shift in focus to saloon owners as a group in one particular place can provide a fuller appreciation of the realistic possibilities of the trade.

The silver-mining town of Leadville, high in the Colorado Rockies near the source of the Arkansas River, was by far the largest gold- or silver-mining town in the mountains. Its great rush began in 1878, and by 1881 the "cloud city" held perhaps 15,000 persons, while another few thousand living in the surrounding hills looked to Leadville for supplies and recreation. Early visitors remarked on the vigorous liquor trade, but little can be said of the first saloonmen and their success or failure. A correspondent for *Harper's Weekly* in 1879 listed the names of the first six men to settle on land that would become Leadville, and three of these, George Harris, D. H. Houghton, and William Nye, appeared as saloonmen in the *Colorado State Business Directory* for 1878.[42] If nothing else, the fact that half of the first six arrivals turned to the liquor trade testifies to the appeal of that line of work. All three, furthermore, amassed considerable property over the next two years. In 1880, Harris's assessed property totaled $7,850; Houghton's, $12,825; and Nye's, $14,700.

These figures suggest that these early liquor dealers did quite well for themselves, but of the many others who sold rotgut out of tents and cabins during the first weeks, there is little hard evidence concerning their identities and none on their success or lack of it. Beginning in 1879, however, Leadville began publishing its own city directory, which included a listing of saloons and their proprietors. In the same year, Lake County officials began assessing the personal property, real estate, and buildings of Leadville citizens, although the procedure remained somewhat casual for the first two years. These sources and the federal manuscript census of 1880 provide some information on the identity and economic holdings of a great many of the men involved in the saloon business, especially during the town's maturing years after 1880.

During the 1880s, any frequent patron of Leadville's saloons would have recognized distinct regions in the city's drinking life. The plushest and best-known drinking places were found on the first three blocks of Harrison Avenue. Here was the center of Leadville's economic life. Horses, pack trains, and heavy ore wagons filled this

21. The crowd outside the canvas-and-plank saloon suggested Leadville's social diversity—roughly clad workmen, some dandies in derbies, two women, and a young boy. *Courtesy of the Amon Carter Museum, Fort Worth, Texas*

ninety-foot-wide main business street, and a surging mass of miners, businessmen, housewives, speculators, vagrants, and soldiers of fortune crowded its sidewalks and stood talking in groups along its edges. Among the hardware stores, tailor shops, restaurants, and groceries of Harrison Avenue were the largest barrooms of the community. Spacious, well-constructed, and elegantly furnished, these saloons often featured gambling casinos and concert stages in addition to facilities for drinking.

Had he turned east or west off Harrison Avenue's first three blocks, a miner on the town would have entered narrower side streets lined with smaller, seedier businesses—laundries, cigar stores, shooting galleries, and lodging houses—and here he would have found barrooms a definite cut below those on Harrison. Along one such street, West Second, was Leadville's "whiskey row." There, among twenty-four buildings on one side of a single block, fourteen groggeries operated at full blast. There was little to distinguish these places. Going from one to another of these frame saloons, a customer would have seen in each a cramped, smoke-filled interior and, in the light of kerosene lamps, men drinking at a bar or around small tables. The scene rarely changed all night, for most owners remained open nearly until sunrise, trying to garner enough business to survive the competition.

Several blocks east of Harrison, near the mining district, other small frame saloons served the workingmen who chose not to walk down to the center of the city's night life. Farther to the north another group of barrooms clustered around the depot of the Denver and Rio Grande Railroad on North Poplar. The remainder of the saloons were sprinkled throughout the residential blocks and among the shanties of the poorest miners and laborers on the fringes of the city.

Compared to many other mining regions, Leadville enjoyed good connections with the outside world, and its barkeepers would have had plenty of liquor to sell. But the town's rapid growth meant that the cost of property and rents for business houses were quite high. A building of moderate size might rent for $500 a month, and a large drinking and gambling saloon for up to $2,000 in the early years. Though the rates eventually leveled off, they remained high even after the boom. In addition to the high cost of housing for their businesses, saloonmen paid substantial license fees, which provided much of the city's income. The city council, in one of its first actions, levied an annual license fee of $200 on liquor dealers in February 1878, an amount soon raised to $500, then $600 per year.[43]

By all accounts, the competition was stiff. It is impossible to determine exactly how many saloon owners plied their trade in Leadville during the 1880s. The number declined as the city's population fell somewhat and gradually stabilized after about 1882, but in any year there were probably many who did not appear in official records. The city directory for 1880, for example, lists 129 owners, but the *Leadville Democrat* claimed that 249 saloons had operated during that year.[44] Apparently many would-be owners tried their hand for a few weeks or months and moved on without ever appearing in the official listing of the city's businesses. In 1880, approximately 20,000 persons lived in and around Leadville. If the more conservative figure of 129 proprietors is used, then there was one saloon for every 155 persons, while if the larger number is accepted, the ratio of barrooms-to-people drops to one for every 80 individuals. At no time during the 1880s did Leadville's population drop below about 8,000, and by the most cautious estimates, its legion of barkeepers never numbered fewer than about 85. Thus there was probably one saloon for about every 100 Leadvilleites throughout the decade, and this figure includes not only the city's confirmed carousers but also women, children, and nondrinkers, however rare. At any rate, the number of customers available to each Leadville barkeeper appears to have been perilously small.

What can be said of the men engaged in this competitive struggle? When all Leadville saloonmen listed on the census for 1880 are compared with a 10 percent sample of the adult population, few differences between the two groups are apparent.[45] Both liquor sellers and the general population were predominantly white and male. Most members of both groups were in their early thirties and were slightly more likely to be single than married. The two groups differed most markedly in place of birth. Saloonmen were far more likely to have been born abroad (43.9 percent to 32 percent), and of these immigrant keepers of the bars, well over half hailed from Germany or Ireland. As was apparently true of saloonmen throughout the Rockies, they were somewhat more cosmopolitan than the society around them, but apart from this, little can be learned from the census alone.

Other information, however, reveals more. In the material that follows, only the proprietors included in Leadville directories will be considered. The names of 656 saloonmen appear in these volumes between the years 1878 and 1890. Many of the transient barkeepers are surely not part of this roster, and so it represents a conservative tally of the more stable businesses. Nonetheless, when these proprietors are followed over time, the first, and inescapable, impression is one of extreme instability. A large majority of owners appear as saloonmen in only one or two volumes. Over the years between 1878 and 1890, roughly 70 percent of all owners appear in only one issue of the directories, a figure even more striking when it is recalled that these lists probably represent only the better-established liquor dealers. Some show up again later engaged in other occupations, but most

Wealth and Persistence of Saloonmen in Leadville, Colorado Related to Values of Assessed Property in 1882, 1884, and 1887

WEALTH DISTRIBUTION OF LEADVILLE OPERATORS

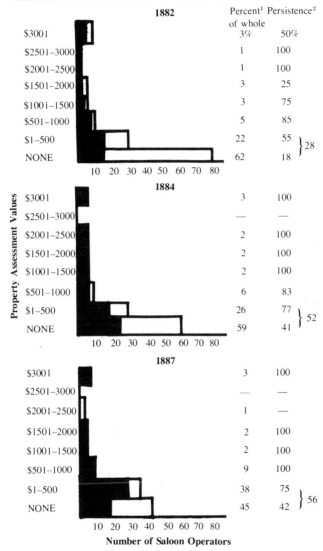

1. Percent of all saloon operators during sample year
2. Percent of economic category that remained in operation for more than two years

simply disappear. Only thirty-two saloonmen, or about 5 percent, remained in business for six years or more.

Local tax and property records quickly yield a second conclusion, that there were great differences in the economic resources of those practicing the liquor trade. The graphs show the number of saloon operators and their assessed wealth for the sample years of 1882, 1884, and 1887. In each graph, the saloonmen of each year are grouped according to the assessment of their personal property and real estate. The number of barkeepers declined during these years from 124 to 87, reflecting the drop in and relative stabilization of the general population. Regardless of how many barkeepers were in operation, however, between 80 and 85 percent of all dealers either had no assessable personal property or real estate, or had property totaling less than $500. At the top, 3 percent of the saloonmen commanded property valued at more than $3,000. Between these two extremes were others, between 12 and 14 percent, whose property was assessed at between $500 and $3,000.

To say the least, the saloon business was somewhat bottom-heavy. Not surprisingly, furthermore, operators in the lower economic category were far more transient than those above them. Most of the decline in the total number of saloonkeepers was among those in the bottom ranks, with the least amount of property, and many of those who did go into business remained in operation only a relatively short time. In the graphs, the darker portion of the columns represents those owners who remained in business for more than two years. In 1882, fewer than three out of ten (28 percent) of those with less than $500 in property were in this category. As the city passed from its highly speculative early stage, all groups became a bit more stable, but even in 1884 and 1887, barely half of those in the lower rank (52 percent and 56 percent) remained in operation three years or longer. Especially after 1882, however, virtually all owners of the middle and upper ranks stayed past the two-year mark.

When these facts are considered, three categories can be suggested for the entire roster of Leadville saloonmen who operated between 1878 and 1890. At the bottom were 563 operators, the most transient group, who rarely stayed in business for more than one or two seasons and who showed little evidence of economic success. Only a few of these men were located close to the most desirable part of the trade district, those first three prestigious blocks of Harrison Avenue, where the city's mercantile traffic was the heaviest. Most instead were to be found on the periphery of this section, particularly among the many frame doggeries on West Second and along the side streets east of Harrison, the first an area marked by blistering competition and the second somewhat removed from the main arena of recreational action.

Little can be said of these men's economic resources. Of them all, only 68 (12 percent) are listed as owners of any real estate, and barely half of these (35 persons, or 6 percent) can be clearly shown to have owned the building in which they did business. What of the background of these operators? Previous occupations of 112 can be identified through city directories. Exactly half were workingmen before they turned to dealing in liquor, some of them skilled laborers but most miners, porters, railroad yardmen, or common laborers. About one in five (18 percent) had been employed in some aspect of the whiskey business, primarily as bartenders. Most of the rest seem to have been small businessmen who decided to abandon their butcher shops and groceries to seek their wealth as lords of the liquor trade. And what of their futures following their short tenures as saloonmen? The great majority seem to have left the city, for only 83 appear in the directories after abandoning their barrooms. This minority apparently turned to the same sort of work done by others prior to going into the liquor business. Almost eight out of ten became either workers or bartenders (55 percent and 23 percent), and the rest either opened small businesses or became clerical or city employees. Certainly there is no indication of a substantial improvement in their positions.

These hopeful entrepreneurs, the largest portion by far of saloon-keepers, apparently came to the business with little and left with the same. Leaving their jobs in the mines or other small businesses, they probably rented their simple barrooms and competed with many others of their kind for an adequate share of the town's drinking crowd. And the evidence suggests strongly that most of these saloonmen either failed utterly or decided that the rewards were not worth the effort. Some returned to doing what they had done before, but most seem to have shaken off the dust and snow of Leadville and headed elsewhere, presumably in search of a new dream.

A second, far smaller group of thirty-eight held down the choicest spots of the saloon trade. Their most noticeable common characteristic was that they all began their businesses with considerable amounts of capital, for their first property assessments averaged more than $4,300. Most of these men operated the grand saloons along and immediately off Harrison Avenue. Particularly during the years between 1879 and 1881, several of them remained in the saloon business only a short time. A few then turned to other lucrative enterprises in Leadville. The Baer brothers and Adolph Hirsch opened wholesale liquor houses, for example, and another man invested in successful mining properties. Most of these well-to-do transient owners, however, disappeared entirely from the directories, probably having left with their profits after those first flush years. Yet eight of these operators stayed with the trade for several years, running grandiose halls like the Board of Trade, St. Anne's Rest, Texas House, and Wyman's Place among the restaurants, jewelers' shops, and large mercantile firms along the city's main street. These men were the barroom elite, the most publicized of their fraternity, who held forth nightly over the milling, noisy crowds who packed their places to drink and gamble.

They arrived at their enviable positions by a variety of routes. Some, like Daniel Shaw of St. Anne's Rest, arrived early enough to occupy strategic locations. Others had been successful saloonmen elsewhere; Phil Golding, for instance, had run a popular resort in Denver for several years before opening a branch operation in Leadville in 1880. For yet another type, the saloon business was just one of several enterprises. Charles E. "Pap" Wyman, he of the change purse made from a human scrotum, was an investor, auctioneer, and the agent for the state lottery, a position that probably required some political backing, before opening his famous saloon and theater at 124 Harrison Avenue. Joe Gavin's background was particularly intriguing. This Irish immigrant appeared in the city directory as a miner and prospector in the early 1880s, and a later biographical sketch mentioned the development of unnamed business interests. Then in 1889 he suddenly emerged as part owner of the prosperous Board of Trade Saloon and possessor of more than $4,000 in property. After moving on to Denver he eventually became master of a $25,000 home and president of Cripple Creek's Consolidated Gold Mining Company. About Joe Gavin there is clearly the scent of the plunger and speculator.[46]

Between these two groups was a third, composed of fifty-five men who were more successful than saloonmen of the bottom ranks but less so than the barons of Harrison Avenue. In some ways, there was little to distinguish these operators from the large number who lasted only a year or two. About half of both groups seem to have been miners or laborers before turning to the saloon trade, although a slightly higher percentage—about a third—of the more successful group had worked previously as bartenders or brewery employees. Similarly, both groups apparently began their careers with only limited economic resources. Of the fifty-five, forty-four either had no assessed property during their first two years of operation or had property valued at less than $1,000. Finally, the men in these two categories operated side-by-side, for their shops could all be found in the trenches of the trade along West Second, East Fifth, and other side streets lined with rows of gin mills.

Yet saloon owners of this third category survived. They were, in fact, the least transient of the groups, for they remained in business at least five years and some continued for more than a decade. Most of them, moreover, managed to make modest economic gains. About two out of three (thirty-six, or 65 percent) had assessable property valued at between $500 and $2,500 during their peak years, and thirty-two (58 percent) eventually gained clear title to their places of business.

Included in their number were a few real success stories. The Polish immigrant Goulder Janowitz, for instance, began selling whiskey on West Chesnut in 1880, then rented a saloon on Harrison Avenue two years later. Within the next five years he had bought a new saloon located next to the county courthouse up the street and had acquired three other lots and a considerable amount of personal property. His total assessment came to just under $5,000. Patrick Riley opened a barroom with Thomas Flood on East Third, and during the next seven years he acquired personal and residential property valued at $1,600 and took over two prominent corner saloons on Harrison Avenue.

Most, however, remained where they began. With a couple of exceptions, none accumulated property approaching the holdings of men like Charles Wyman, Phil Golding, or the others of the barroom elite. Their improvement was gradual and apparently won with determination. Why these men were able to remain and to succeed to a degree when so many around them failed is a matter for speculation. More of them had had experience as bartenders, and perhaps this training gave them an advantage. It seems more likely, though, that some element of personality—perseverance and an ability to deal with their public—accounted for their survival and limited success.

One further point is suggested by the names of the hardiest few among this group, those who remained in business between nine and thirteen years, longer than all the rest: John Mauss, Rudolf Wenger, W. H. Jones, T. J. Burke, Daniel W. Meskill, Bernard Fanning, Matthew Dee, A. F. Grundel, Goulder Janowitz, Gottlieb Mack, Charles Mierendorf, and John C. Ryan. The impression is clear. The list is dominated by names of German, Irish, and East European origin. The one apparently old-stock Anglo-Saxon name, W. H. Jones, was in fact that of a black who turned from barbering to barkeeping in 1880 and ran a successful State Street saloon for a decade. Obviously, their origins did not guarantee these men success, for many of those who tried and failed were of similar background. Rather this roster emphasizes that the liquor trade was an enterprise especially inviting to urban frontiersmen of these ethnic groups and that, if the circumstances were right and their abilities met the challenge, it was one in which they might hope to make their mark.

Despite the lack of detailed personal information on the lives of all but a few of the hundreds of Leadville saloon operators, some general conclusions seem clear enough. To the great majority of these men, the mountains did not prove an easy and bountiful land. Most saloon-keepers, men with backgrounds as workers or small businessmen, entered the liquor trade with little if any investment of their own and stayed in business only a year or two before moving on to something else. A handful came to their trade with a large amount of capital in hand, occupied the most prominent spots in the city's adult playground, and apparently prospered. A third group shared with the vast majority obscure and humble beginnings, but its members persisted and often made for themselves a reasonably secure place in the town's financial life. If the mining frontier was a source of hefty profits for a few and a modest advance for some, for most it was hardly a place of plenty.

If the figures seem somewhat cold and lifeless, it should be remembered that they represent the realities of men's hopes. The thousands of men who handed whiskey across bars throughout the Rockies were expectant capitalists, and the persistence of their dream is not so hard to understand. Simple observation and a little ciphering would have shown that a lot of people were willing to pay a good price for something that the seller could acquire easily and inexpensively. What else was there to worry about? As it turned out, there was plenty. The saloonman quick to a new strike and the wealthier operator in an older camp may have done well, but most owners in maturing towns seem to have been caught in a cruel squeeze between growing competition and increasing costs. A business slump, seasonal fluctuation, or flaw of personality might well have spelled the difference between marginal survival and failure. Faced with difficulties that frustrated one dream, most saloonmen apparently struck off in search of another.

None of this should be particularly surprising, for the story of the saloonkeeper ran parallel to that of the independent prospector. Just as the placer miner usually found the most lucrative opportunities already controlled by well-heeled capitalists, so the small time barkeeper quickly learned to measure the gap between expectations and reality. The field was left to those who owned resplendent drinking houses and to the few who began with little but managed to hold on through some combination of tenacity, good fortune, hard work, and the kind of personality that appealed to customers. Such were the limits of the economic miracle of the saloon.

6

The Morning After

JANUARY 1879: George Elder, twenty-three years old and fresh from law school, had joined the flood of immigrants coming to Leadville to find their fortunes. The penny-pinching Pennsylvanian was paying an outrageous rent for a single ill-heated room that served as both office and living quarters. Nonetheless, when he first arrived Elder was excited by the vitality around him and somewhat intrigued with the raucous night life so alien to his Quaker upbringing of simplicity and good works. "All is push and bustle," he wrote his parents. "The streets are crowded and every other house is a saloon or dance hall." But one frigid night his feelings changed. A fire on Harrison Avenue drove into the street the tenderloin's gamblers, dissipated vagrants, and prostitutes. As they stood gazing at the flames, he saw in their drawn and haggard faces the cost of the camp's well-publicized wickedness: "I shall carry the feelings of disgust and contempt for my race . . . to my dying day."[1]

May 1888: The reporter from *Harper's Weekly* had come prepared for depravity. Few cities in America had reputations as scarlet as Leadville's, and the journalist expected to find vice and fleshpots to rival those of the Barbary Coast and the French Quarter. Instead he discovered that hard-working and respectable citizens had transformed the town into a community "as steady-going as Salem or Plymouth Rock." Not all, however, were pleased by what had happened. Some older inhabitants who had been there from the start longed for the excitement of the past. "Leadville!" one of them snorted. "No, stranger; this ain't Leadville. It's only some infernal Sunday-school town that ain't been named yet."[2]

130

The different sources of disgust to the two men, the proper Quaker and the crusty veteran are a measure of the changes that came to the cloud city and to other mining towns that managed to survive past their first hectic months. As the towns changed, so did the place of the saloon within them. The appearance of other businesses and institutions relieved the barroom of some of its functions. The arrival of a new type of immigrant, one who brought a family and who hoped to build a respectable life, encouraged a set of values different from those of earlier days. These developments rarely if ever threatened the saloon with extinction. They did, however, foster criticism of the more sordid barroom behavior, and they limited the saloon's role in the society of the town.

Because mining camps grew so suddenly, the normal mechanism of supply and demand was thrown temporarily out of sync. Argonauts needed places to sleep, but hostelers had not had time to build them. The religiously inclined wanted churches, the bored wanted theaters, and all needed public halls for discussion of common problems, but these places required at least some proof of a town's permanence and some time for construction. It was during this period that the saloon's functions were the most varied and its place in the camp the most important.

Where deposits of precious metals proved too scanty or too expensive to extract and process, the towns that had sprung up around them disappeared or dwindled to a handful of diehards. But where the strikes proved more enduring, the camps underwent important changes. Businessmen felt secure enough to invest in hotels, banks, and newspapers. Even in towns of moderate size someone usually bought a downtown lot and constructed a hall to rent for dances, traveling entertainers, and political gatherings. Incorporation brought taxes for public buildings. A larger population justified the founding of a church, if only a one-room cabin for interdenominational services. These businesses and institutions were fitted specifically for sleeping, hoedowns, theatricals, worship, lectures, harangues, the dissemination of information, and the deposit of money. Once they had filled the void, the saloon was left to its fundamental function—to provide a place where men could drink, talk, and perhaps find the diversions of dancing and gambling.

Other changes in the town also modified the role of the saloon. Despite its social contributions, there were always individuals who were willing to point out the association of the consumption of alcohol with violence and disorder. Those guilty of homicide and assault, whether a back-alley biting match or a full-scale riot, frequently were found to have been drinking heavily prior to the action. The most common and irritating offenses—the nocturnal caterwauling of miners and prostitutes, the random shooting of pistols and rifles, and all the other misdemeanors gathered under the category of "disturbing the peace"—followed even more clearly from mass drinking. It cannot be said whether drinking was a cause of this social disorder, or whether drinking and crime were both part of the effect of deeper forces and problems. For most of those on the scene, however, the situation probably invited a simple explanation: men murdered and maimed and raised hell because they were drunk.

Any serious attempt to limit crime and disorder by limiting the liquor trade, however, waited upon a change in the makeup of mining town society. Many in the early camps might have agreed readily that drinking bred many problems, but because they rarely planned to remain, they had little interest in stability and order. To the law-abiding prospector, crime was primarily nothing more than an irritant unless it affected him personally. If drink seemed to drive some of the strangers around him to dissipation or suicide, that was little of his concern.

If a town survived, it attracted other immigrants, who considered it not a way station but a prospective home. These new immigrants often brought with them their wives and children, and they were more concerned about the quality of life in the town both in the present and for the indefinite future. They could be expected to look critically upon those places that challenged most blatantly their concept of morality and decorum, particularly the bordello, the dance hall, and the saloon.

This change within the mining towns, moreover, came at a time when the American temperance movement was gaining momentum in many parts of the nation. Between the Civil War and the turn of the century, a growing number of organizations promoted the voluntary decision of individuals to reject the bottle for a life of abstinence. By the latter years of the century, temperance groups were orienting their efforts more and more toward governmental prohibition of the manufacture and sale of intoxicants through local option and state law, especially following the formation of the Anti-Saloon League in 1896.

Recent interpretations of the American prohibition movement have emphasized that temperance reform during these years attracted particularly strong support because it represented a "symbolic crusade" to protect older values threatened by the social forces of urbanization, industrialization, geographical mobility, and the "new" immigration of non-Protestants from southern and eastern Europe. These developments appeared to threaten especially the stability of the nuclear family and the values of self-discipline, responsibility, sexual rectitude, and community stability, the bourgeois ideals of the Victorian home and the evangelical Protestant churches. The public drinking house became a symbol of permissiveness, irreverence, errant fathers, and self-indulgence. To eliminate the saloon was to strike a blow at much that seemed to be going awry in America.[3]

The maturation of the mining town therefore forecast trouble for the drinking house on two counts. New arrivals who came to stay often considered restrictions on the saloon a practical weapon against crime and for public order. Beyond that, they seemed to share a broader national concern that the cherished values of old-stock America were under siege, and they directed their alarm against the liquor trade.

The clearest evidence of this change could be seen in the appearance of institutions and structures associated with "civilized" behavior. Most obvious were the church and the schoolhouse. In the fall of 1865 residents of Ruby City in southern Idaho formed the Union Church and School Society. The time had come, they resolved, for those concerned about the future to buy a lot and build a meeting place proper for public functions. For several weeks religious services and a children's Sunday school had been held in Holgate's news depot, but citizens needed a permanent building for a place of worship, a school, lecture room, and public meeting hall—but not, the Society emphasized, as "a place of amusement." This emerging attitude was typical of most other surviving towns. The pealing of the first church and school bells announced, as one Colorado editor expounded, "the advancement of the humanizing influence of Christianity and healthy progress."[4]

Almost as important in the minds of some was a place where young men could relax and yet avoid the moral pitfalls of the dance hall or saloon. In an open letter published in Ouray's *Solid Muldoon*, in fact, a local minister suggested that before constructing buildings for worship and education, the citizenry should provide a free reading room for men who were living without the restraints and comforts of domestic life. Moral spokesmen considered equally necessary a lyceum for public lectures and, to avoid the raucous dance hall, some building where sedate parties and dances could be conducted with due decorum. The appearance of these facilities revealed the thrust of the changing society. When the Methodist women of Tombstone opened a club in the former Miner's Exchange Saloon and offered miners a lunch of Boston baked beans, profound changes surely were afoot.[5]

Not surprisingly, groups opposed to the liquor trade often played an active role in the promotion of these new facilities. Leadville's chapter of the Woman's Christian Temperance Union and the Young Men's Christian Association sponsored a free reading room that opened with the new year of 1881. There miners who wanted to avoid the temptations of the grogshop could relax, read, or hear lectures on "Life in Japan" or "Hygiene." Alarmed when a young man in Ouray told her that a saloon was the only place where he could find a warm place to sit, a leader of that town's WCTU led a successful campaign to establish such a room in her town.[6]

Reading rooms, lyceums, schools, and churches all represented attempts to encourage wholesome alternatives to the miner's morally dubious way of life. In a similar impulse, some residents founded and promoted temperance movements to reduce the consumption of alcohol and thus its ill effects. Both developments frequently were given strong support by mining town editors anxious to project the proper image to outsiders. Even as they admitted that some rowdiness persisted in their midst, these journalists usually insisted that such "eccentricities" of society as brawling, open prostitution, and rampant drunkenness were being displaced rapidly by the family, religion, innocent entertainments, and the rule of law. Newcomers could expect a "well ordained, decent, reading, visiting, and praying community." But as part of this urban evolution, one figure, the habitual drunkard, had to be eliminated. "The death of such a one is looked on as a relief and not as a loss to a community," a Central City, Colorado, editor wrote. "They are the excrescence of society, and like the fungus which fastening itself upon the trunk of a living, thriving tree, must be speedily removed else they will communicate decay and rottenness to every thing with which they come into contact."[7]

This opinion was more brutal than most, but it expressed a general concern that drunkenness posed a genuine threat to the town's emerging respectability. To meet this challenge, voluntary temperance movements appeared in many towns. Some were impromptu episodes, lectures by local ministers and by traveling evangelists. Others were more permanent. Occasionally, residents spontaneously organized local groups unaffiliated with national organizations. The Pale Noses of Lake City, Colorado, retained a frontier sense of humor as they promised to shun any "succulent juices of the grape, apple, peach, bug, and tarantula."[8] More often, men and women banded together to form chapters of associations that spanned the nation. The most prominent of these during the early years of the mining frontier was the Independent Order of Good Templars. This organization, founded in Oneida, New York, in 1850, languished during the Civil War, but afterwards it enjoyed phenomenal growth and by 1868 boasted a national membership of more than 400,000. Local Good Templar lodges could be found in Colorado as early as 1861, but not until 1866 did members form a Grand Lodge for the territory. Three years later more than one thousand men and women had joined, most of them residents of mountain mining towns. By the latter 1860s, anyone so inclined could join chapters of the IOGT in Montana, Idaho, and Arizona camps as well.[9]

At least until the 1880s, the IOGT emphasized the conversion of individuals through persuasion and education. They recognized the lure of their opponent, the liquor seller. "The enemy is fascinating and armed with sophistry,'' warned one of their leaders, ''but at last biteth like a serpent, and stingeth like an adder.'' To offset the appeal of the saloon, members sponsored lectures, held dances and Fourth of July celebrations with no tempting intoxicants, organized ''juvenile temples'' for the young, published their own newspapers, and produced stereoptican shows on the evils of the grape. That these activities reflected a concern for public order and respectability among the middle class of merchants and professionals is suggested by the fact that while a few officers of the Colorado lodges in Nevadaville, Georgetown, and Central City were miners, most were ministers, engineers, lawyers, tailors, journalists, or the wives of professional men.[10]

The Murphy ''blue ribbon'' movement also stressed the voluntary reformation of drinkers, but unlike the IOGT it had no permanent local organization.[11] Instead, its backers in a town would hold a series of rallies and sermons, often over a period of weeks, to build popular momentum for their cause. The crusade of Lake City, Colorado, began in early December, 1877, when the Presbyterian minister George Darley delivered as his opening salvo a sermon with the provocative title, ''Come, and Take a Drink.'' By the end of the first week, Darley and other speakers were attracting large crowds, who heard demon rum denounced in fiery speeches and joined in singing ''Hold the Fort,'' ''Crowded Awfully,'' and other hymns of temperate self-determination. At the end of each service, converts came forward to sign pledges of nonindulgence and to receive small blue ribbons to pin on their lapels as symbols of their new lives. The local editor did his part by encouraging attendance and publishing poems, one of which told of a tough, dedicated sot who came to town determined to disrupt the meetings. He was, of course, converted instead, and after thanking God he strode to the front of the crowd:

> Then he signed his name to the Murphy man's pledge,
> And, holding it high, said he—
> ''I came yer to bust that Murphy man,
> But I reckon he's busted me!''

By the time the movement sputtered and died in late February, its sponsors had gathered a few hundred promises of alcoholic abstinence.[12]

The arguments presented by Murphyites in Georgetown, Colorado, the same autumn showed how the movement appealed specifically to those interested in long-term community growth and morality. The featured speaker, a former saloonkeeper and pardoned murderer turned temperance evangelist, pleaded emotionally for the salvation of souls. But local civic leaders followed with shrewd arguments stressing that drinking not only weakened the homes, health, and morality of Georgetown, but, equally important, it kept taxes high by encouraging crime, while by diverting money into grogshops it reduced merchants' income and stunted economic growth. In response, just under a thousand persons, including virtually all the town's merchant and professional classes, signed pledges during the six-week campaign.[13]

No other groups attracted as much attention and support as the Good Templars and the Murphy "blue-ribboners," but these two organizations did not hold the field alone. The Woman's Christian Temperance Union typically drew its strongest support from agricultural regions and market towns, but its sympathizers organized chapters in at least some of the larger mining communities, and Frances Willard herself, founder of the organization, lectured Leadville on its errant ways in 1880. The Father Mathew Total Abstinence Society attracted Irish Catholics who chose to swear off the bottle. Other lesser groups, like the Sons of Temperance and an occasional antitreating society, gave some solace to those concerned over the human cost of the whiskey business.[14]

Just how effective these groups were in reforming a town's drinking habits is highly uncertain. Supporters often considered organizations like the Good Templars designed primarily to cultivate among the young a knowledge of debate, a talent for elocution, and an appreciation of polished manners. Hostility to the whiskey trade appeared to be a secondary concern. Suspiciously, temperance campaigns usually occurred during the dull winter months, and many of those attending may well have been looking as much for entertainment as for personal reformation. The Reverend Mr. Darley reported seeing men reeling drunkenly about the streets, still bedecked in their Murphy ribbons, only hours after their supposed conversion. In the course of a single year, the Black Hawk, Colorado, lodge of the IOGT expelled half of its members for breaking their temperance vows.

Nonetheless, even when backsliders are taken into account, the number of people who attended rallies and meetings represented a significant minority in the mining towns. These men and women appear to have been dedicated not so much to drying out their communities completely as to promoting the values of personal restraint, public order, and generally "civilized" behavior. They saw the saloon as a threat to this broader concern.[15]

These movements promoted a more respectable community life through the voluntary conversion of individuals. Other efforts tried to use the rule of law to restrict some of the bawdier types of recreation. Legislative charters for mining communities usually granted the civil authority the power to regulate or prohibit saloons, gambling halls, bordellos, and dance halls. Citizens concerned with their town's image tried to use this authority for their own ends. In particular, houses of prostitution and dance houses, or hurdy-gurdies, attracted the wrath of the guardians of public morality. Such places directly threatened the home by luring the father from his hearthside and by seducing curious youths, they charged, and the frequent fights that broke out there emphasized their challenge to civic order.[16]

To discourage these "institutions for the dissemination of moral leprosy," reformers usually adopted one of two strategies. To minimize the effect of these houses, local ordinances might confine them to one part of town or require that they keep a certain distance from schools and churches. Efforts to secure and enforce such legislation were not always successful. Despite petitions on its behalf, a proposed ordinance to confine dance halls in Silverton, Colorado, failed by one vote to pass the town board of trustees. In other communities, however, campaigns for segregation were more successful.[17]

As a second line of attack, opponents of dance halls and bawdy houses urged the imposition of high licensing fees to eradicate or at least severely reduce the numbers of those institutions. The sum of $100 per month was commonly suggested, though others argued for a charge of several dollars per night for each girl. Supporters of these schemes argued that because much of the town's police expenses could be traced to the rows erupting in places of drunken revelry, those businesses should pay the bill. Furthermore, miners spent most of their money in those sinks of folly, and come winter they relied upon charity for support. In any case, the argument ran, their squandering ways left the local economy sluggish and retarded healthy economic growth.[18]

Morally concerned citizens often associated the saloon with the hurdy-gurdy and the house of prostitution. Though serious movements to confine the drinking place to one part of town or to restrict it by high license fees were rare and almost always unsuccessful, activities in the barroom did not proceed totally unrestrained. With formal incorporation of a town, the first government usually moved quickly to pass ordinances restricting at least some of the more objectionable aspects of saloon life. Silverton, Colorado, provides a typical example. After passing as its first ordinance a prohibition of public drunkenness, the newly formed board of trustees in the fall of 1879 proceeded to forbid saloonmen to allow loud noises or disorderly conduct in their places of business, sell liquor to minors, idiots, or habitual drunkards, or employ a prostitute as a singer or "carrier of beer." In other cases, owners were forbidden to permit women of any kind to consort within their doors and were threatened with fines unless they stopped patrons from dancing and making music during the early morning hours.[19]

While these restrictions inspired relatively little opposition, another issue could provoke a bitter public debate. Citizens concerned about their town's moral climate were particularly appalled by the general disregard of the Sabbath. The crowds of men shopping for supplies were bad enough; worse were those who spent Sunday afternoons and evenings drinking and carousing in saloons. In the early days of the camp, the few open complaints against conducting business on the Sabbath went largely ignored, but as the town matured, well-organized and vocal movements might appear to demand Sunday closing. These groups called for all shops to observe a day of rest, but it was clear the barroom was their principal target.

Advocates of Sunday closing might call for voluntary agreements among merchants and saloonmen to shut down operations, or, when territorial or local laws were on the books, they might seek redress

22. Readers of J. Ross Browne's travel account, *Adventures in Apache Country*, could see a rather overdramatized view of a dance hall, or "hurdy-gurdy," and a barroom brawl the author witnessed in an Arizona mining camp. *Courtesy of the Arizona Historical Society*

through the courts. Usually they organized sympathizers to petition town governments to pass and enforce Sunday closing statutes. In 1880 and 1881 supporters of a Sabbath ordinance in Leadville gathered petitions, one being eighty feet long and another including more than four thousand names. Their opponents, led by two liquor wholesalers and organized into the Merchants Protective Association, attacked the reformers as fanatics driven by intolerance, and they condemned Sunday closing as a threat to property rights. Despite several acrimonious debates in the city council chambers, the Sabbath ordinance was not passed.[20]

Leadville's experience was not unusual. To reformers, the Sunday saloon symbolized a contempt for the values of home and church essential for a proper town. Defenders of the status quo argued that only on Sunday could miners come to town to refill their larders and to meet and relax with friends. To barkeepers and their patrons, the issue was one of economic rights and personal liberty. When Sabbath laws were passed in mining towns, they usually were enforced half-heartedly, if at all. But the presence of such movements, unprecedented during the early months of the camps, showed that some were questioning the predominance of the saloon in the social life of their communities and suggesting a harsher, more restrictive look at its activities.

During the early 1880s, temperance sympathizers across the nation, the mountain West included, campaigned to reduce the number of saloons by raising substantially the local license fee. As early as 1870, an Idaho editor endorsed expensive licenses as a means of eliminating the lowest deadfalls and reducing crimes of assault and brawling.[21] Reformers in the 1880s echoed such arguments and added others pitched to the interests of the respectable middle class. In general, however, their efforts fared even less well in mining towns than those for Sunday closing.

A decade after the excitement of the Murphy "blue ribbon" crusade, Georgetown temperance advocates tried to elect one of their own as police judge as part of a campaign to raise the town's saloon license fee from $200 to $500 a year. Had Georgetown changed from a rough mining camp to a settlement of families? High license would protect the morals of youth by squeezing out all but the most staid drinking places. Most saloon revenue, furthermore, was said to be diverted from local channels of trade to faraway brewers and distillers. Opponents replied that only barrooms with illegal gambling would survive the new rates. Moreover, higher license fees would reduce the town's income as saloons closed down, so that property owners could expect to pay higher taxes. In the end, these arguments held the day, and the reform candidate ran third in a field of three, garnering a little more than 20 percent of the vote.[22]

No one could claim seriously that temperance and reform movements worked a moral revolution in the mining camps. These communities remained workingmen's towns that generated a strong demand for liquor. Reducing the number of barrooms and the hours they operated, as one Utah editor pointed out, would be like damming a river at its mouth to stop it flowing from its source. Most young, hard-working men would drink whatever, whenever, and wherever they could.[23]

Rather, movements of moral reform and civil improvement showed that the saloon no longer stood almost unopposed as the social center of the town. Backers of the IOGT and Murphy movements, deacons of the churches, lyceum sponsors, and advocates of Sunday closing, high license, and eradication of prostitution all believed that the values of the church and the hearth were essential to any genuinely civilized town. They appealed both for a Victorian morality and for the economic needs of merchants and professionals worried over local taxes and the flow of trade. Both lines of argument attracted those who wanted to remain in the mountains and to build the right sort of life there, men and women who hoped for a future both prosperous and proper.

This clash of values was similar to that found in the Kansas cattle towns by historian Robert Dykstra.[24] Unlike their brethren in the towns of the plains, however, reformers in the mining communities almost never succeeded in imposing prohibition ordinances, probably because there was no alternative economic base to replace mining, as farming replaced the cattle drives, and because working miners demanded their liquor. Nonetheless, if criticism of the barroom usually remained a minority opinion, it still represented a change in the social composition of the town and the growth of a moral self-consciousness.

With the appearance of institutions that performed the functions previously fulfilled by the saloon, the barroom's place in its community changed, becoming very much like that of drinking places elsewhere in urban America. It remained an important part of the town's recreational life, but its role was not as varied nor its social dominance as unchallenged as during the flush times of the first rush. Time and maturity had done their work.

The swinging doors, the gilt mirror, the white-shirted barkeep, the boots on the bar rail—today all would be recognized immediately throughout America and much of the world. The Western saloon remains an indelible part of the popular image of the American frontier. As part of our national mythology, the barroom of celluloid images and pulp novels is an exciting place, peopled with steely-eyed heroes, oily villains, and fair-but-frail sisters. Its main purpose seems to be to provide a setting for demonstrations of virility or cowardice.

The saloon of reality was in some ways different from the saloon of myth, but the barroom's prominence in the popular vision of the frontier is justified. Apart from their sheer abundance and impressive volume of trade, the drinking house played an important part in the life of the Rocky Mountain mining towns.

At the outset, however, two points should be made to put the saloon of the mining camp in its proper perspective. First, if it helped miners to cope with the peculiar problems of the mountains, in other ways it was hardly unique. Much of what can be said of drinking places in Silver City and Rico no doubt holds true both for barrooms that served Western cowboys, farmers, and loggers and for saloons in those parts of Eastern cities dominated by young workingmen. Differences in the economic bases and social compositions of these places would have produced some variations, but the similarities would have been just as striking. The story of the Rocky Mountain barroom tells something both of the special conditions of the mining frontier and of the saloon as a national institution.

Second, the saloon never monopolized the social activities of most mining towns. It catered mainly to workingmen without families, but there were others—engineers, mine managers, ministers, teachers, and some merchants, the better educated and the better-to-do—who enjoyed a social life that centered on the home and, eventually, the church. They passed their leisure hours talking in parlors, reading, riding, picnicking, and dancing the schottische or quadrille in the larger homes of friends. Miners and other workers who had brought their families with them might also prefer the comforts of the home to the barroom. The elite might sip madeira at their gatherings, and the workingman might send his son to "rush the growler" from the nearest tavern, but to these members of the community the saloon was just another local business.

Even given these circumstances, however, the saloon's place in the mining town was still an important one. In some ways it contributed to the economic development of mountain communities. Because they were often the most numerous of all retail businesses, barrooms provided employment, however tentative, for many persons, and these saloonkeepers, bartenders, and other workers in turn spent their incomes on the goods and services of other businessmen in the camps. Certainly the saloonman was a boon to the freighter and muleteer who made room for barrels and casks of whiskey in their wagons and on the pack animals. Critics of the barroom might point out that saloonkeepers bought most of their liquor, furnishings, and ornaments elsewhere, but this charge, while largely true, could be leveled as well at most other businesses of the towns, including mining. Saloons, moreover, did help sustain some local production, particularly of the small mountain breweries, but also of artisans who sometimes built bars, tables, false fronts, and other furnishings and improvements. The saloons' most important economic contribution was as a critically important source of public revenue. Their licenses might account for more than half of a town's income, money needed for services and construction in a town built from scratch. Presumably these fees also kept property taxes lower than they might have been and thus indirectly attracted the investors and settlers who would help transform a crude camp into a maturing community.

In the final analysis, however, the saloon had its greatest impact on the social life of the town. The many saloons that lined the streets were there to give the public what it wanted and seemed to require. Among the materialistic, competitive, mobile gatherings of lonely men from many lands in the early-day camps, there were many who needed alcohol to help them cope with the turn their lives had taken. By supplying it the saloon performed what those on the scene considered to be an important service. Without a doubt, the liquor sold in these places contributed to many problems. Alcohol played a part in the disorder and suffering brought about by the frustrated and the naturally troublesome, and the saloon was the site of much of the violent behavior and human degradation to be found in the diggings. Many of the lowest barrooms became primarily places where men met to drink whiskey of the cheapest and rawest kind, and the uglier side of the liquor trade was clear to anyone who wished to see.

Whatever the personal sorrows and social woes caused by drunkenness, however, the barroom's positive contributions are equally clear. The saloon was more than a store where men bought a chemical that helped them deal with the world around them. To be fully understood the functions of the drinking house must be considered from several perspectives. The saloon was a setting, an experience, a scene of many activities, and a business. All of these various aspects—and the interrelationship among them—must be taken into account, for each influenced and in turn depended upon the others.

The changes in the structure of the saloon paralleled the evolution of the town, from its primitive beginnings through its maturity. If a settlement took root, its drinking places became more substantial, and in the more prosperous communities, the grander halls became monuments to civic success and boasts of permanence. Because there were so many of them, the barrooms revealed far more vividly than other businesses the economic and social diversity of the community. A tour from the posh palaces with paneled clubrooms located on prominent business corners to the rows of gin mills set apart from the main region of trade would have revealed to an observer the financial strata and the occupational and ethnic components of the large mining town. No other sort of enterprise could tell so much.

Beyond that, the setting of the saloon fit it admirably for functions at once more varied and more subtle than those of most other businesses. Its open floor space provided room for men to meet and try to solve common problems. As gathering places for much of the populace, the saloons served as funnels of information and as forums for politics and even religion. Early on, the saloon floor frequently was the only resting place for men of all backgrounds and wealth, and even after hotels had been built, the barroom continued to offer some protection for vagrants who otherwise would have lived their days and nights in one of the harshest environments the country could offer.

Most of these functions would be assumed in time by other businesses and institutions. The saloon, however, began as and remained primarily a place of amusement and relaxation; as such, it met an important need in an isolated and demanding land. Men gathered there to forget their troubles and be entertained by boxers, plank-walkers, and champion pie-eaters, by dances, lotteries, bearbaiting, and a variety of activities that taxed the imagination of the most resourceful owner.

Aside from its value as a place of diversion, the saloon provided a male sanctuary that fulfilled an emotional need for young bachelors and married men living apart from their families. Again its setting, accentuated by a masculine, virile decor, fit it well for its role. Particularly in the smaller "drinking saloons" with no facilities for music and dancing, a customer could choose between sipping quietly at the bar, talking with others at a table, or playing a bit of billiards or poker. The saloonman of the Rockies sought to duplicate the structure and furnishings of the traditional saloon—its distinctive bar, sitting and playing area, and artwork—to create a unique and familiar atmosphere that would recall similar places back home. This emphasis on the recognizable was reinforced by the vernacular and customs of the barroom, most of them common to drinking spots throughout the country.

Social historians of the West often have concentrated on the ways that Eastern institutions changed to meet the demands of the frontier. Initially the drinking house did adapt to its new environment by assuming new roles and coping with new conditions. The saloon, however, was in another sense essentially conservative. Like other institutions, such as the church and the fraternal lodge, the barroom fulfilled the needs of the frontier precisely by not changing and by providing familiar settings and experiences in a strange land. To the immigrant surrounded by the new and the unknown, it gave the expected.

Interestingly, temperance critics of the saloon understood part of its function and appeal. Leaders of the national movement for prohibition stressed the need for institutions in the city where young men could meet together and find wholesome, "uplifting" entertainment. Temperance groups on the frontier often called for reading rooms, YMCA chapters, lyceums, and the like. Given these alternatives, their argument ran, workingmen would forsake the saloon, and the liquor traffic would wither away.

23. The Cosmopolitan Saloon in Telluride, Colorado, featured all the masculine comforts—gambling, plenty of bar space, tables for talk, and an assortment of saloon art. *Courtesy of the Homer E. Reid Collection*

This insight into the barroom's function was essentially correct but incomplete. An article by a temperance-minded minister in the *Rocky Mountain Presbyterian* illustrated the limits of the prohibitionists' understanding. His particular complaint was against the practice of treating. He applauded the impulse of men to share with their fellows, but he argued that they need not buy liquor. Why not, he urged, treat one's friends to chocolate drops at a candy store? Better yet, an expansive miner should invite his cohorts into the local post office and set up a round of stamps.[25]

This suggestion, made in perfect seriousness, assumed that alcohol was only an addictive poison and the saloon only a building in which to drink it. In fact, if liquor could kill it could also make men happier and more companionable. The agreeable customs of group drinking and the institution in which the customs were pursued were rooted deep in the culture of the common folk of America and Europe.

Tradition, atmosphere, and the physical effect of alcohol together explain the powerful appeal of the saloon as a place of escape and male companionship. Just as the intricate interweaving of these factors could never be unraveled, so the saloon could never be eliminated entirely in societies of unattached workingmen. After ten hours of laboring underground, treating one's fellows to stamps would not do.

The most prominent saloon owners seem to have understood well the unique attraction of the barroom experience and, consequently, to have placed great emphasis upon projecting the desired image. Through their actions and their advertisements they portrayed themselves as generous and genial fellows, men's men who could guarantee a good time and provide protection from the unruly. They personified the allure of the saloon as a haven of good fellowship, a place of action for the restless and relaxation for the weary.

The saloonman obviously had to have some understanding of his business's appeal and the desires of his patrons if he were to succeed. Not surprisingly, most barkeepers had backgrounds similar to those of their customers. Men of limited education, they usually had worked as miners, laborers, or proprietors of small businesses before entering the whiskey trade. The fact that a large percentage had come from other countries, especially Germany and Ireland, emphasizes both the ethnic diversity of the camps and the special attraction of the saloon business for the foreign-born. Other immigrant groups present in fairly substantial numbers in the mountains—the Chinese and Latin Americans, for instance—apparently found the saloon trade closed to them, along with most of the other businesses of the mining camps. Nonetheless, liquor selling apparently was one line of commerce in which the public might accept and reward ambitious aliens. The more successful saloonmen often had one other thing in common as well. Many of them had traveled extensively in the American West and had worked at a great variety of occupations. Their experiences probably left these men with insights into their clientele that would have made success more likely. The competition among saloonmen was the most intense in town, and such an edge was not insignificant.

In any case, it was an uphill struggle. Despite the common belief that the saloon business virtually guaranteed a comfortable income, the evidence indicates that mounting costs, erratic seasonal peaks and troughs of trade, problems of credit, and, especially the great number of competitors caught most owners in a squeeze between increasing expenses and declining income. The saloonman quick to the scene of a rush did well enough, but unless he began with sufficient capital to invest in a good location and lavish furnishings, the newcomer to an established town probably needed a combination of personality, savvy, perseverance, and luck to survive. Most owners proved as transient as the men they served and soon moved on to other places and jobs.

Successful or not, barkeepers and their businesses played a part in the life of the camps that historians should not ignore. The saloon was a breeding place for trouble and a magnet for mischief. It was also a public space available for common needs, a place where men could meet and sit and laugh, a gathering ground for human contact in a land where men's lives were often solitary and always trying. The barroom was not only the most numerous but also the most complex and versatile retail business of the Rockies. Above all, it was a natural outgrowth of the social environment of the mining town. Its surviving descendants stand as reminders of its role in the history of those isolated settlements sprinkled along the spine of the continent.

A Census Profile of Saloon Owners and the Adult Mining Town Population

RACE

	White	Black	Chinese
Saloon Owners	99.8%	.2%	—
General Sample	91.0	.8	8.2
miners/unskilled	85.4	.8	13.8
skilled	98.9	.4	.7
merchants	93.6	1.2	5.2
professional	100.0	—	—

SEX

	Male	Female
Saloon Owners	98.7%	1.3%
General Sample	78.8	21.2
miners/unskilled	100.0	—
skilled	99.3	.7
merchants	85.1	14.9
professional	92.5	7.5

MEDIAN AGE

Saloon Owners	34.2 years
General Sample	33.2
miners/unskilled	32.8
skilled	33.9
merchants	34.9
professional	35.5

MARITAL STATUS

	Single	Married	Divorced or Widowed
Saloon Owners	56.5%	41.0%	2.5%
General Sample	48.3	46.7	5.0
miners/unskilled	61.4	36.0	2.6
skilled	48.7	47.2	4.1
merchants	39.9	51.7	8.4
professional	44.7	49.0	6.3

ORIGIN

	U.S.	Foreign	(Germany)	(Ireland)
Saloon Owners	54.3%	45.7%	18.0%	9.2%
General Sample	55.9	44.1	7.4	8.6
miners/unskilled	47.5	52.5	4.6	11.0
skilled	73.1	26.9	5.3	5.6
merchants	54.5	45.5	17.0	5.5
professional	77.4	22.6	4.8	1.4

LEADVILLE ONLY

RACE

	White	Black	Chinese
Saloon Owners	99.6%	0.4%	—
General Sample	98.5	1.5	—

SEX

	Male	Female
Saloon Owners	98.0%	2.0%
General Sample	82.4	17.6

MEDIAN AGE

Saloon Owners	33.2 years
General Sample	32.3

MARITAL STATUS

	Single	Married	Divorced or Widowed
Saloon Owners	54.2%	43.8%	2.0%
General Sample	52.7	42.7	4.6

ORIGIN

	U.S.	Foreign	(Germany)	(Ireland)
Saloon Owners	56.1%	43.9%	16.5%	10.2%
General Sample	68.0	32.0	6.4	9.8

These figures are based upon the federal manuscript census returns taken in the following towns for 1870 and 1880:

	1870	1880
Arizona	Prescott	Globe
		Tombstone
		Tip-Top
Colorado	Central City	Central City
	Georgetown	Black Hawk
	Idaho Springs	Leadville
	Black Hawk	
Montana	Virginia City	Virginia City
	Deer Lodge	
Idaho	Centerville	Centerville
	Idaho City	Idaho City
	Pioneerville	Pioneerville
	Placerville	Placerville

All saloon owners were recorded and compared with a sample of 10 percent of the population of seventeen years of age or older.

A Biographical Profile of Saloon Owners

ORIGIN

U.S.	57%
Foreign	43
Germany	20
Ireland	7
Canada	7
France	4
Other	5

PREVIOUS OCCUPATION*

mercantile	45 persons
mining	41
farm/ranch	25
unskilled labor	11
professional	10
skilled labor	5
investments	5
other	13

Below is an alphabetical listing of the saloon owners included among the biographical sketches and the state or territory in which they operated.

James D. Agnew, Idaho
Ben Anderson, Idaho
T. C. Bail, Idaho
Louis Beaupre, Montana
Charles Bemis, Idaho
Charles F. Bennett, Arizona
H. D. Blossom, Montana
Augustus Brichta, Arizona

Charles O. Brown, Arizona
Michael Burns, Montana
John D. Butler, Montana
John Cady, Arizona
John Carten, Montana
John Carter, Montana
A. P. Carter, Montana
James D. Chesnut, Montana

P. B. Cheyney, Colorado
William Coleman, Colorado
J. M. Colson, Montana
Benjamin Cook, Arizona
M. D. Cooper, Montana
John H. Cornwall, Montana
Andrew Coyle, Idaho
Ernest Cramer, Idaho
E. R. Dean, Montana
Frank Dierman, Montana
Alonzo Davis, Arizona
William A. Dingee, Montana
Charles Douglas, Idaho
Leon Dupont, Montana
Daniel Floweree, Montana
W. E. Fuller, Montana
Joe Gavin, Colorado
Henry Glassman, Arizona
Jacob Goetz, Idaho
Phil Golding, Colorado
Isadore Goldtree, Arizona
Nicholas Gredel, Montana
I. Greenwood, Montana
John Grete, Idaho
A. F. Grundel, Colorado
George Hand, Arizona
James H. Hart, Idaho
Peter Hauck, Montana
Nicholas Haug, Idaho
M. P. Haynes, Idaho
Chris Hehli, Montana
W. A. Helm, Colorado
George Herendeen, Montana
John E. Higgins, Montana
Green Holland, Idaho
John H. Hovey, Arizona
J. W. Jones, Montana
Christian Kenck, Montana
E. A. Kenney, Montana
Billy King, Arizona
John Kircher, Montana
J. H. Locke, Montana
I. Marks, Montana

T. Marquis, Montana
Peter Martin, Montana
J. S. McAndrews, Montana
W. R. McComas, Montana
James McKay, Idaho
Thomas J. McNamara, Montana
George McKenzie, Arizona
J. L. Melgren, Arizona
W. M. Mellon, Arizona
Frank Miller, Idaho
H. A. Milot, Montana
Conrad Mockel, Montana
Matthias Mounts, Montana
Peter Neth, Idaho
T. J. Noble, Montana
John P. Nolan, Montana
Sank Owens, Idaho
Louis Payette, Montana
Abraham Peeples, Arizona
Johnston Pratt, Montana
Charles Reahm, Montana
M. Roth, Montana
Charles Rouleau, Montana
H. C. Riggs, Idaho
Edward Ryan, Montana
George B. Silverberg, Montana
Jefferson R. Smith, Colorado
Madison C. Smith, Idaho
Jacob F. Soieth, Montana
John Taylor, Idaho
William H. Tichner, Idaho
Isham L. Tiner, Idaho
Ira Tingley, Idaho
J. A. Vail, Arizona
Peter Valiton, Montana
James Wardner, Idaho
M. T. Watrous, Colorado
William F. Wentworth, Montana
Menton Wetzstein, Montana
C. F. White, Montana
Green White, Idaho
P. P. Worsham, Montana

In addition to the files of various newspapers, the biographical material on the
saloon owners in the above list was taken from the following sources: H. H.
Bancroft Collection, Western Historical Collection, University of Colorado
Library, Boulder, Colo.; Charles F. Bennett Reminiscence, Arizona Histori-
cal Society, Tucson, Ariz.; John H. Cady, *Arizona's Yesterday* (Los Angeles:
Los Angeles Times-Mirror Printing Co., 1916); Colorado Writers Project
Interviews, State Historical Society of Colorado, Denver, Colo.; Alonzo E.
Davis, *Pioneer Days in Arizona*, microfilm, Henry E. Huntington Library,
San Marino, Calif.; Byron Defenbach, *Idaho, the Place and Its People*
(Chicago: American Historical Society, 1933); Thomas G. Donaldson, *Idaho
of Yesterday* (Caldwell, Idaho: Caxton Printers, Ltd., 1941); Hiram T.
French, *History of Idaho* (Chicago: The Lewis Publishing Co., 1914);
Thomas Edwin Farish, *History of Arizona* (Phoenix: Filmer Brothers, 1915);
James Hawley Manuscript, Idaho State Historical Society, Boise, Idaho;
Frank Hall, *History of the State of Colorado* (Chicago: Blakely Printing
Co., (1889–95); George Herendeen Reminiscence, Montana Historical Society,
Helena, Mont.; *History of Idaho Territory* (San Francisco: Wallace W. Elliott
and Co., 1884); *An Illustrated History of the State of Idaho* (Chicago: Lewis
Publishing Co., 1899); Orion E. Kirkpatrick, *History of Leesburg Pioneers*
(Salt Lake City: Pyramid Press, 1934); Michael A. Leeson, *History of Mon-
tana, 1739–1885* (Chicago: Warner, Beers, and Co., 1885); *Portrait and
Biographical Record of Arizona* (Chicago: Chapman Publishing Co., 1901);
Bob Powell Reminiscence, Montana Historical Society, Helena, Mont.;
Progressive Men of Southern Idaho (Chicago: A. W. Bowen and Co., 1904);
Progressive Men of the State of Montana (Chicago: A. W. Bowen and Co.,
1903); C. L. Sonnichsen, *Billy King's Tombstone, The Private Life of an
Arizona Boom Town* (Tucson: University of Arizona Press, 1972); James F.
Wardner, *Jim Wardner, of Wardner, Idaho* (New York: Anglo-American
Publishing Co., 1900).

*Previous occupation can be determined for 92 of the 101 saloon owners. Because many
of them engaged in more than one occupation before becoming owners of saloons, the
total number in the table above is 155.

Notes

Abbreviations

AHS	Arizona Historical Society, Tucson, Arizona
CU	University of Colorado Library, Boulder, Colorado
HEH	Henry E. Huntington Library, San Marino, California
IHS	Idaho State Historical Society, Boise, Idaho
MHS	Montana Historical Society, Helena, Montana
SHSC	State Historical Society of Colorado, Denver, Colorado

Preface

1. For a brief discussion of the literature on saloons, see Bibliography.

2. See, for instance, Hubert Howe Bancroft, *The Works of Hubert Howe Bancroft*, vol. 31, *History of Washington, Idaho, and Montana, 1845–1889* (San Francisco: The History Company, 1890), p. 420; Duane A. Smith, *Rocky Mountain Mining Camps: The Urban Frontier* (Lincoln: University of Nebraska Press, 1974), pp. 222–24; Harold E. Briggs, *Frontiers of the Northwest: A History of the Upper Missouri Valley* (New York: Peter Smith, 1950), pp. 82–86.

3. Norman H. Clark, *Deliver Us from Evil: An Interpretation of American Prohibition* (New York: W. W. Norton and Co., 1976), pp. 14–24; James H. Cassedy, "An Early American Hangover: The Medical Profession and Intemperance, 1800–1860," *Bulletin of the History of Medicine* 50 (Fall 1976): 405–13; William F. Bynum, "Chronic Alcoholism in the First Half of the 19th Century," *Bulletin of the History of Medicine* 42 (March–April 1968): 160–85.

4. E. M. Jellinek, "Recent Trends in Alcoholism and in Alcohol Consumption," *Quarterly Journal of Studies on Alcohol* 8 (June 1947): 1–47; Board of Trade, Great Britain, "Alcoholic Beverages. Statement 'showing the Production and Consumption of Alcoholic Beverages (Wine, Beer, and Spirits) in the Various Countries of Europe, in the United States, and in the principal British Colonies,' " (London, 1901).

5. Mrs. James D. Agnew, "Idaho Pioneer of 1864," *Washington Historical Quarterly* 15 (January 1924): 45.

6. (Leadville, Colo.) *Carbonate Weekly Chronicle*, 3 January 1880; Julian Ralph, *Our Great West: A Study of the Present Conditions and Future Possibilities of the New Commonwealths and Capitals of the United States* (Freeport, New York: Books for Libraries Press, 1970), p. 205; Anne Ellis, *The Life of an Ordinary Woman* (Boston: Houghton Mifflin Co., 1929), p. 24.

Chapter 1

1. Albert D. Richardson, *Beyond the Mississippi: From the Great River to the Great Ocean* (Hartford: American Publishing Co., 1869), pp. 493–500.

2. George N. Fenin and William K. Everson, *The Western: From Silents to the Seventies* (New York: Grossman Publishers, 1973), p. 47. For a brief discussion of drinking excesses on the mining frontier, see Allan M. Winkler, "Drinking on the American Frontier," *Quarterly Journal of Studies on Alcohol* 29 (June 1968): pt. A, pp. 413–45.

3. (Central City, Colo.) *Tri-Weekly Miner's Register*, 6 January 1863; William Larimer, *Reminiscences of General William Larimer and of His Son William H. H. Larimer, Two of the Founders of Denver City* (Lancaster: New Era Publishing Company, 1918), p. 168; John Henry Cady, *Arizona's Yesterday, Being the Narrative of John H. Cady, Pioneer* (Los Angeles: Times-Mirror Co., 1916), pp. 76–77.

4. John W. Grannis Diary, 1864, bk. 2, 44, small collection #301, MHS; Unidentified ledger [1869], Helena Bankers Group Papers, MHS; Allen Grant Wallihan Diary, SHSC; Thomas Conrad to Mary Conrad, 6 September 1864, 2 October 1864, 6 November 1864, Box 1, Thomas Conrad Papers, MHS; Sallie R. Herndon Diary, 21 January 1866, MHS.

5. (Silver City, Idaho) *Owyhee Avalanche*, 3 February 1866.

6. Nolie Mumey, *Creede: History of a Colorado Silver Mining Town* (Denver: Artcraft Press, 1949), p. 10; W. A. Goulder, *Reminiscences of a Pioneer* (Boise: Timothy Regan, 1909), pp. 194–95; Elladean Pierce, "Early Days of Craig, Colorado," *Colorado Magazine* 5 (1928): 156; Michael A. Leeson, *History of Montana, 1739–1885* (Chicago: Warner, Beers and Co., 1885), pp. 1035–36.

7. Lola M. Homsher, ed., *South Pass, 1868: James Chisholm's Journal of the Wyoming Gold Rush* (Lincoln: University of Nebraska Press, 1960), pp. 156–59.

8. *Leadville* (Colo.) *Weekly Herald*, 19 June 1880.

9. Samuel Bowles, *Across the Continent* (Springfield: Samuel Bowles, 1866); Rev. William H. Goode, *Outposts of Zion with Limnings of Mission Life* (Cincinnati: Poe and Hitchcock, 1864), pp. 421–22; Maurice O'Conner Morris, *Rambles in the Rocky Mountains* (London: Smith, Elder and Co., 1864), pp. 86–87; Ellen Fletcher to Blanche, 23 September 1866, copy, Ellen Fletcher Papers, small collection #78, MHS; Thomas Maitland Marshall, ed., *Early Records of Gilpin County, Colorado, 1859–1861* (Boulder: W. F. Robinson, 1920), pp. 139, 172, 176; Cornelius Hedges to mother, 2 May 1866, Hedges Papers, box 2, MHS; Myron Eells Journal, 8 April 1872, copy, MS2/Ee5, IHS.

10. Much research on the causes of drinking in various societies has

tested and often challenged the findings of David Horton in his "The Function of Alcohol in Primitive Societies: A Cross-Cultural Study," *Quarterly Journal of Studies on Alcohol* 4 (September 1943): 199–320. For examples of research suggesting the reasons for drinking stressed in my discussion, see *First Report to the U.S. Congress on Alcohol and Health* (Washington: G.P.O., 1971), pp. 619–46; Rudolf Kalin, David McClelland, and Michael Kahn, "The Effects of Male Social Drinking on Fantasy," *Journal of Personality and Social Psychology* 1 (May 1965): 441–52; Peter Nathan et al., "Comparative Studies of the Interpersonal and Affective Behavior of Alcoholics and Non-Alcoholics during Prolonged Experimental Drinking," in *Recent Advances in Studies of Alcoholism: An Interdisciplinary Symposium*, ed. Nancy K. Mello and Jack H. Mendelson (Washington: G.P.O., 1971), pp. 619–46; Allan F. Williams, "Social Drinking, Anxiety and Depression," *Journal of Personality and Social Psychology* 3 (June 1966): 689–93; David C. McClelland, "The Power of Positive Drinking," *Psychology Today* 4 (January 1971): 40–41, 78–79; Don Cahalan, Ira H. Cisin, and Helen Crossley, *American Drinking Patterns: A National Study of Drinking Behavior and Attitudes* (New Brunswick: Rutgers Center of Alcohol Studies, 1969), pp. 71–99; Margaret K. Bacon, "The Dependency-Conflict Hypothesis and the Frequency of Drunkenness," *Quarterly Journal of Studies on Alcohol* 35 (September 1974): 863–76; Harold Fallding, *Drinking, Community and Civilization: The Account of a New Jersey Interview Study* (New Brunswick: Rutgers Center of Alcohol Studies, 1974), pp. 3–9; William Madsen and Claudia Madsen, "The Cultural Structure of Mexican Drinking Behavior," *Quarterly Journal of Studies on Alcohol* 30 (September 1969): 701–18.

On the ill effects of excessive drinking and social restraints on those effects, see Richard M. Bennett, Arnold H. Buss, and John A. Carpenter, "Alcohol and Human Physical Aggression," *Quarterly Journal of Studies on Alcohol* 30 (December 1969): 870–76; Donald W. Goodwin, "Alcohol in Suicide and Homicide," *Quarterly Journal of Studies on Alcohol* 34 (March 1973): 144–56; A. R. Nicol et al., "The Relationship of Alcoholism to Violent Behavior Resulting in Long-Term Imprisonment," *British Journal of Psychiatry* 123 (July 1973): 47–51; James Pierce, "Blood Alcohol Levels Following Successful Suicide," *Quarterly Journal of Studies on Alcohol* 27 (March 1966): 23–29; Craig MacAndrew and Robert B. Edgerton, *Drunken Comportment: A Social Explanation* (Chicago: Aldine Publishing Co., 1969); Peter Field, "A New Cross-Cultural Study of Drunkenness," in *Society, Culture and Drinking Patterns*, ed. David J. Pittman and Charles R. Snyder (New York: John Wiley and Sons, Inc., 1962), pp. 48–74; John J. Honigmann, "Dynamics of Drinking in an Austrian Village," *Ethnology* 2 (Spring 1963): 157–69.

11. *Deer Lodge* (Mont.) *Independent*, 6 March 1868.

12. See Appendix A. Occasional informal censuses showed similar results. One conducted in Tombstone, Arizona, in 1882 showed 54 percent of the population native born; of the rest 21 percent were from England, Ireland, or Germany. (Tombstone, Ariz.) *Weekly Epitaph*, 8 July 1882.

13. *Denver Rocky Mountain News*, 29 August 1861.

14. (Boise) *Idaho Tri-Weekly Statesman*, 8 September 1864. The verse can be found in *Tri-Weekly Miner's Register*, 28 July 1862.

15. Duane A. Smith, *Rocky Mountain Mining Camps: The Urban Frontier* (Lincoln: University of Nebraska Press, 1974), p. 22; William Joseph Trimble, *The Mining Advance into the Inland Empire* (Madison, Wis.: Bulletin of the University of Wisconsin, 1914), pp. 164–65; Goode, *Outposts of Zion*, p. 438; Frank Hall, *History of the State of Colorado*, 4 vols. (Chicago: Blakely Printing Co., 1889), 1:206–207.

16. The *Oregonian* is quoted in Trimble, *Inland Empire*, p. 158. See also Smith, *Rocky Mountain Mining Camps*, pp. 10, 22, 57; Ralph Mann, "The Decade after the Gold Rush: Social Structure in Grass Valley and Nevada City, California, 1850–1860," *Pacific Historical Review* 41 (November 1972): 492–96; *Leadville* (Colo.) *Daily Democrat*, 11 February 1880.

17. Elizabeth Chester Fisk to Fannie, 24 July 1867, box 6, Fisk Family Papers, MHS; Daniel Tuttle, *Reminiscences of a Missionary Bishop* (New York: T. Whittaker, 1906), p. 120; (Prescott) *Arizona Miner*, 23 May 1866; Stephen Smart, *Leadville, Ten Mile, Eagle River, Elk Mountain, Tin Cup and All Other Noted Colorado Mining Camps* (Kansas City: Ramsey, Millett and Hudson, 1879), p. 7; H. H. [Helen Hunt Jackson] "To Leadville," *Atlantic Monthly* 43 (May 1879): 575.

18. Rodman W. Paul, ed., *A Victorian Gentlewoman in the Far West: The Reminiscences of Mary Hallock Foote* (San Marino, Calif.: The Huntington Library, 1972), p. 205.

19. Demas Barnes, *From the Atlantic to the Pacific, Overland* (New York: D. Van Nostrand, 1866), p. 17.

20. (Central City, Colo.) *Daily Miner's Register*, 22 December 1863.

21. C. Aubrey Angelo, *Idaho: A Descriptive Tour, and Review of Its Resources and Route* (San Francisco: H. H. Bancroft and Co., 1865), p. 46; E. Lafayette Bristow to Mrs. Rachael Jones, 4 June 1862, copy, E. Lafayette Bristow Papers, MS2/B77, IHS.

22. Clyde McLemore, ed., "Bannack and Gallatin City in 1862–63: A Letter by Mrs. Emily R. Meredith," *Sources of Northwest History*, no. 24, p. 5.

23. Daniel Tuttle to "My own dear wifie," 11 August 1867, 30 January 1868, Daniel Tuttle Papers, MHS.

24. N. S. Slater, "A Winter Journey in Colorado," *Atlantic Monthly* 48 (January 1881): 52.

25. *Idaho Tri-Weekly Statesman*, 14 January 1865.

26. The quotations are from Alva J. Noyes, "Gilbert Benedict," 7, Gilbert Benedict Papers, MHS, and William Larned Diary, 10 September 1864, reprinted in Helen White, ed., *Ho! For the Gold Fields: Northern Overland Wagon Trains of the 1860s* (St. Paul: Minnesota Historical Society, 1966), p. 117. See also Jack J. Detzler, ed., *Diary of Howard Stillwell Stanfield* (Bloomington: Indiana University Press, 1969), p. 63; *Leadville Weekly Herald*, 3 April 1880; James W. Watts, "Experiences of a Packer in Washington Territory Mining Camps During the Sixties," *Washington Historical Quarterly* 20 (January 1929): 47; Gilbert Benedict, "Trip to Montana," verse form, 4–5, Gilbert Benedict Papers, MHS; Andrew F. Rolle, ed., *The Road to Virginia City: The Diary of James Knox Polk Miller* (Norman: University of Oklahoma Press, 1960), p. 70; William D. Dibb Diary, 4 July 1862, 31 July 1862, MHS.

27. Richardson, *Beyond the Mississippi*, p. 162.

28. Libeus Barney, *Early-day Letters from Auraria* (Denver: Luddett Press, 1907), p. 81. For a description of production of mescal, see Samuel Woodworth Cozzens, *The Marvellous Country; or, Three Years in Arizona, and New Mexico, the Apaches' Home* (Boston: Shepard and Gill, 1873), pp. 152–53. See also Iris H. Wilson, ed., "Pineda's Report on the Beverages of New Spain," *Arizona and the West* 5 (Spring 1963): 79–90; Edwin L. Sabin, *Kit Carson Days, 1809–1868* (New York: Press of the Pioneers, 1928), pp. 27–28; Richard Charles Deus Reminiscence, SHSC.

29. Robert Thoroughman Reminiscence, MHS. Also Granville Stuart, *Forty Years on the Frontier*, 2 vols. (Cleveland: Arthur Clark, 1925), 1:265; Goulder, *Reminiscences*, pp. 240–41.

30. Henry Miller, "Letters From the Upper Columbia," *Idaho Yesterdays* 4 (Winter 1960–61): 24.

31. *Laws of the Territory of Idaho, First Session* (Lewiston, 1864), p. 467; *Colorado [Territory] General Assembly. General Laws, Joint Resolutions and Private Acts* (Denver, 1861), p. 314; Leroy R. Hafen, ed., *Colorado Gold Rush: Contemporary Letters and Reports, 1858–1859* (Glendale: Arthur H. Clark, 1941), pp. 359–60, 191–92.

32. George Ade, *The Old Time Saloon, Not Wet—Not Dry, Just History* (New York: Ray Long and Richard R. Smith, Inc., 1931), p. 50; Peter Tamony, "Western Words," *Western Folklore* 26 (April 1967): 124–27; (Globe) *Arizona Silver Belt*, 14 February 1880; *Lake City* (Colo.) *Silver World*, 27 May 1876; *Leadville Daily Democrat*, 17 April 1880; *Deer Lodge Independent*, 14 August 1868; (Hailey, Idaho) *Wood River Times*, 25 January 1882; (Idaho City) *Idaho World*, 16 June 1870.

33. Katherine Dunlap Diary, 1 June 1864, copy, MHS; Thomas Josiah Dimsdale, *The Vigilantes of Montana* (Virginia City, Mont: D. W. Tilton, 1866), p. 265; Joseph Horsky Reminiscence, MHS; (Bonanza, Idaho) *Yankee*

Fork Herald, 29 May 1880, 12 June 1880; *Gunnison* (Colorado) *Review*, 4 December 1880; *Idaho World*, 25 May 1867.

34. Leroy R. Hafen, ed., *Colorado and Its People: A Narrative and Topical History of the Centennial State*, 4 vols. (New York: Lewis Historical Publishing Co., 1948), 1:233; Stanley Baron, *Brewed in America: A History of Beer and Ale in the United States* (Boston: Little, Brown and Co., 1962), pp. 247–49.

35. Daniel Tuttle to "My own dear wifie," 19 July 1867, Daniel Tuttle Papers, MHS; *Leadville Daily Herald*, 19 February 1881; (Park City, Utah) *Park Record*, 1 October 1881; Julian Ralph, *Our Great West: A Study of the Present Conditions and Future Possibilities of the New Commonwealths and Capitals of the United States* (Freeport, New York: Books for Libraries Press, 1970), p. 205.

36. Account books of Virginia City Tavern, 128, MHS; Mollie Dorsie Sanford, *Mollie: The Journal of Mollie Dorsey Sanford in Nebraska and Colorado Territories, 1857–1866* (Lincoln: University of Nebraska Press, 1959), p. 149; Charles D. Poston Reminiscence, 8, HEH.

37. W. R. Sellew to mother, 31 December 1884, W. R. Sellew Papers, MHS.

38. Poem is in *Wood River Times*, 6 July 1881. See also *Idaho World*, 8 July 1865; *Park Record*, 7 July 1883; Edward J. Lewis Diary, 4 July 1860, SHSC.

39. Daniel Tuttle to "My own dear wifie," 11 August 1867, Daniel Tuttle Papers, MHS. For comments on prominence of liquor in political and government affairs, see *Yankee Fork Herald*, 16 October 1880; (Ouray, Colo.) *Solid Muldoon*, 3 September 1880; *Leadville Daily Democrat*, 2 April 1880; *Park Record*, 7 August 1880; *Creede* (Colo.) *Candle*, 21 April 1893; *Owyhee Avalanche*, 21 October 1865, 28 October 1865; Samuel William Carvoso Whipps Reminiscence, 111, MHS.

40. *Wood River Times*, 28 September 1881; *Creede* (Colo.) *Chronicle*, quoted in (Denver) *Colorado Sun*, 3 April 1892; Henry J. Bose Reminiscence, 9–10, MHS.

41. *Solid Muldoon*, 12 September 1879; *Deer Lodge Independent*, 26 October 1867, 3 April 1868; *Owyhee Avalanche*, 19 August 1865; *Lake City Silver World*, 31 July 1875; Henry J. Bose Reminiscence, 4, MHS; James G. Wolf Reminiscence, AHS; James W. Watts, "Experiences as a Packer," 288; Ethelbert Talbot, *My People of the Plains* (New York and London: Harper and Brothers, 1946), pp. 58–59.

42. *Frank Leslie's Illustrated Newspaper*, 12 April 1879.

43. *Lake City Silver World*, 19 June 1875.

44. Louis L. Simonin, "Colorado in 1867 as Seen by a Frenchman," trans. Wilson O. Clough, *Colorado Magazine* 14 (March 1937): 57.

45. Ralph, *Our Great West*, pp. 263–64.

46. Rolle, ed., *Road To Virginia City*, pp. 85–92, 106.

47. *Colorado Sun*, 25 February 1892; *Creede Candle*, 1 April 1892.

48. *Leadville Weekly Herald*, 6 March 1880, 13 March 1880, 3 April 1880, 10 April 1880, 17 April 1880, 19 June 1880, 26 June 1880, 10 July 1880, 24 July 1880, 11 September 1880.

49. *Creede Candle*, 10 June 1892; (Virginia City) *Montana Post*, 17 December 1864, 24 December 1864; *Yankee Fork Herald,* 22 May 1880; *Leadville Daily Democrat*, 8 February 1880; *Leadville Daily Herald*, 4 February 1881; *Idaho World*, 8 April 1865, 3 November 1866; *Tri-Weekly Miner's Register*, 8 October 1862; *Wood River Times*, 29 November 1882; *Park Record*, 13 August 1881; *Helena* (Mont.) *Herald*, 7 August 1867, 19 September 1867, 10 October 1867; Lin B. Feil, "Helvetia: Boom Town of the Santa Ritas," *Journal of Arizona History* 9 (Summer 1968): 85–86.

50. *Idaho World*, 8 April 1865; City Record Book I, 10, 7 June 1888, Telluride, Colorado, Town Hall; Police Docket, Georgetown, Colorado, Town Hall; Justice Docket, July 1876 to August 1883, Silverton, Colorado, Town Hall. Information on Virginia City is from police dockets published in *Montana Post* between February 1865 and March 1866.

51. McLemore, ed., "Bannack and Gallatin City;" Alfreda Elsensohn, *Pioneer Days in Idaho County*, 2 vols. (Caldwell, Idaho: Caxton Printers, 1947–51), 1:56; (Silverton, Colo.) *LaPlata Miner*, 2 August 1879; *Park Record*, 24 March 1883.

52. *Idaho Tri-Weekly Statesman,* 9 September 1871.

53. *Weekly Epitaph*, 10 April 1882; *Leadville Daily Herald*, 5 January 1881; *Gunnison Review*, 18 September 1880; *Tri-Weekly Miner's Register*, 22 September 1862; *Leadville Daily Democrat*, 8 January 1880, 8 February 1880, 25 February 1880; Eugene Irey, "A Social History of Leadville, Colorado, During the Boom Days, 1877–1881," (Ph.D. diss., University of Minnesota, 1951), pp. 256–59.

54. *Yankee Fork Herald*, 10 January 1880; *Solid Muldoon*, 19 March 1880.

55. *Leadville Daily Herald*, 15 January 1881; Goulder, *Reminiscences*, p. 241; *Idaho Tri-Weekly Statesman*, 10 January 1884; *Leadville Weekly Herald*, 29 November 1879; *Wood River Times*, 4 January 1882; *Leadville Daily Democrat*, 10 January 1880, 17 February 1880.

56. *Leadville Daily Herald*, 19 January 1881; *Leadville Daily Democrat*, 23 January 1880, 21 March 1880, 25 May 1880; *Montana Post*, 11 February 1865; *Yankee Fork Herald*, 21 August 1880; *Creede Candle*, 11 February 1892; *Owyhee Avalanche*, 23 June 1866; *Lake City Silver World*, 10 November 1877.

57. Rev. James Joseph Gibbons, *In the San Juan Colorado* (Chicago: Calumet Book and Engraving Co., 1898), pp. 142–46; Nels C. Jensen Diary, 16 June 1881, MS2/J45, IHS; Alonzo Boardman to Nancy, 2 April 1863,

Alonzo Boardman Papers, SHSC; *Leadville Daily Democrat*, 22 January 1880; *Leadville Weekly Herald*, 13 March 1880; *Montana Post*, 16 September 1865; *Owyhee Avalanche*, 15 September 1866; *Idaho Tri-Weekly Statesman*, 4 April 1865; *Yankee Fork Herald*, 21 August 1880; *Idaho World*, 8 April 1865.

Chapter 2

1. David Macrae, *The Americans at Home* (New York: E. P. Dutton Co., 1952), p. 530.

2. Mihaly Csikszentmihalyi, "A Cross-Cultural Comparison of Some Structural Characteristics of Group Drinking," *Human Development* 2 (1968): 201–209.

3. Dean Albertson, "Puritan Liquor in the Planting of New England," *New England Quarterly* 23 (December 1950): 477–90; Walter B. Stevens, "The Missouri Tavern," *Missouri Historical Review* 68 (October 1973): 94–130; A. E. Richardson and H. Donaldson Eberlein, *The English Inn Past and Present: A Review of Its History and Social Life* (New York: Benjamin Blom, 1968); Carl Bridenbaugh, *Cities in Revolt: Urban Life in America, 1743–1776* (New York: Oxford University Press, 1971), pp. 157–62, 358–60.

4. George Philip Krapp, *The English Language in America*, 2 vols. (New York: Frederick Ungar Publishing Co., 1960), 1:144–45; Mitford M. Mathews, ed., *A Dictionary of Americanisms on Historical Principles*, 2 vols. (Chicago: University of Chicago Press, 1951), 2:1448.

5. The quotation is from Clara Spaulding Brown, "An Arizona Mining District," *Californian* 4 (July 1881): 57.

6. Quotations are in (Silverton, Colo.) *LaPlata Miner*, 8 November 1879, and *Leadville* (Colo.) *Weekly Herald*, 14 February 1880. See also description of Leesburg, Idaho, in *Helena* (Mont.) *Herald*, 3 July 1867.

7. H. H. [Helen Hunt Jackson], "To Leadville," *Atlantic Monthly* 43 (May 1879): 575.

8. (Globe) *Arizona Silver Belt*, 9 May 1878; (Corinne) *Utah Reporter*, 28 April 1870; *Denver Rocky Mountain News*, 24 October 1861; Virginia City, Mont., Livery Stable Records, small collection #254, MHS; Charles M. Clark, *A Trip to Pike's Peak and Notes along the Way* (Chicago: S. P. Rounds, 1861), p. 95.

9. Richens L. Wootton, *"Uncle Dick" Wootton, the Pioneer Frontiersman of the Rocky Mountain Region* (Chicago: W. E. Dibble, 1890).

10. Charles F. Bennett Reminiscence, AHS.

11. Henry Miller, "Letters From the Upper Columbia," *Idaho Yesterdays* 4 (Winter 1960–61): 20.

12. *Coeur d'Alene* (Idaho) *Nugget*, 15 March 1884; (Aspen, Colo.) *Rocky Mountain Sun*, 30 July 1881.

13. (Boise) *Idaho Tri-Weekly Statesman*, 5 January 1884.

14. C. Eric Stoehr, *Bonanza Victorian: Architecture and Society in Colorado Mining Towns* (Albuquerque: University of New Mexico Press, 1975), pp. 10–13; Albert D. Richardson, *Beyond the Mississippi: From the Great River to the Great Ocean* (Hartford: American Publishing Co., 1869), pp. 181, 504–505; *Leadville* (Colo.) *Daily Democrat*, 17 April 1880.

15. Comment on Virginia City in Jack J. Detzler, ed., *Diary of Howard Stillwell Stanfield* (Bloomington: Indiana University Press, 1969), pp. 72–73. See also *Leadville Daily Democrat*, 9 January 1880; *Idaho Tri-Weekly Statesman*, 22 November 1864; E. W. Carpenter, "A Glimpse of Montana," *Overland Monthly* 2 (April 1869): 282–83.

16. *Red Mountain* (Colo.) *Review*, 26 May 1883; *Helena Herald*, 12 December 1867; (Park City, Utah) *Park Record*, 10 March 1883; *Leadville Daily Democrat*, 17 April 1880; Rev. J. R. Fisher, *Camping in the Rocky Mountains* (New York: Holt Brothers, 1880), p. 52; Mrs. James D. Agnew, "Idaho Pioneer in 1864," *Washington Historical Quarterly* 15 (January 1924): 47–48.

17. E. L. Bristow to W. P. Jones, 4 April 1863, E. L. Bristow Papers, MS2/B77, IHS.

18. Richardson, *Beyond the Mississippi*, pp. 187–88; Alexander J. Davidson Reminiscence, 2, AHS; D. S. Chamberlain Manuscript, AHS; *Chicago Tribune*, 7 February 1880, copy in Adolphus Henry Noon Papers, AHS.

19. *Idaho Tri-Weekly Statesman*, 5 January 1884.

20. William Shepherd, *Prairie Experiences in Handling Cattle and Sheep* (London: Chapman and Hall, 1884), p. 69.

21. (Hailey, Idaho) *Wood River Times*, 29 June 1881; (Virginia City) *Montana Post*, 20 May 1865; *Leadville Daily Democrat*, 1 February 1880; *Park Record*, 18 February 1882.

22. Duane A. Smith, *Rocky Mountain Mining Camps: The Urban Frontier* (Lincoln: University of Nebraska Press, 1974), especially chaps. 6, 7, 9, and 10.

23. *Gunnison* (Colo.) *Review*, 25 September 1880; (Ouray, Colo.) *Solid Muldoon*, 23 August 1880; *Deer Lodge* (Mont.) *Independent*, 14 December 1867; (Bonanza, Idaho) *Yankee Fork Herald*, 4 September 1880; Stoehr, *Bonanza Victorian*, pp. 61–65, 103.

24. *Yankee Fork Herald*, 3 April 1880; (Idaho City) *Idaho World*, 7 January 1865; *Creede* (Colo.) *Candle*, 4 January 1892; (Central City, Colo.) *Tri-Weekly Miner's Register*, 6 August 1863; (Central City, Colo.) *Daily Miner's Register*, 7 December 1863; *Silver Reef* (Utah) *Miner*, 14 October 1882; *Park Record*, 6 May 1882.

25. *Idaho World*, 25 May 1867; (Prescott) *Arizona Miner*, 9 May 1866.

26. The description that follows in text is a composite from several

accounts of such saloons. See *Wood River Times*, 29 March 1882; *Lake City Silver World*, 30 June 1877; *Montana Post*, 14 January 1865; (Flagstaff) *Arizona Champion*, 12 July 1884; *Silverton* (Colo.) *Democrat*, 5 May 1883, 19 May 1883; *Yankee Fork Herald*, 3 July 1880; Richard Harding Davis, "The West From a Car Window, III. At a New Mining Camp," *Harper's Weekly*, 9 April 1892, p. 343; *Idaho World*, 5 October 1867; Charles Liftchild Reminiscence, AHS; Hal Dickey, "The Famous Crystal Palace, Tombstone, Arizona," n.p., n.d., pamphlet, AHS.

27. F. L. Kirkaldie to wife, 30 August 1866, Franklin L. Kirkaldie Papers, small collection #160, MHS.

28. (Tombstone, Ariz.) *Weekly Nugget*, 6 May 1880; William Henry Barneby, *Life and Labour in the Far, Far West* (London: Cassell and Co., 1884), p. 25. See also (Mineral Park) *Alta Arizona*, 11 February 1882; (Tombstone, Ariz.) *Daily Nugget*, 15 October 1880; (Leadville, Colo.) *Carbonate Weekly Chronicle*, 3 January 1880; *Solid Muldoon*, 14 May 1880; *Silverton Democrat*, 5 May 1883; *Montana Post*, 15 October 1864; *Deer Lodge Independent*, 2 November 1867.

29. *Montana Post*, 14 January 1865; *Arizona Champion*, 1 January 1887; *Yankee Fork Herald*, 25 October 1879, 13 March 1880; *Idaho World*, 5 October 1867.

30. *Red Mountain Review*, 28 April 1883; *Deer Lodge Independent*, 18 January 1868, 15 May 1868.

31. *Chicago Tribune*, 7 February 1880, in Adolphus Henry Noon Papers, AHS; Anne Ellis, *The Life of an Ordinary Woman* (Boston: Houghton Mifflin Co., 1929), pp. 44–45; G. W. McPherson, *A Parson's Adventures* (Yonkers, N.J.: Yonkers Book Co., 1925), p. 151.

32. *Lake City Silver World*, 28 April 1877; *Red Mountain* (Colo.) *Pilot*, 30 June 1883; *Park Record*, 3 December 1881.

33. Foster Rhea Dulles, *America Learns to Play: A History of Popular Recreation, 1607–1940* (Gloucester, Mass.: Peter Smith, 1959), p. 36; "Billiards," *Harper's Weekly*, 8 March 1890, pp. 186–87; "The Annals of Billiards," *Cornhill Magazine* (July–December 1886): 180–88; Richard Henry Edwards, *Popular Amusements* (New York: Association Press, 1915), pp. 82–85.

34. Julian Ralph, *Our Great West: A Study of the Present Conditions and Future Possibilities of the New Commonwealths and Capitals of the United States* (Freeport, New York: Books for Libraries Press, 1970), p. 265.

35. For quotations see *Yankee Fork Herald*, 11 September 1879, and *Montana Post*, 25 February 1865. See also *Denver Rocky Mountain News*, 20 September 1861; *LaPlata Miner*, 26 April 1879; *Leadville Daily Herald*, 18 February 1881; *White Pine* (Colo.) *Cone*, 7 September 1883; *Tri-Weekly*

Miner's Register, 21 January 1863; *Lake City Silver World*, 1 December 1877; *Montana Post*, 10 September 1864, 3 December 1864, 10 June 1865; (Silver City, Idaho) *Owyhee Avalanche*, 24 February 1866; *Idaho World*, 10 December 1864, 22 June 1867; *Yankee Fork Herald*, 3 April 1880.

36. Record Book I, 15 April 1872, 381–85, Boise County Clerk's Office, Idaho City, Idaho; *Yankee Fork Herald*, 3 August 1880; *Idaho World*, 2 November 1867; (Tombstone, Ariz.) *Weekly Epitaph*, 22 July 1882; *Montana Post*, 24 September 1864.

37. Paul A. Hutton, "From Little Bighorn to Little Big Man: The Changing Image of a Western Hero in Popular Culture," *Western Historical Quarterly* 7 (January 1976): 29–30; Don Russell, *Custer's Last* (Fort Worth: Amon Carter Museum of Western Art, 1968), pp. 31–35.

38. Frank Robertson and Beth Kay Harris, *Soapy Smith, King of the Frontier Con Men* (New York: Hastings House, 1961), pp. 48–49; "Comments on an Article in the *Saturday Evening Post*," James C. Hancock Collection, AHS; Robert Ray Latta, *Reminiscences of Pioneer Life* (Kansas City: Franklin Hudson Publishing Co., 1912), pp. 158–59; James W. Callaway, Colorado Writers' Project Interviews, Chaffee County, p. 2, SHSC.

39. Daniel Ellis Conner, *A Confederate in the Gold Fields*, ed. Donald J. Berthrong and Odessa Davenport (Norman: University of Oklahoma Press, 1970), p. 117. See also *Owyhee Avalanche*, 9 June 1866; *Daily Miner's Register*, 24 November 1863; Harry Drachman Reminiscence, 12–15, AHS; James G. Wolf Reminiscence, AHS.

40. Tim Kinerk Reminiscence, small collection #175, MHS; John Henry Cady, *Arizona's Yesterday, Being the Narrative of John H. Cady, Pioneer* (Los Angeles: Times-Mirror Co., 1916), p. 83; Richardson, *Beyond the Mississippi*, pp. 479–80.

41. *Idaho World*, 10 December 1864; Harry Drachman Reminiscence, 12–15, AHS; Dan de Lara Hughes, *South From Tombstone: A Life Story by Dan de Lara Hughes* (London: Methuen and Co., 1938); Alexander Ziede, "The Territorial History of the Globe Mining District, Arizona," (M.A. thesis, University of Southern California, 1939), pp. 88–89.

42. Lola M. Homsher, ed., *South Pass, 1868: James Chisholm's Journal of the Wyoming Gold Rush* (Lincoln: University of Nebraska Press, 1960), p. 114.

43. *Owyhee Avalanche*, 31 March 1866.

44. George Hand Diary, 10 March 1875, 14 March 1875, AHS. The entry for 2 August 1876 indicates that not all bummers were men: "Had several lady callers. All wanted to bum drinks. No go." See also *Leadville Weekly Herald*, 8 November 1879; *Leadville Daily Democrat*, 10 July 1880; *Silverton Democrat*, 9 June 1883.

Chapter 3

1. Thomas C. Donaldson, *Idaho of Yesterday* (Caldwell, Idaho: Caxton Printers, Ltd., 1941), pp. 113–19; John Hailey, *The History of Idaho* (Boise: Press of Syms-York Co., 1910), p. 89; James H. Hawley Manuscript, 123, IHS.

2. See Appendix A.

3. See Appendix B.

4. These individuals were James D. Chesnut and E. A. Kenney, both of Montana. See Michael A. Leeson, *History of Montana, 1739–1885* (Chicago: Warner, Beers and Co., 1885), pp. 1110–11, 1311.

5. James F. Wardner, *Jim Wardner, of Wardner, Idaho. By Himself* (New York: The Anglo-American Publishing Co., 1900).

6. Leeson, *History of Montana*, pp. 1196, 1236; Charles F. Bennett Reminiscence, AHS; John Henry Cady, *Arizona's Yesterday, Being the Narrative of John H. Cady, Pioneer* (Los Angeles: Times-Mirror Co., 1916).

7. Bob Powell Reminiscence, MHS.

8. (Idaho City) *Idaho World*, 5 May 1866; *Lake City* (Colo.) *Silver World*, 6 November 1875; *Red Mountain* (Colo.) *Pilot*, 30 June 1883; *Deer Lodge* (Mont.) *Independent*, 28 February 1868; J. J. and W. J. Boyer Reminiscence, William Bertsche Collection, MHS.

9. (Denver, Colo.) *Western Mountaineer*, 7 December 1859; (Central City, Colo.) *Tri-Weekly Miner's Register*, 29 August 1862.

10. Bob Powell Reminiscence, MHS.

11. George Herendeen to sister, 4 March 1878, George Herendeen Papers, small collection #16, MHS; George Hand Diary, 17 March 1875, AHS.

12. (Hailey, Idaho) *Wood River Times*, 17 August 1881; *White Pine* (Colo.) *Cone*, 1 June 1883; (Boise, Idaho) *Idaho Tri-Weekly Statesman*, 14 February 1865; *Creede* (Colo.) *Candle*, 5 May 1893; *Helena* (Mont.) *Herald*, 18 April 1867; (Bonanza, Idaho) *Yankee Fork Herald*, 17 January 1880.

13. George Hand Diary, 19 January 1875, 24 May 1877, AHS; Charles Liftchild Reminiscence, AHS.

14. George Hand Diary, 1 June 1875, 9 July 1876, AHS.

15. Alexander Davidson recalled that Billy George of Total Wreck, Arizona, allowed no disorder in his saloon and therefore did more business than all other competitors in the camp combined. Alexander J. Davidson Reminiscence, AHS.

16. *Fairplay* (Colo.) *Flume*, 1 May 1879. See also *Silver Reef* (Utah) *Miner*, 17 March 1882; (Park City, Utah) *Park Record*, 19 August 1882; *Silverton* (Colo.) *Democrat*, 11 August 1883; (Ouray, Colo.) *Solid Muldoon*, 18 June 1880; *Red Mountain* (Colo.) *Review*, 3 March 1883; *Deer Lodge Independent*, 24 October 1868.

17. Albert D. Richardson, *Beyond the Mississippi: From the Great River to the Great Ocean* (Hartford: American Publishing Co., 1869), p. 186.

18. William John McConnel, "Idaho Inferno," Bancroft manuscript, microfilm copy, IHS; *Idaho Tri-Weekly Statesman*, 22 December 1870, 14 November 1871, 14 June 1881; James Hawley Manuscript, 123, IHS; Donaldson, *Idaho of Yesterday*, pp. 43, 211–13; *An Illustrated History of the State of Idaho* (Chicago: Lewis Publishing Co., 1899), pp. 92–94; (Boise) *Idaho Daily Statesman*, 26 November 1933; Martin Duggan interview, H. H. Bancroft Collection, CU; *Leadville* (Colo.) *Daily Democrat*, 4 February 1880, 8 February 1880; Samuel William Carvoso Whipps Reminiscence, 117, MHS; Orion E. Kirkpatrick, *History of the Leesburg Pioneers* (Salt Lake City: Pyramid Press, 1934), pp. 65–66; Platt Cline, *They Came to the Mountain, The Story of Flagstaff's Beginnings* (Flagstaff: Northland Press, 1976), pp. 145–46.

19. W. R. Sellew to mother, 10 December 1884, W. R. Sellew Papers, MHS.

20. Samuel William Carvoso Whipps Reminiscence, 95, MHS.

21. Ethelbert Talbot, *My People of the Plains* (New York and London: Harper and Brothers, 1946), pp. 67–69.

22. For editor's comment, see (Silverton, Colo.) *LaPlata Miner*, 11 October 1879. See also Mrs. Vance Cornell Reminiscence, MS2/Cor81, IHS; (Tombstone, Ariz.) *Daily Nugget*, 3 December 1880; (Globe) *Arizona Silver Belt*, 8 August 1878; *Idaho World*, 1 April 1865; *Yankee Fork Herald*, 31 July 1879; Talbot, *My People of the Plains*, pp. 90–91; *Idaho World*, 5 August 1865, 1 September 1866, 20 November 1867.

23. *Park Record*, 1 October 1881, 14 October 1881, 29 October 1881, 19 November 1881, 10 December 1881.

24. *Tri-Weekly Miner's Register*, 2 May 1863, 23 January 1863.

25. John A. Rockfellow Reminiscence, AHS.

26. James Hancock Reminiscence, Frank C. Lockwood Collection, AHS. For a similar reference to another town, see Anne Ellis, *The Life of an Ordinary Woman* (Boston: Houghton Mifflin Co., 1929), pp. 106–107. Also D. S. Chamberlain Reminiscence, AHS; (Tucson) *Arizona Weekly Citizen*, 8 March 1884; *Leadville Weekly Herald*, 2 October 1880.

27. Carlyle Channing Davis, *Olden Times in Colorado* (Los Angeles: Philips Publishing Co., 1916), pp. 115–16; Henry W. Lucy, *East by West, a Journey in the Recess* (London: Richard Bentley and Son, 1885), pp. 88–90; George F. Willison, *Here They Dug the Gold* (New York: Reynal and Hitchcock, 1946), pp. 220–21.

28. *Yankee Fork Herald*, 11 September 1879; (Virginia City) *Montana Post*, 11 November 1864. Other examples: (Silver City, Idaho) *Owyhee Avalanche*, 2 September 1865; *Idaho World*, 9 September 1865; *Lake City Silver World*, 19 June 1875; *Helena Herald*, 31 July 1867; *Deer Lodge*

Independent, 26 October 1867; *Tri-Weekly Miner's Register*, 20 August 1863.

29. *Owyhee Avalanche*, 7 July 1866; *Solid Muldoon*, 10 October 1879.

30. *Boise City* (Idaho) *Republican*, 27 February 1886.

Chapter 4

1. William Joseph Trimble, *The Mining Advance into the Inland Empire* (Madison, Wis.: Bulletin of the University of Wisconsin, 1914), p. 143; Board of Directors Minutes, 15 November 1858, 17 January 1859, Auraria Town Company Papers, SHSC.

2. *White Pine* (Colo.) *Cone*, 17 August 1883.

3. Eugene Floyd Irey, "A Social History of Leadville, Colorado, During the Boom Days, 1877–1881," (Ph.D. diss., University of Minnesota, 1951), pp. 63–66; (Hailey, Idaho) *Wood River Times*, 12 October 1881.

4. Quotation in *Frank Leslie's Illustrated Weekly Newspaper*, 7 June 1879. See also George Romspert, *The Western Echo: A Description of the Western States and Territories of the United States as Gathered in a Tour by Wagon* (Dayton, Ohio: United Brethren Publishing House, 1881), pp. 289–91; Charles Boettcher, "The Flush Times of Colorado," H. H. Bancroft Collection, CU; Samuel D. Silver Interview, H. H. Bancroft Collection, CU.

5. Daniel Ellis Conner, *A Confederate in the Colorado Gold Fields*, ed. Donald J. Berthrong and Odessa Davenport (Norman: University of Oklahoma Press, 1970), pp. 95–96; Fitz Brind, *Colorado, the Land of Sunshine, Health and Wealth* (London: Caines and Co., 1882), p. 10; Ernest Ingersoll, *The Crest of the Continent: A Record of a Summer's Ramble in the Rocky Mountains and Beyond* (Chicago: R. R. Donnelley and Sons, 1885), pp. 213–14; (Tombstone, Ariz.) *Weekly Nugget*, 6 May 1880; (Globe) *Arizona Silver Belt*, 4 July 1878.

6. *Weekly Nugget*, 23 September 1880; *Arizona Silver Belt*, 16 May 1878; *White Pine Cone*, 21 September 1883; *Wood River Times*, 29 March 1882; *Leadville* (Colo.) *Daily Democrat*, 10 February 1880; (Bonanza, Idaho) *Yankee Fork Herald*, 16 October 1880.

7. *White Pine Cone*, 8 June 1883; (Idaho City, Idaho) *Idaho World*, 31 March 1866; (Boise, Idaho) *Idaho Tri-Weekly Statesman*, 10 January 1865, 2 March 1865; (Virginia City) *Montana Radiator*, 12 October 1866; *Helena* (Mont.) *Herald*, 11 April 1867, supplement; A. J. Fisk Diary, 23 October 1866, Fisk Family Papers, MHS.

8. (Tucson) *Arizona Weekly Citizen*, 8 March 1884; *Wood River Times*, 1 November 1882; D. S. Chamberlain Manuscript, AHS; George A. Bancroft, "Chinese Polly, A Reminiscence," MS2/Chi43, IHS.

9. Peterson and Anderson's Saloon Day Book, CU; (Mineral Park) *Alta Arizona*, 25 February 1882. See also *Wood River Times*, 11 October 1882.

10. Ethelbert Talbot, *My People of the Plains* (New York and London: Harper and Brothers, 1946), p. 96.

11. Trimble, *Inland Empire*, p. 175; Isaac Haight Beardsley, *Echoes from Peak and Plain; or, Tales of Life, War, Travel, and Colorado Methodism* (Cincinnati: Curts and Jennings, 1898), p. 247; Bennett E. Seymour, "A Continuation of the Diary Written by His Father, Edward Seymour, 1861," SHSC; *Leadville* (Colo.) *Weekly Herald*, 3 January 1880; *Gunnison* (Colo.) *Review*, 19 June 1880; *Creede* (Colo.) *Candle*, 18 February 1892.

12. D. S. Chamberlain Manuscript, AHS; Richard Harding Davis, "The West From a Car Window, III. At a New Mining Camp," *Harper's Weekly*, 9 April 1892, p. 343.

13. *Creede Candle*, 11 February 1892; (Virginia City) *Montana Post*, 26 November 1864; *Red Mountain* (Colo.) *Review*, 10 March 1883.

14. *Wood River Times*, 1 March 1882; *Idaho World*, 24 December 1864, 20 May 1865, 20 October 1866, 30 March 1867, 18 May 1867; *Montana Post*, 17 September 1864; *Lake City* (Colo.) *Silver World*, 17 November 1877.

15. For the quotations, see Harold E. Briggs, *Frontiers of the Northwest: A History of the Upper Missouri Valley* (New York: Peter Smith, 1950), p. 84, and on the trial in Hell's Gate, see Granville Stuart, *Forty Years on the Frontier*, 2 vols. (Cleveland: Arthur H. Clark, 1925), 1:200. For other instances of these uses, see *Idaho World*, 7 January 1865, 8 September 1879; (Peach Springs) *Arizona Champion*, 5 January 1884; (Central City, Colo.) *Tri-Weekly Miner's Register*, 23 February 1863; *Leadville* (Colo.) *Daily Democrat*, 6 March 1880; (Silverton, Colo.) *LaPlata Miner*, reprinted in *Lake City Silver World*, 18 August 1877; (Prescott) *Arizona Miner*, 10 August 1864; (Silver City, Idaho) *Owyhee Avalanche*, 17 February 1866, 28 October 1865; (Boise) *Idaho Tri-Weekly Statesman*, 2 March 1865; *Montana Post*, 4 March 1865. Miners' use of the saloon as a meeting place sometimes preceded the opening of a camp, for they might use its facilities to organize an expedition to a new boom. See (Salem) *Oregon Statesman*, 2 September 1861.

16. Quoted in Duane A. Smith, *Rocky Mountain Mining Camps: The Urban Frontier* (Lincoln: University of Nebraska Press, 1974), p. 155.

17. John Adams, *The Works of John Adams*, ed. Charles Francis Adams, 10 vols. (Boston: Charles C. Little and James Brown, 1850), 2:85.

18. *Owyhee Avalanche*, 28 July 1866.

19. Libeus Barney, *Early-day Letters from Auraria* (Denver: Luddett Press, 1907), p. 42; Proceedings of the Alturas County Commissioners, 25,

Blaine County Courthouse, Hailey, Idaho; *Arizona Miner*, 16 May 1868; *Arizona Weekly Miner*, 30 July 1880; *Arizona Silver Belt*, 18 September 1880; *Leadville Daily Democrat*, 27 January 1880; *Lake City Silver World*, 11 August 1877; *Creede Candle*, 8 April 1892; *Wood River Times*, 6 September 1882; *Idaho World*, 12 November 1864, 4 March 1865, 6 July 1867; *Idaho Tri-Weekly Statesman*, 22 July 1865.

20. *Lake City Silver World*, 18 August 1877; Virginia City, Montana, Tavern Account Book, 166, 180–81, MHS. For an account of the legislative session see Robert G. Athearn, *Thomas Francis Meagher: An Irish Revolutionary in America* (Boulder: University of Colorado Press, 1949), pp. 145–55 and Clark C. Spence, *Territorial Politics and Government in Montana, 1864–1889* (Urbana: University of Illinois Press, 1975), pp. 35–56.

21. Alexander J. Davidson Reminiscence, 10, 12, AHS.

22. Charles Edward Young, *Dangers of the Trail in 1865* (Geneva, New York: W. F. Humphrey, 1912), pp. 91–92; George Hand Diary, 4 January 1875, 6 November 1878, 9 November 1878, AHS; Nels C. Jensen Diary, 19 June 1881, MS2/J45, IHS; *Daily Nugget*, 9 October 1880; *Idaho World*, 3 December 1864; *Idaho Tri-Weekly Statesman*, 17 November 1864; *Montana Post*, 10 February 1866.

23. *Owyhee Avalanche*, 19 May 1866.

24. For quotations, see *Idaho World*, 4 March 1865. Also, *Yankee Fork Herald*, 13 December 1879.

25. Daniel Pidgeon, *An Engineer's Holiday, Or Notes of a Round Trip from Long. 0° to 0°* (London: Kegan Paul, Trench, and Co., 1883), p. 154.

26. On Idaho City, see *Idaho World*, 8 July 1865, 15 July 1865, 19 August 1865. For other material on raffles, see Stuart, *Forty Years*, 1:221–22; *Daily Nugget*, 18 November 1880; *Tri-Weekly Miner's Register*, 30 March 1863; *Leadville Daily Herald*, 31 January 1880; (Ouray, Colo.) *Solid Muldoon*, 19 December 1879; *Fairplay* (Colo.) *Flume*, 10 April 1879; (Park City, Utah) *Park Record*, 9 December 1882; *Helena* (Mont.) *Herald*, 24 August 1867, 3 October 1867.

27. *Leadville Daily Herald*, 3 February 1881, 11 January 1881; *Leadville Daily Democrat*, 6 January 1880, 11 January 1880; *LaPlata Miner*, 12 July 1879; *Park Record*, 3 March 1883; *Idaho World*, 10 December 1864, 31 December 1864, 2 February 1867, 25 December 1867; *Yankee Fork Herald*, 6 December 1879; *Wood River Times*, 20 July 1881; *Montana Post*, 7 October 1865.

28. *Daily Miner's Register*, 10 December 1863. On prizefighting popularity, see Alexander Johnston, *Ten—And Out! The Complete Story of the Prize Ring in America* (New York: Ives Washburn, 1947), pp. 1–11.

29. On the Orem-O'Neil fight, see *Montana Post*, 15 October 1864, 29 October 1864, 7 January 1865. For others, *Denver Rocky Mountain News*, 2 September 1861; *Tri-Weekly Miner's Register*, 29 August 1862; *Creede*

Candle, 21 January 1892, 3 March 1893, 10 March 1893; (Virginia City) *Montana Radiator*, 1 September 1866; *Owyhee Avalanche*, 5 May 1866. Saloons also sponsored wrestling matches, though wrestling never reached the popularity of sparring exhibitions. See (Tombstone, Ariz.) *Weekly Epitaph*, 27 April 1884; *Leadville Daily Democrat*, 10 June 1880; *Montana Post*, 19 November 1864.

30. The quotation is in *Wood River Times*, 11 January 1882. On saloons and bands, see *Red Mountain* (Colo.) *Review*, 28 April 1883; *Solid Muldoon*, 2 July 1880; *Park Record*, 22 July 1882; *Helena Herald*, 25 April 1867; *Owyhee Avalanche*, 12 May 1866.

31. Daniel Tuttle to "My own dear wifie," 3 August 1867, Daniel Tuttle Papers, MHS.

32. *Wood River Times*, 11 January 1882; *Montana Post*, 29 October 1864, 12 November 1864; *Daily Nugget*, 9 October 1880.

33. Douglas D. Martin, *Tombstone's Epitaph* (Albuquerque: University of New Mexico Press, 1951), p. 31; *Arizona Silver Belt*, 23 May 1878; *Lake City Silver World*, 1 September 1877; *Park Record*, 7 October 1882; *Montana Radiator*, 8 September 1866; *Helena Herald*, 14 August 1867; *Idaho World*, 1 September 1866, 1 June 1867.

34. Archie L. Clark, "John McGuire, Butte's First 'Belasco,' " *The Montana Magazine of History* 2 (January 1952): 34; *Leadville Daily Democrat*, 5 March 1880; *Park Record*, 7 April 1883; *Montana Radiator*, 27 January 1866; *Boise* (Idaho) *News*, 13 October 1863; *Owyhee Avalanche*, 30 June 1866; *Wood River Times*, 1 February 1882.

35. Peterson and Anderson's Saloon Day Book, CU.

36. Mihaly Csikszentmihalyi, "A Cross-Cultural Comparison of Some Structural Characteristics of Group Drinking," *Human Development* 2 (1968): 201–209.

37. John C. Bell, *The Pilgrim and the Pioneer: The Social and Material Developments of the Rocky Mountains* (Lincoln: International Publishing Association, 1906), p. 195; Richard Baxter Townshend, *A Tenderfoot in Colorado* (Norman: University of Oklahoma Press, 1968), pp. 108–109; Frederick W. Hackwood, *Inns, Ales, and Drinking Customs of Old England* (New York: Sturgis and Walton Co., 1909), pp. 141–52.

38. *White Pine Cone*, 17 August 1883.

39. A reporter for the *Idaho World* set out to test the validity of this timeless question. For an hour-by-hour account of his experiment, conducted by a tour of local saloons, see *Idaho World*, 22 September 1866.

40. Editors sometimes published brief glossaries of local slang to aid the bewildered newcomer. See *Wood River Times*, 10 August 1881; *Owyhee Avalanche*, 30 September 1865, 29 September 1866.

41. The opinion is that of Daniel J. Boorstin in *The Americans: The National Experience* (New York: Random House, 1965), pp. 286–87. Of

several studies and dictionaries of American slang, the most helpful regarding the historical development of drinking terms are H. L. Mencken, *The American Language: An Inquiry into the Development of the English in the United States* (New York: Alfred A. Knopf, 1945), pp. 149, 568, and Mencken's *Supplement I* of that work (New York: Alfred A. Knopf, 1945), pp. 252–69; Mitford M. Mathews, ed., *A Dictionary of Americanisms on Historical Principles*, 2 vols. (Chicago: University of Chicago Press, 1951); Richard H. Thornton, *An American Glossary, Being an Attempt to Illustrate Certain Americanisms upon Historical Principles* (Philadelphia: J. B. Lippincott, 1912); Ramon F. Adams, *Western Words: A Dictionary of the American West* (Norman: University of Oklahoma Press, 1968).

42. For mention of such slang terms see Trimble, *Inland Empire*, p. 158; Henry J. Bose Reminiscence, MHS; *Owyhee Avalanche*, 25 November 1865, 17 February 1866, 27 October 1866; *Idaho Tri-Weekly Statesman*, 13 May 1865, 25 February 1865; *Lake City Silver World*, 3 July 1875; Charles Liftchild Reminiscence, AHS.

Chapter 5

1. *Red Mountain* (Colo.) *Review*, 19 May 1883.

2. (Boise) *Idaho Tri-Weekly Statesman*, 5 October 1867.

3. *Progressive Men of the State of Montana* (Chicago: A. W. Bowen and Co., 1903), p. 158; Helen F. Sanders, *A History of Montana*, 3 vols. (Chicago: Lewis Publishing Co., 1913), 2:951–52; Tom Stout, *Montana, Its Story and Biography*, 3 vols. (Chicago: American Historical Society, 1921), 2:582–83; Samuel William Carvoso Whipps Reminiscence, 105, MHS.

4. Bob Powell Reminiscence, MHS.

5. Emma Hildreth Adams, *To and Fro in Southern California: With Sketches in Arizona and New Mexico* (Cincinnati: Cranston and Stowe, 1888), pp. 53–54.

6. (Idaho City) *Idaho World*, 20 May 1865, 18 May 1867; (Flagstaff) *Arizona Champion*, 12 July 1884, 27 February 1886; *Deer Lodge* (Mont.) *Independent*, 24 April 1868; *Tombstone* (Ariz.) *Weekly Epitaph*, 1 July 1882; (Prescott) *Arizona Miner*, 4 May 1867; *Lake City* (Colo.) *Silver World*, 20 October 1877, 5 January 1878.

7. Charles F. Bennett Reminiscence, 20–21, AHS; Bob Powell Reminiscence, MHS.

8. Granville Stuart, *Forty Years on the Frontier*, 2 vols. (Cleveland: Arthur H. Clark, 1925), 1:238; Henry F. Woode Diary, 25 March 1867, small collection #138, MHS.

9. Record Book I, 284–85, Boise County Clerk's Office, Idaho City, Idaho; Charles F. Bennett Reminiscence, 20–21, AHS.

10. James G. Wolf Reminiscence, part 6, AHS; Duane A. Smith,

Rocky Mountain Mining Camps: The Urban Frontier (Lincoln: University of Nebraska Press, 1974), p. 171; (Silverton, Colo.) *LaPlata Miner*, 13 September 1879.

11. (Central City, Colo.) *Daily Miner's Register*, 5 December 1863; Record Book I, 188–89, Boise County Clerk's Office, Idaho City, Idaho.

12. For mention of prices of such saloons, see (Hailey, Idaho) *Wood River Times*, 1 November 1882; *Creede* (Colo.) *Candle*, 11 February 1892; *Arizona Miner*, 4 May 1867; *Weekly Epitaph*, 1 July 1882; Colorado Writers' Project Interviews, Chaffee County, 4, SHSC.

13. (Tombstone, Ariz.) *Weekly Nugget*, 25 March 1880, 24 June 1880. The Leadville city directory of 1887 lists a John Condon of Chicago as part owner of the Board of Trade.

14. On the various types of transportation used in the Rockies, see Henry P. Walker, *The Wagonmasters: High Plains Freighting from the Earliest Days . . . to 1880* (Norman: University of Oklahoma Press, 1966), chap. 9; Henry P. Walker, "Wagon Freighting in Arizona," *The Smoke Signal* 28 (Fall 1973): 182–204; Henry P. Walker, "Wagon Freighting from Guaymas to Tucson, 1850–1880," *Western Historical Quarterly* 1 (July 1970): 291–304; Oscar Osburn Winther, *The Old Oregon Country: A History of Frontier Trade, Transportation, and Travel* (Lincoln: University of Nebraska Press, 1969), pp. 202–13, 216–27; W. A. Goulder, *Reminiscences of a Pioneer* (Boise: Timothy Regan, 1909), pp. 239–40; James W. Watts, "Experiences of a Packer in Washington Territory Mining Camps During the Sixties," *Washington Historical Quarterly* 19 (July 1928): 287–92, and 20 (January 1929): 45–46, 48, 50; John Hailey, *The History of Idaho* (Boise: Press of Syms-York Co., 1910), pp. 95–99; Hiram Martin Chittenden, *History of Early Steamboat Navigation on the Missouri River*, 2 vols. (Minneapolis: Ross and Haines, Inc., 1962), 1:218–21, 273–76; Robert Edgar Riegel, *The Story of the Western Railroads* (Lincoln: University of Nebraska Press, 1963), chaps. 6, 12, and 14.

15. For examples of the variety of freight rates, see Walker, *Wagonmasters*, pp. 187–88; Clyde McLemore, ed., "Bannack and Gallatin City in 1862–63: A Letter by Mrs. Emily R. Meredith," *Sources of Northwest History*, no. 24; Winther, *Old Oregon Country*, pp. 216–21; (Silver City, Idaho) *Owyhee Avalanche*, 2 September 1865; Smith, *Rocky Mountain Mining Camps*, pp. 68–70.

16. Daniel Ellis Conner, *A Confederate in the Colorado Gold Fields*, ed. Donald J. Berthrong and Odessa Davenport (Norman: University of Oklahoma Press, 1970), p. 95; (Walla Walla) *Washington Statesman*, 22 March 1862.

17. Goulder, *Reminiscences*, pp. 239–40; Tim Kinerk Reminiscence, small collection #175, MHS; Watts, "Experiences of a Packer," 48.

18. The amounts of liquor sent to the wholesale firm of E. S. Mansfield

of Helena are contained in listings of freight found in the *Corinne* (Utah) *Reporter* between 19 May 1871 and 16 June 1871.

19. *Saguache Chronicle* reprinted in *Lake City Silver World*, 23 October 1875. See also *Wood River Times*, 29 November 1882; (Virginia City) *Montana Post*, 16 September 1865; *Helena* (Mont.) *Herald*, 28 May 1867; (Bonanza, Idaho) *Yankee Fork Herald*, 10 July 1880, 9 October 1880, 8 November 1879, 6 December 1879.

20. *Fairplay* (Colo.) *Flume*, 13 March 1879; *Denver Rocky Mountain News*, 26 August 1861; *Tri-Weekly Miner's Register*, 1 August 1862, 28 July 1863; *Daily Miner's Register*, 20 November 1863; *Leadville* (Colo.) *Democrat*, 6 May 1880; *Leadville* (Colo.) *Daily Herald*, 21 October 1880, 13 January 1881; *Weekly Nugget*, 25 March 1880; *Daily Nugget*, 12 November 1880; (Peach Springs) *Arizona Champion*, 3 November 1883; *Creede Candle*, 7 January 1892; *Red Mountain Review*, 14 April 1883; *Idaho World*, 28 October 1865, 18 November 1865, 16 December 1865; *Owyhee Avalanche*, 20 October 1866; *Idaho Tri-Weekly Statesman*, 16 August 1864, 27 June 1865; *Yankee Fork Herald*, 11 October 1879; *Helena Herald*, 26 December 1867; *Silverton* (Colo.) *Democrat*, 5 May 1883.

21. Virginia Brewery Ledgers, November 1864 to July 1865, March 1866 to 1869, MHS; "History of the Nicholas Kessler Brewery of Helena, Montana," and Brewer's Record of Fermented Liquors Made and Sold, November 1868 to November 1870, January 1871 to February 1873, Kessler Brewery Papers, MHS; Stanley Baron, *Brewed in America: A History of Beer and Ale in the United States* (Boston: Little, Brown and Co., 1962), chap. 28; Michael A. Leeson, *History of Montana, 1739–1885* (Chicago: Warner, Beers and Co., 1885), p. 1095; *Fairplay Flume*, 27 March 1879; *Arizona Quarterly Illustrated* (Tucson, Arizona), July 1880.

22. Record book of unidentified liquor distributor, Helena Bankers Group Papers, MHS; *Weekly Nugget*, 3 June 1880; *Leadville Weekly Herald*, 13 December 1879; *Yankee Fork Herald*, 12 June 1880; *Wood River Times*, 3 May 1882. For examples of advertisements, see *Leadville* (Colo.) *Chronicle*, 7 April 1879, 9 July 1879.

23. *Idaho World*, 17 December 1864.

24. John Franklin Graff, *"Graybeard" 's Colorado; or, Note of the Centennial State* (Philadelphia: J. B. Lippincott, 1882), p. 71; *Idaho Tri-Weekly Statesman*, 25 October 1883.

25. For some examples of listings of wholesale prices of liquor in various supply centers, see *Idaho World*, 2 December 1865; (Park City, Utah) *Park Record*, 25 February 1882; (Helena) *Montana Radiator*, all issues between January and October, 1866; (Tucson) *Arizona Quarterly Illustrated*, July 1880; *Idaho Tri-Weekly Statesman*, 19 November 1864, 24 June 1865, 29 June 1865; *Tri-Weekly Miner's Register*, 3 September 1862. On rare occa-

sions whiskey was distilled in the region of the Rockies, and its price was significantly lower. "Valley Tan" whiskey, produced in the Salt Lake valley, for instance, was available there for seventy-five cents per gallon wholesale. See (Corinne) *Utah Semi-Weekly Reporter*, 16 October 1869.

26. The advertisement is in *Wood River Times*, 22 June 1881. See also (Ouray, Colo.) *Solid Muldoon*, 19 September 1879; Mark D. Ledbetter to Will Mitchell, 26 October 1862, in Helen White, ed., *Ho! For the Gold Fields: Northern Overland Wagon Trains of the 1860s* (St. Paul: Minnesota Historical Society, 1966), p. 47; *Leadville Daily Democrat*, 17 April 1880; *Lake City Silver World*, 3 July 1875; A. J. Fisk Diary, 6 October 1866, Fisk Family Papers, MHS.

27. *Solid Muldoon*, 3 October 1879.

28. *Helena Herald*, 26 June 1867; *Lake City Silver World*, 28 April 1877, 3 November 1877; *Silverton Democrat,* 14 July 1883, 11 August 1883.

29. See, for instance, inventory in Virginia City, Montana, Tavern Account Book, small collection #143, MHS; Bill of Sale, Book 18, 277, Clear Creek County Clerk's Office, Georgetown, Colorado; Record Book I, 225–27, 381–85, Boise County Clerk's Office, Idaho City, Idaho; *Wood River Times*, 4 January 1882; *Yankee Fork Herald*, 6 December 1879; *Idaho World*, 18 November 1865, 26 August 1865; *Creede Candle*, 21 January 1892; *Helena Herald*, 14 March 1867; *Park Record*, 11 March 1892.

30. George Hand Diary, 21 December 1875, AHS; *Wood River Times*, 15 June 1881; *Helena Herald*, 7 November 1867; *Leadville Daily Democrat*, 26 May 1880; George Herendeen to sister, 4 March 1878, George Herendeen Papers, small collection #16, MHS; Leeson, *History of Montana*, p. 1230; *Tri-Weekly Miner's Register*, 2 February 1863.

31. Eugene Floyd Irey, "A Social History of Leadville, Colorado, during the Boom Days, 1877–1881," (Ph.D. diss., University of Minnesota, 1951), p. 122; "Journal of N. H. Webster," *Contributions to the Historical Society of Montana*, 3, p. 324; *Wood River Times*, 3 August 1881; *Silverton Democrat*, 5 May 1883; Frank Robertson and Beth Kay Harris, *Soapy Smith, King of the Frontier Con Men* (New York: Hastings House, 1961), pp. 107–108.

32. License issued in Shoshone County, Idaho, 5 June 1863, copy, MS2/Sho7, IHS.

33. For examples of this license legislation, see *Colorado General Assembly. General Laws, Joint Resolutions and Private Acts. First Session, 1861*, p. 70; *The Charter Ordinances of the City of Central* (Central City: Register-Call Book and Printing Office, 1879), pp. 108–109; Ordinance Book A, Silverton, Colorado, Town Hall; Record Book 1, 46–50, Telluride, Colorado, Town Hall; *Laws of the Territory of Idaho, Second Session* (Boise: Frank Kenyon, 1866), pp. 331, 355–56; *The Compiled Laws of the Territory*

of Arizona, Including the Howell Code and the Session Laws From 1864 to 1871 Inclusive (New York: Weed, Parsons, and Co., 1871); *Denver Rocky Mountain News*, 5 December 1861; *Creede Candle*, 15 April 1892; *Montana Post*, 17 December 1864; *Deer Lodge Independent*, 11 January 1868; *Weekly Nugget*, 15 April 1880; (Flagstaff, Ariz.) *Coconino Sun*, 22 March 1894; *Park Record*, 1 April 1882.

34. *Tri-Weekly Miner's Register*, 26 September 1862.

35. George Hockderffer Autobiography, 152–53, AHS; *Tri-Weekly Miner's Register*, 16 July 1863; *Helena Herald*, 14 May 1880. For examples of importance of license income in county and city finances, see *Fairplay Flume*, 20 February 1879; *Daily Miner's Register*, 7 November 1863; *Arizona Miner*, 17 August 1867, 21 September 1867; *Owyhee Avalanche*, 14 October 1865, 13 January 1866; *Idaho Tri-Weekly Statesman*, 16 June 1883; *Deer Lodge Independent*, 15 February 1868; *Leadville Daily Democrat*, 2 April 1880, 20 April 1880, 11 June 1880, 12 June 1880; Register of Licenses, 1886–1891, Leadville, Colorado, City Hall; *Weekly Epitaph*, 13 February 1882; *LaPlata Miner*, 25 January 1879.

36. Watts, "Experiences of a Packer," 40; *Idaho Tri-Weekly Statesman*, 27 October 1864; *Owyhee Avalanche*, 20 October 1866; Libeus Barney, *Early-day Letters from Auraria* (Denver: Luddett Press, 1907), p. 55; Stuart, *Forty Years*, 1:266; Mollie Dorsey Sanford, *Mollie: The Journal of Mollie Dorsey Sanford in Nebraska and Colorado Territories, 1857–1866* (Lincoln: University of Nebraska Press, 1959), p. 135; Henry J. Bose Reminiscence, 7, MHS; J. J. and W. J. Boyer Reminiscence, William Bertsche Collection, MHS; *Montana Post*, 12 November 1864; *Idaho World*, 27 October 1866; *Yankee Fork Herald*, 17 January 1880.

37. *Montana Post*, 23 September 1865; *Solid Muldoon*, 12 September 1879; *Park Record*, 1 April 1882; George Hand Diary, 31 July 1875, 27 December 1875, AHS.

38. Peter Herbert Saloon Records, MHS; Virginia City, Montana, Tavern Account Book, MHS; Meyer and Koerner Saloon Ledgers, MHS; Peterson and Anderson's Saloon Day Book, CU; John Bruce Collection, SHSC.

39. *Idaho World*, 3 June 1865, 11 September 1867; *Park Record*, 24 March 1883; *Laws and Resolutions Passed by the Sixth Legislative Assembly of the Territory of Idaho* (Boise: James S. Reynolds, 1871), p. 75; George Hand Diary, 3 June 1875, 27 July 1877, AHS.

40. *Owyhee Avalanche*, 2 September 1865; Rocky Bar, Idaho, Account Book, MS2/Rock59, IHS; *Wood River Times*, 13 December 1882; *Idaho Tri-Weekly Statesman*, 25 October 1864, 19 January 1865; *LaPlata Miner*, 1 November 1879; *Red Mountain Review*, 24 November 1883; *Lake City Silver World*, 15 December 1877.

41. George Hand Diary, 4 and 5 October 1875, AHS.

42. *Harper's Weekly*, 21 June 1879, p. 485.

43. Charles Mater interview, H. H. Bancroft Collection, CU; Irey, "History of Leadville," pp. 84, 214–15; Register of Licenses, Leadville, Colorado, City Hall.

44. (Leadville, Colo.) *Carbonate Weekly Chronicle*, 3 January 1880.

45. See Appendix A.

46. Frank Hall, *History of the State of Colorado*, 4 vols. (Chicago: Blakely Printing Co., 1889), 4:524.

Chapter 6

1. Robert L. Elder, George R. Elder Letters, Lake County Library, Leadville, Colorado.

2. William Willard Howard, "The Modern Leadville," *Harper's Weekly*, 1 December 1888, p. 928.

3. See, for instance, Joseph R. Gusfield, *Symbolic Crusade: Status Politics and the American Temperance Movement* (Urbana: University of Illinois Press, 1963), and Norman H. Clark, *Deliver Us from Evil: An Interpretation of American Prohibition* (New York: W. W. Norton and Co., 1976).

4. (Silver City, Idaho) *Owyhee Avalanche*, 9 September 1865, 7 October 1865; *Georgetown* (Colo.) *Weekly Miner*, 25 January 1872.

5. (Ouray, Colo.) *Solid Muldoon*, 19 November 1880. See also *Leadville* (Colo.) *Weekly Herald*, 27 March 1880; (Park City, Utah) *Park Record*, 19 August 1882; (Tombstone, Ariz.) *Weekly Epitaph*, 14 January 1882.

6. *Leadville* (Colo.) *Daily Herald*, 4 January 1881, 9 January 1881; Annie Fairbanks manuscript and Colorado WCTU Annual Report, 1888, 30, in Colorado State Woman's Christian Temperance Union Collection, CU.

7. (Central City, Colo.) *Daily Miner's Register*, 18 December 1863; *Creede* (Colo.) *Candle*, 6 January 1893; (Virginia City) *Montana Post*, 28 January 1865; (Hailey, Idaho) *Wood River Times*, 7 December 1881.

8. *Weekly Epitaph*, 3 April 1882; *Leadville Weekly Herald*, 10 January 1880; *Leadville Daily Democrat*, 7 January 1880, 20 March 1880; *Lake City* (Colo.) *Silver World*, 26 January 1878. Probably the first formal temperance society in the Rockies was formed in Auraria, Colorado, late in 1858. See Leroy R. Hafen, ed., *Colorado Gold Rush: Contemporary Letters and Reports, 1858–1859* (Glendale: Arthur H. Clark, 1941), p. 186.

9. Ernest Hurst Cherrington, ed., *Standard Encyclopedia of the Alcohol Problem*, 6 vols. (Westerville, Ohio: American Issue Publishing Co., 1926), 3:1332–38; *One Hundred Years of Temperance* (New York: National Temperance Society and Publication House, 1886), pp. 488–90; (Denver, Colo.) *Rocky Mountain News*, 10 April 1861, reprinted in Thomas Maitland

180 NOTES

Marshall, ed., *Early Records of Gilpin County, Colorado, 1859–1861* (Boulder: W. F. Robinson, 1920), p. 143; *Journal of the Proceedings of the Third Annual Session of the Grand Lodge of the Colorado IOGT* (Georgetown: Jesse S. Randall, 1869), p. 9; (Idaho City) *Idaho World*, 2 February 1867, 6 April 1867; *Deer Lodge* (Mont.) *Independent*, 27 March 1868, 1 May 1868; Myron Eells Journal, 3 September 1873, copy, MS2/Ee5, IHS.

10. Quotation is in *Journal of the Proceedings of the Ninth Annual Session of the Grand Lodge of the Colorado IOGT* (Georgetown: Jesse S. Randall, 1875), p. 7. See as well *Journal of Proceedings of IOGT, 1869*, pp. 7, 25; (Boise) *Idaho Tri-Weekly Statesman*, 9 February 1871; Myron Eells Journal, 27 November 1871, IHS.

11. The Irish immigrant Francis Murphy, a former barkeeper, led and inspired a series of national temperance campaigns during the 1870s. An untutored but effective orator, Murphy emphasized voluntary abstinence from alcohol through religious conversion. Converts to the movement signed a pledge card and were given a small blue ribbon to wear. Cherrington, ed., *Standard Encyclopedia*, 4:1838–40.

12. The poem is found in *Lake City Silver World*, 29 December 1877. For an account of the crusade, see issues of the paper for 1 December 1877, 15 December 1877, 22 December 1877, 23 February 1878. Also George M. Darley, *Pioneering in the San Juan* (Chicago: Fleming H. Revell Co., 1899), pp. 53–56.

13. John Willard Horner, *Silver Town* (Caldwell, Idaho: The Caxton Printers, 1950), pp. 257–58; (Georgetown) *Colorado Miner*, 6 October 1877; *Georgetown* (Colo.) *Courier*, 20 September 1877, 27 September 1877, 18 October 1877, 1 November 1877, 8 November 1877. The Georgetown crusade was successful enough to draw the applause of the national convention of the WCTU. See copy of the national WCTU minutes, 1878, 196, in Colorado State Woman's Christian Temperance Union Collection, CU.

14. Colorado WCTU Minutes, 1889, p. 40, Colorado State Woman's Christian Temperance Union Collection, CU. Also *Leadville Daily Democrat*, 28 April 1880; *Park Record*, 24 June 1882; *Constitution and By-laws of the Father Mathew Total Abstinence and Beneficial Union of Georgetown, Colorado* (Georgetown: Jesse S. Randall, 1877); W. H. Daniels, *The Temperance Reform and Its Great Reformers* (New York: Nelson and Phillips, 1878), pp. 212–46; *Colorado Miner*, 9 February 1871; *Leadville Daily Democrat*, 4 May 1880.

15. See, for example, *Deer Lodge Independent*, 1 May 1868; Darley, *Pioneering in the San Juan*, p. 56; *Journal of the Proceedings of the IOGT, 1869*, p. 9.

16. *Charter of the City of Tombstone, County of Cochise, Territory of*

Arizona (Tombstone: Commercial Job Printing Office, 1881), p. 3; *Montana Post*, 11 February 1865.

17. Quotation is from (Tucson) *Arizona Citizen*, 23 May 1874. See also Minute Book 1, 19 May 1877 and 21 May 1877, 42–44, Silverton Town Hall, Silverton, Colorado; City Record Book 1, 13 September 1889, 78–79, Telluride, Colorado, Town Hall; *Weekly Epitaph*, 7 March 1882.

18. *Montana Post*, 14 January 1865, 24 December 1865; *Idaho World*, 19 June 1867; *Idaho Tri-Weekly Statesman*, 22 November 1864; *Owyhee Avalanche*, 14 April 1866.

19. Ordinance Book A, 63, 66, 68, Silverton, Colorado, Town Hall; (Tombstone, Ariz.) *Weekly Nugget*, 13 May 1880; *Creede Candle*, 29 July 1892.

20. *Leadville Daily Democrat*, 20 January 1880, 28 April 1880, 12 May 1880, 18 May 1880; *Leadville Daily Herald*, 11 February 1881, 13 February 1881, 16 February 1881, 25 February 1881.

21. *Idaho World*, 7 July 1870.

22. *Georgetown Courier*, 20 December 1883, 3 April 1884, 10 April 1884; *Colorado Miner*, 12 April 1884.

23. *Park Record*, 7 July 1883.

24. Robert R. Dykstra, *The Cattle Towns* (New York: Alfred A. Knopf, 1968), chap. 7.

25. (Denver, Colo.) *Rocky Mountain Presbyterian*, September 1872.

Bibliography

MOST published works on Western saloons have been sensationalized accounts consisting mainly of anecdotes that stress the
bawdiness and violence of frontier drinking houses. Only rarely do
they offer any analysis of the social importance of the saloon. A
notable exception is Thomas J. Noel's excellent "The Multifunctional
Frontier Saloon: Denver, 1858–1876," *Colorado Magazine* 52
(Spring 1975): 114–36. Noel discusses the various roles played by the
barrooms in Colorado's capital and how these roles changed as Denver
evolved from a raw frontier village to a major urban center. His
doctoral dissertation on Denver saloons should be an important contribution to Western urban history. For two other more analytical
treatments of Western saloons, see Elliott West, "The Saloon in
Territorial Arizona," *Journal of the West* 13 (July 1974): 61–73, and
Ann Burk, "The Mining Camp Saloon as a Social Center," *Red River
Valley Historical Review* 2 (Fall 1975): 381–92. For examples of
popularized works on Western drinking places, the reader should
consult Jim Marshall, *Swinging Doors* (Seattle: Frank McCaffrey
Publishers, 1949); Cy Martin, *Whiskey and Wild Women: An Amusing
Account of the Saloons and Bawds of the Old West* (New York: Hart
Publishing Co., Inc., 1974); Robert L. Brown, "Saloons of the
American West," *The Denver Westerners Roundup* 29 (March–April
1973): 3–19; and Gerald Carson, "The Saloon," *American Heritage*
14 (April 1963): 24–31, 103–107, part of which is devoted to Western
saloons.

Saloons of Eastern cities have attracted a bit more serious attention from scholars. For an insightful examination of Chicago saloons
written near the turn of the century, see E. C. Moore, "The Social
Value of the Saloon," *American Journal of Sociology* 3 (July 1897):
1–12. Two recent works consider the same general topic from a
modern perspective: Perry R. Duis, "The Saloon and the Public City:
Chicago and Boston, 1880–1920," (Ph.D. diss., University of
Chicago, 1975), and Jon M. Kingsdale, "The 'Poor Man's Club':
Social Functions of the Urban Working-Class Saloon," *American
Quarterly* 25 (October 1973): 472–89.

Several recent studies have concentrated on the behavior and attitudes to be found in modern drinking places, and on the place and function of the barroom in modern society. Of these some of the more interesting are E. E. LeMasters, *Blue Collar Aristocrats: Life-Styles at a Working Class Tavern* (Madison: University of Wisconsin Press, 1975); Sherri Cavan, *Liquor License: An Ethnography of Bar Behavior* (Chicago: Aldine Publishing Co., 1966); Matthew P. Dumont, "Tavern Culture, The Sustenance of Homeless Men," *American Journal of Orthopsychiatry* 37 (October 1967): 938–45; and David Gottlieb, "The Neighborhood Tavern and the Cocktail Lounge: A Study in Class Differences," *American Journal of Sociology* 62 (May 1957): 559–62. In addition to these works, there is an extensive literature on the causes, functions, and effects of group drinking. For the books and articles on this subject that I found most useful, see note ten of chapter 1.

What follows is a selected bibliography of the primary and secondary sources I found most useful in studying the mining town saloons and the social conditions on the Rocky Mountain mining frontier.

I. Unpublished Diaries, Letters, Records, and Reminiscences

Arizona Historical Society, Tucson, Arizona.
    Charles F. Bennett Reminiscence.
    D. S. Chamberlain Manuscript.
    Alexander J. Davidson Reminiscence.
    Harry Drachman Reminiscence.
    James C. Hancock Reminiscence, Frank C. Lockwood Collection.
    George Hand Diary.
    George Hockderffer Autobiography (typescript).
    Charles Liftchild Reminiscence.
    Adolphus Henry Noon Papers.
    John A. Rockfellow Reminiscence.
    James G. Wolf Reminiscence.
State Historical Society of Colorado, Denver, Colorado.
    Auraria Town Company Records.
    Alonzo Boardman Papers.
    John Bruce Collection.
    Elmer R. Burkey Collection.

Colorado Writers' Project Interviews.
Richard Charles Deus Reminiscence.
Edward J. Lewis Diary.
Bennett E. Seymour Diary.
Allen Grant Wallihan Diary.
University of Colorado Library, Western Historical Collection,
Boulder, Colorado.
Hubert Howe Bancroft Collection.
Colorado State Woman's Christian Temperance Union Collection.
Peterson and Anderson's Saloon Day Book.
Henry E. Huntington Library, San Marino, California.
Charles D. Poston Reminiscence.
Idaho State Historical Society, Boise, Idaho.
E. Lafayette Bristow Papers.
Myron Eells Journal (copy).
James H. Hawley Manuscript.
Nels C. Jensen Diary.
Rocky Bar, Idaho, Account Book.
Montana Historical Society, Helena, Montana.
Gilbert Benedict Papers.
William Bertsche Collection.
Henry J. Bose Reminiscence.
Thomas Conrad Papers.
William Dibb Diary.
Katherine Dunlap Diary.
Fisk Family Papers.
Ellen Fletcher Papers.
John W. Grannis Diary.
Cornelius Hedges Papers.
Helena Bankers Group Papers.
Peter Herbert Saloon Records.
George Herendeen Papers.
Sallie R. Herndon Diary.
Joseph Horsky Reminiscence.
Kessler Brewery Papers.
Tim Kinerk Reminiscence.
Franklin L. Kirkaldie Papers.
Meyer and Koerner Saloon Ledgers.
Bob Powell Reminiscence.
W. R. Sellew Papers.
Z. E. Thomas Reminiscence.
Robert Thoroughman Reminiscence.

Daniel Tuttle Papers.
Virginia Brewery Ledgers.
Virginia City, Montana, Livery Stable Records.
Virginia City, Montana, Tavern Account Book.
Samuel William Carvoso Whipps Reminiscence.
Henry F. Woode Diary.

II. Unpublished Government Records

United States Bureau of the Census. Manuscript Reports, 1870, 1880.
Georgetown, Colorado, Town Hall. Police Docket.
Clear Creek County Courthouse. Georgetown, Colorado. Deeds, Property, and Tax Assessment Records.
Leadville, Colorado, City Hall. Register of Licenses.
Lake County Courthouse. Leadville, Colorado. Property and Tax Assessment Records.
Silverton, Colorado, Town Hall. Justice Docket and Ordinances.
Telluride, Colorado, Town Hall. Town Record Books.
Blaine County Courthouse. Hailey, Idaho. Alturas County Commissioners Proceedings.
Boise County Courthouse. Idaho City, Idaho. County Record Books.

III. Published Diaries, Letters, Reminiscences,
and Autobiographies.

Adams, Emma Hildreth. *To and Fro in Southern California: With Sketches in Arizona and New Mexico*. Cincinnati: Cranston and Stowe, 1888.
Agnew, Mrs. James D. "Idaho Pioneer in 1864." *Washington Historical Quarterly* 15 (January 1924):44–48.
Angelo, C. Aubrey. *Idaho: A Descriptive Tour, and Review of Its Resources and Route*. San Francisco: H. H. Bancroft and Co., 1865.
Barneby, William Henry. *Life and Labour in the Far, Far West*. London: Cassell and Co., 1884.
Barnes, Demas. *From the Atlantic to the Pacific, Overland*. New York: D. Van Nostrand, 1866.
Barney, Libeus. *Early-day Letters from Auraria*. Denver: Luddett Press, 1907.
Beardsley, Isaac Haight. *Echoes From Peak and Plain; or, Tales of Life, War, Travel, and Colorado Methodism*. Cincinnati: Curts and Jennings, 1898.
Bell, John C. *The Pilgrim and the Pioneer: The Social and Material Developments of the Rocky Mountains*. Lincoln: International Publishing Association, 1906.
Bowles, Samuel. *Across the Continent*. Springfield: Samuel Bowles, 1866.

Brind, Fitz. *Colorado, The Land of Sunshine, Health and Wealth*. London: Caines and Co., 1882.

Brown, Clara Spaulding. "An Arizona Mining District." *Californian* 4 (July 1881).

Cady, John Henry. *Arizona's Yesterday, Being the Narrative of John H. Cady, Pioneer*. Los Angeles: Times-Mirror Co., 1916.

Carpenter, E. W. "A Glimpse of Montana." *Overland Monthly* 2 (April 1869):378–86.

Clark, Charles M. *A Trip to Pike's Peak and Notes along the Way*. Chicago: S. P. Rounds, 1861.

Conner, Daniel Ellis. *A Confederate in the Colorado Gold Fields*. Edited by Donald J. Berthrong and Odessa Davenport. Norman: University of Oklahoma Press, 1970.

Cozzens, Samuel Woodworth. *The Marvellous Country; or, Three Years in Arizona, and New Mexico, the Apaches' Home*. Boston: Shepard and Gill, 1873.

Darley, George M. *Pioneering in the San Juan*. New York: Fleming H. Revell Co., 1899.

Davis, Carlyle Channing. *Olden Times in Colorado*. Los Angeles: Phillips Publishing Co., 1916.

Davis, Richard Harding. "The West From a Car Window, III. At a New Mining Camp." *Harper's Weekly* (9 April 1892):341–44.

Detzler, Jack J., ed. *Diary of Howard Stillwell Stanfield*. Bloomington: Indiana University Press, 1969.

Dimsdale, Thomas Josiah. *The Vigilantes of Montana*. Virginia City: D. W. Tilton, 1866.

Ellis, Anne. *The Life of an Ordinary Woman*. Boston: Houghton Mifflin Co., 1929.

Fisher, Rev. J. R. *Camping in the Rocky Mountains*. New York: Holt Brothers, 1880.

Gibbons, Rev. James Joseph. *In the San Juan Colorado*. Chicago: Calumet Book and Engraving Co., 1898.

Goode, Rev. William H. *Outposts of Zion with Limnings of Mission Life*. Cincinnati: Poe and Hitchcock, 1864.

Goulder, W. A. *Reminiscences of a Pioneer*. Boise: Timothy Regan, 1909.

Goulder, W. A. "Rocky Bar and Atlanta in 1876." *Idaho Yesterdays* 17 (Spring 1973):12–25.

Graff, John Franklin. *"Graybeard"'s Colorado; or, Note of the Centennial State*. Philadelphia: J. B. Lippincott, 1882.

Hafen, Leroy R., ed. *Colorado Gold Rush: Contemporary Letters and Reports, 1858–1859*. Glendale: Arthur H. Clark, 1941.

Homsher, Lola M., ed. *South Pass, 1868: James Chisholm's Journal of the Wyoming Gold Rush*. Lincoln: University of Nebraska Press, 1960.

Howard, William Willard. "The Modern Leadville." *Harper's Weekly* (1 December 1888):925–28.

Hughes, Dan de Lara. *South From Tombstone: A Life Story by Dan de Lara Hughes*. London: Methuen and Co., 1938.

Ingersoll, Ernest. *The Crest of the Continent: A Record of a Summer's Ramble in the Rocky Mountains and Beyond*. Chicago: R. R. Donnelley and Sons, 1885.

Larimer, William Henry Harrison. *Reminiscences of General William Larimer and of His Son William H. H. Larimer, Two of the Founders of Denver City*. Lancaster, Pennsylvania: Press of the New Era, 1918.

Latta, Robert Ray. *Reminiscences of Pioneer Life*. Kansas City: Franklin Hudson Publishing Co., 1912.

Lewis, William S. "Reminiscences of Joseph H. Boyd, An Argonaut of 1857." *Washington Historical Quarterly* 15 (October 1924):243–62.

Lucy, Henry W. *East by West, a Journey in the Recess*. London: Richard Bentley and Son, 1885.

Macrae, David. *The Americans at Home*. New York: E. P. Dutton and Co., 1952.

Marshall, Thomas Maitland, ed. *Early Records of Gilpin County, Colorado, 1859–1861*. Boulder: W. F. Robinson, 1920.

McLemore, Clyde, ed. "Bannack and Gallatin City in 1862–63: A Letter by Mrs. Emily R. Meredith." *Sources of Northwest History*, no. 24.

McPherson, G. W. *A Parson's Adventures*. Yonkers, New Jersey: Yonkers Book Co., 1925.

Miller, Henry. "Letters From the Upper Columbia." *Idaho Yesterdays* 4 (Winter 1960–61):19–24.

Morris, Maurice O'Conner. *Rambles in the Rocky Mountains*. London: Smith, Elder and Co., 1864.

Paul, Rodman W., ed. *A Victorian Gentlewoman in the Far West: The Reminiscences of Mary Hallock Foote*. San Marino, California: The Huntington Library, 1972.

Pidgeon, Daniel. *An Engineer's Holiday; or, Notes of a Round Trip from Long. 0° to 0°*. London: Kegan Paul, Trench, and Co., 1883.

Pierce, Elladean. "Early Days of Craig, Colorado." *Colorado Magazine* 5 (1928):152–58.

Pumpelly, Raphael. *Across America and Asia: Notes of a Five Years' Journey around the World and of Residence in Arizona, Japan and China*. New York: Leypoldt and Holt, 1870.

Ralph, Julian. *Our Great West: A Study of the Present Conditions and Future Possibilities of the New Commonwealths and Capitals of the United States*. Freeport, New York: Books for Libraries Press, 1970.

Richardson, Albert D. *Beyond the Mississippi: From the Great River to the Great Ocean*. Hartford: American Publishing Co., 1869.

Rolle, Andrew F., ed. *The Road to Virginia City: The Diary of James Knox Polk Miller*. Norman: University of Oklahoma Press, 1960.

Romspert, George. *The Western Echo: A Description of the Western States and Territories of the United States as Gathered in a Tour by Wagon*. Dayton, Ohio: United Brethren Publishing House, 1881.

Sanford, Mollie Dorsey. *Mollie: The Journal of Mollie Dorsey Sanford in Nebraska and Colorado Territories, 1857–1866*. Lincoln: University of Nebraska Press, 1959.

Shepherd, William. *Prairie Experiences in Handling Cattle and Sheep*. London: Chapman and Hall, 1884.

Simonin, Louis L. "Colorado in 1867 as Seen by a Frenchman." Translated by Wilson O. Clough. *Colorado Magazine* 14 (March 1937):56–63.

Smart, Stephen F. *Leadville, Ten Mile, Eagle River, Elk Mountain, Tin Cup and All Other Noted Colorado Mining Camps*. Kansas City: Ramsey, Millett and Hudson, 1879.

Stuart, Granville. *Forty Years on the Frontier*. 2 vols. Cleveland: Arthur H. Clark, 1925.

Talbot, Ethelbert. *My People of the Plains*. New York and London: Harper and Brothers, 1946.

Toponce, Alexander. *Reminiscences of Alexander Toponce*. Salt Lake City: By the Author, 1923.

Townshend, Richard Baxter. *A Tenderfoot in Colorado*. Norman: University of Oklahoma Press, 1968.

Tuttle, Daniel S. *Reminiscences of a Missionary Bishop*. New York: T. Whittaker, 1906.

Wardner, James F. *Jim Wardner, of Wardner, Idaho. By Himself*. New York: The Anglo-American Publishing Co., 1900.

Watts, James W. "Experiences of a Packer in Washington Territory Mining Camps During the Sixties." *Washington Historical Quarterly* 19 (July 1928):206–13, (October 1928):285–93; 20 (January 1929):36–53.

White, Helen, ed. *Ho! For the Gold Fields: Northern Overland Wagon Trains of the 1860s*. St. Paul: Minnesota Historical Society, 1966.

Wilson, Iris H., ed. "Pineda's Report on the Beverages of New Spain." *Arizona and the West* 5 (Spring 1963):79–90.

Wootton, Richens L. *"Uncle Dick" Wootton, the Pioneer Frontiersman of the Rocky Mountain Region*. Chicago: W. E. Dibble, 1890.

Young, Charles Edward. *Dangers of the Trail in 1865*. Geneva, New York: W. F. Humphrey, 1912.

IV. Newspapers

Alta Arizona (Mineral Park, Arizona)
Arizona Champion (Flagstaff, Arizona)

Arizona Miner (Prescott, Arizona)
Arizona Quarterly Illustrated (Tucson, Arizona)
Arizona Silver Belt (Globe, Arizona)
Arizona Weekly Citizen (Tucson, Arizona)
Boise City Republican (Boise, Idaho)
Carbonate Weekly Chronicle (Leadville, Colorado)
Coconino Sun (Flagstaff, Arizona)
Coeur d'Alene Nugget (Coeur d'Alene, Idaho)
Colorado Miner (Georgetown, Colorado)
Colorado Sun (Denver, Colorado)
Corinne Reporter (Corinne, Utah)
Creede Candle (Creede, Colorado)
Daily Miner's Register (Central City, Colorado)
Daily Nugget (Tombstone, Arizona)
Deer Lodge Independent (Deer Lodge, Montana)
Fairplay Flume (Fairplay, Colorado)
Georgetown Courier (Georgetown, Colorado)
Gunnison Review (Gunnison, Colorado)
Helena Herald (Helena, Montana)
Idaho Tri-Weekly Statesman (Boise, Idaho)
Idaho World (Idaho City, Idaho)
Lake City Silver World (Lake City, Colorado)
LaPlata Miner (Silverton, Colorado)
Leadville Daily Chronicle (Leadville, Colorado)
Leadville Daily Democrat (Leadville, Colorado)
Leadville Daily Herald (Leadville, Colorado)
Leadville Weekly Herald (Leadville, Colorado)
Montana Post (Virginia City, Montana)
Montana Radiator (Virginia City, Montana)
Owyhee Avalanche (Silver City, Idaho)
Park Record (Park City, Utah)
Red Mountain Pilot (Red Mountain, Colorado)
Red Mountain Review (Red Mountain, Colorado)
Rocky Mountain News (Denver, Colorado)
Rocky Mountain Presbyterian (Denver, Colorado)
Rocky Mountain Sun (Aspen, Colorado)
Santa Fe New Mexican (Santa Fe, New Mexico)
Silver Reef Miner (Silver Reef, Utah)
Silverton Democrat (Silverton, Colorado)
Solid Muldoon (Ouray, Colorado)
Tri-Weekly Miner's Register (Central City, Colorado)
Utah Reporter (Corinne, Utah)
Utah Semi-Weekly Reporter (Corinne, Utah)

Washington Statesman (Walla Walla, Washington)
Weekly Epitaph (Tombstone, Arizona)
Weekly Nugget (Tombstone, Arizona)
Western Mountaineer (Denver, Colorado)
White Pine Cone (White Pine, Colorado)
Wood River Times (Hailey, Idaho)
Yankee Fork Herald (Bonanza, Idaho)

V. Secondary Books

Adams, Ramon F. *Western Words: A Dictionary of the American West.* Norman: University of Oklahoma Press, 1968.

Athearn, Robert G. *Thomas Francis Meagher: An Irish Revolutionary in America.* Boulder: University of Colorado Press, 1949.

Bancroft, Hubert Howe. *History of Washington, Idaho, and Montana, 1845–1889. The Works of Hubert Howe Bancroft.* 39 vols. San Francisco: History Company, 1890.

Baron, Stanley. *Brewed In America: A History of Beer and Ale in the United States.* Boston: Little, Brown and Co., 1962.

Barsness, Larry. *Gold Camp: Alder Gulch and Virginia City.* New York: Hastings House, 1962.

Boorstin, Daniel J. *The Americans: The National Experience.* New York: Random House, 1965.

Bridenbaugh, Carl. *Cities in Revolt: Urban Life in America, 1743–1776.* New York: Oxford University Press, 1971.

Briggs, Harold E. *Frontiers of the Northwest: A History of the Upper Missouri Valley.* New York: Peter Smith, 1950.

Burkey, Frank J. *The Faded Frontier.* Omaha: Burkey Printing Co., 1935.

Cherrington, Ernest Hurst, ed. *Standard Encyclopedia of the Alcohol Problem.* 6 vols. Westerville, Ohio: American Issue Publishing Co., 1926.

Chittenden, Hiram Martin. *History of Early Steamboat Navigation on the Missouri River.* 2 vols. Minneapolis: Ross and Haines, Inc., 1962.

Clark, Norman H. *Deliver Us from Evil: An Interpretation of American Prohibition.* New York: W. W. Norton and Co., 1976.

Cline, Platt. *They Came to the Mountain: The Story of Flagstaff's Beginnings.* Flagstaff: Northland Press, 1976.

Donaldson, Thomas C. *Idaho of Yesterday.* Caldwell, Idaho: Caxton Printers, 1941.

Dulles, Foster Rhea. *America Learns to Play: A History of Popular Recreation, 1607–1940.* Gloucester, Massachusetts: Peter Smith, 1959.

Dykstra, Robert R. *The Cattle Towns.* New York: Alfred A. Knopf, 1968.

Edwards, Richard Henry. *Popular Amusements.* New York: Association Press, 1915.

Elsensohn, Alfreda. *Pioneer Days in Idaho County*. 2 vols. Caldwell, Idaho: Caxton Printers, 1947–51.

Fenin, George N. and William K. Everson. *The Western: From Silents to the Seventies*. New York: Grossman Publishers, 1973.

Griswold, Don and Griswold, Jean. *A Carbonate Camp Called Leadville*. Denver: University of Denver Press, 1951.

Gusfield, Joseph R. *Symbolic Crusade: Status Politics and the American Temperance Movement*. Urbana: University of Illinois Press, 1963.

Hackwood, Frederick W. *Inns, Ales, and Drinking Customs of Old England*. New York: Sturgis and Walton Co., 1909.

Hafen, Leroy R., ed. *Colorado and Its People, A Narrative and Topical History of the Centennial State*. 4 vols. New York: Lewis Historical Publishing Co., 1948.

Hailey, John. *The History of Idaho*. Boise: Press of Syms-York Co., 1910.

Hall, Frank. *History of the State of Colorado*. 4 vols. Chicago: Blakely Printing Co., 1889.

Hawley, James H. *History of Idaho, the Gem of the Mountains*. Chicago: S. J. Clarke Publishing Co., 1920.

Horner, John Willard. *Silver Town*. Caldwell, Idaho: Caxton Printers, 1950.

An Illustrated History of the State of Idaho. Chicago: Lewis Publishing Co., 1899.

Johnston, Alexander. *Ten—And Out! The Complete Story of the Prize Ring in America*. New York: Ives Washburn, 1947.

Kirkpatrick, Orion E. *History of the Leesburg Pioneers*. Salt Lake City: Pyramid Press, 1934.

Krapp, George Philip. *The English Language in America*. 2 vols. New York: Frederick Ungar Publishing Co., 1960.

Leeson, Michael A. *History of Montana, 1739–1885*. Chicago: Warner, Beers and Co., 1885.

Martin, Douglas D. *Tombstone's Epitaph*. Albuquerque: University of New Mexico Press, 1951.

Mathews, Mitford M., ed. *A Dictionary of Americanisms on Historical Principles*. 2 vols. Chicago: University of Chicago Press, 1951.

Mencken, H. L. *The American Language: An Inquiry into the Development of the English in the United States*. New York: Alfred A. Knopf, 1945.

Mumey, Nolie. *Creede: History of a Colorado Silver Mining Town*. Denver: Artcraft Press, 1949.

Progressive Men of the State of Montana. Chicago: A. W. Bowen and Co., 1903.

Richardson, A. E., and Eberlein, H. Donaldson. *The English Inn Past and Present: A Review of Its History and Social Life*. New York: Benjamin Blom, 1968.

Riegel, Robert Edgar. *The Story of the Western Railroads*. Lincoln: University of Nebraska Press, 1963.

Robertson, Frank and Harris, Beth Kay. *Soapy Smith, King of the Frontier Con Men*. New York: Hastings House, 1961.

Russell, Don. *Custer's Last*. Forth Worth: Amon Carter Museum of Western Art, 1968.

Sabin, Edwin L. *Kit Carson Days, 1809–1868*. New York: Press of the Pioneers, 1928.

Sanders, Helen Fitzgerald. *A History of Montana*. 3 vols. Chicago: Lewis Publishing Co., 1913.

Smith, Duane A. *Rocky Mountain Mining Camps: The Urban Frontier*. Lincoln: University of Nebraska Press, 1974.

Stoehr, C. Eric. *Bonanza Victorian: Architecture and Society in Colorado Mining Towns*. Albuquerque: University of New Mexico Press, 1975.

Stout, Tom. *Montana, Its Story and Biography*. 3 vols. Chicago: American Historical Society, 1921.

Thornton, Richard H. *An American Glossary, Being an Attempt to Illustrate Certain Americanisms upon Historical Principles*. Philadelphia: J. B. Lippincott, 1912.

Trimble, William Joseph. *The Mining Advance into the Inland Empire*. Madison, Wisconsin: Bulletin of the University of Wisconsin, 1914.

Walker, Henry P. *The Wagonmasters: High Plains Freighting from the Earliest Days . . . to 1880*. Norman: University of Oklahoma Press, 1966.

Willison, George F. *Here They Dug the Gold*. New York: Reynal and Hitchcock, 1946.

Winther, Oscar Osburn. *The Old Oregon Country: A History of Frontier Trade, Transportation, and Travel*. Lincoln: University of Nebraska Press, 1969.

VI. Secondary Articles

Albertson, Dean. "Puritan Liquor in the Planting of New England." *New England Quarterly* 23 (December 1950):477–90.

"The Annals of Billiards." *Cornhill Magazine* 54 (July–December 1886):180–88.

"Billiards." *Harper's Weekly* (8 March 1890):186–87.

Clark, Archie L. "John McGuire, Butte's First 'Belasco.' " *The Montana Magazine of History* 2 (January 1954):33–40.

Csikszenmihalyi, Mihaly. "A Cross-Cultural Comparison of Some Structural Characteristics of Group Drinking." *Human Development* 2 (1968):201–209.

Feil, Lin B. "Helvetia: Boom Town of the Santa Ritas." *Journal of Arizona History* 9 (Summer 1968):77–95.

Hutton, Paul A. "From Little Bighorn to Little Big Man: The Changing Image of a Western Hero in Popular Culture." *Western Historical Quarterly* 7 (January 1976):19–45.

Mann, Ralph. "A Decade after the Gold Rush: Social Structure in Grass Valley and Nevada City, California, 1850–1860." *Pacific Historical Review* 41 (November 1972):484–504.

Stevens, Walter B. "The Missouri Tavern." *Missouri Historical Review* 68 (October 1973):94–130.

Walker, Henry P. "Wagon Freighting From Guaymas to Tucson, 1850–1880." *Western Historical Quarterly* 1 (July 1970):291–304.

Walker, Henry P. "Wagon Freighting in Arizona." *The Smoke Signal* 28 (Fall 1973):182–204.

Index